Black Autonomy

Black Autonomy

Race, Gender, and Afro-Nicaraguan Activism

Jennifer Goett

Stanford University Press
Stanford, California

Stanford University Press
Stanford, California

Printed in the United States of America on acid-free, archival-quality paper

Library of Congress Cataloging-in-Publication Data

Names: Goett, Jennifer, author.
Title: Black autonomy : race, gender, and Afro-Nicaraguan activism / Jennifer Goett.
Description: Stanford, California : Stanford University Press, 2016. | Includes bibliographical references and index.
Identifiers: LCCN 2016013231 (print) | LCCN 2016015177 (ebook) | ISBN 9780804799560 (cloth : alk. paper) | ISBN 9781503600546 (pbk. : alk. paper) | ISBN 9781503600553 (ebook) | ISBN 9781503600553 (e-book)
Subjects: LCSH: Blacks—Nicaragua—Monkey Point—Politics and government. | Blacks—Nicaragua—Monkey Point—Government relations. | Women, Black—Political activity—Nicaragua—Monkey Point. | Community activists—Nicaragua—Monkey Point. | Multiculturalism—Political aspects—Nicaragua. | Monkey Point (Nicaragua)—Social conditions.
Classification: LCC F1536.M66 G64 2016 (print) | LCC F1536.M66 (ebook) | DDC 305.896/07285—dc23
LC record available at https://lccn.loc.gov/2016013231

Typeset by Thompson Type in 10/14 Minion

Contents

Acknowledgments

THIS BOOK HAS BEEN A LONG TIME IN THE MAKING, and I owe a debt of gratitude to the many individuals who have helped me bring it to completion. First and foremost, the book would not have been possible without the friendship and solidarity of Monkey Point people. It is with profound gratitude that I dedicate this work to them. Community elders, Miss Bernicia Duncan, Miss Helen Presida, Miss Pearl Marie Watson, Miss Lucille Presida, Mr. Limbert Sambola, and Miss Christina Cooper, shared more knowledge and wisdom about the past than any history book could offer. Allen Clair, Carla Chow, Carla Sinclair, Catherine Clair, Harley Clair, Rolando Clair, Morl Sambola, James Sambola, Gloria Sambola, Leonardo Sambola, George Sambola, Ruby Centeno, Darren Wilson, Charleene Solís, Estelle Duncan, Sullivan Quinn, Edward Duncan, Hubert Duncan, Arleen MacElroy, Isis Lampson, Sandra Morales, Charles Watson, and Robin Archibold each lent me their time and insight over the years.

In Bluefields, I thank my dear friends Carla James, Tavia James, Shirley James, Helen Fenton, Vanesa Almendares, and Brenda Wilson. Galio Gurdián, Maricela Kauffmann, and Fernanda Soto offered camaraderie, intellectual inspiration, and a warm welcome each time I landed in Managua. I hope that I can repay their kindness someday. My respect and admiration go to Maria Luisa Acosta, Dolene Miller, and Nora Newball for their willingness to collaborate and steadfast defense of autonomous rights.

The project first developed under the guidance of faculty at the University of Texas at Austin. I could not have hoped for better mentors than Edmund

T. Gordon and Charles R. Hale. Their intellectual generosity and support for activist scholarship made the research for this book possible. Kamala Visweswaran encouraged me to assertively claim my work as feminist ethnography and offered me countless big and small favors over the years. Juliet Hooker provided inspiration and a rich body of work with which to engage. I am also blessed with a large cohort of brilliant peers from the University of Texas who have challenged me to be a better scholar. Special thanks go to Diya Mehra, Courtney Morris, Shaka McGlotten, Marc Perry, Roosbelinda Cardenas, Keisha-Khan Perry, Pablo González, Melissa Forbis, Nick Copeland, Christine Labuski, Ajb'ee Jiménez, Edwin Matamoros, Melesio Peter, Gilberto Rosas, Korinta Maldonado, Juli Grigsby, Lynn Selby, Mariana Mora, Mohan Ambikaipaker, Ronda Brulotte, Vivian Newdick, Angela Stuesse, Ritu Khanduri, and Teresa Velásquez.

Many other individuals contributed to the project in important ways. Mark Anderson, Ellen Moodie, Brandt Peterson, Christopher Loperena, Miguel González, and Ben Chappell took time out of their busy schedules to read all or parts of the manuscript. I am grateful for their willingness to engage my work and for their sharp insights. Any shortcomings that remain are mine alone. Alicia Estrada, Felipe Pérez, Marilyn Sinkewicz, Cale Layton, Elana Zilberg, Justin Wolfe, Bill Girard, Breny Mendoza, Suyapa Portillo, Dolores Figueroa, Christen Smith, Dána-Ain Davis, Christa Craven, Josh Mayer, Daniel Goldstein, Faye Harrison, Peter Wade, and Karl Offen each offered input or encouragement along the way. At Michigan State University, I extend my gratitude to Laurie Medina, Colleen Tremonte, Gene Burns, Mark Largent, and Peter Murray. I am lucky to have such generous colleagues. I would also like to recognize the National Science Foundation, IIE Fulbright, the University of Texas at Austin, Michigan State University, and James Madison College for funding various stages of research and writing.

Finally, there are a number people who played instrumental roles in bringing the final manuscript to completion. My professorial assistant Ansel Courant did a tremendous amount of hard work organizing and transcribing more than a decade's worth of interviews. Kerry Ann Rockquemore taught me how to get the words on the page and out the door. Michelle Jacob kept me on track with weekly check-in calls and a great deal of sage advice. Robert and Gail Piepenburg provided me with a calm and beautiful place to write. I thank two anonymous readers for Stanford University Press for their helpful comments on the manuscript; my editor Michelle Lipinski for her patience, professionalism, and faith in the project; and editorial assistant Nora Spiegel and copy editor Margaret Pinette for their skillful guidance through the final stages of publication. I owe special thanks to Karen Spencer for granting me permission to use her beautiful painting on the cover of the book. My love and appreciation go to my family for everything they have done for me and to my husband, Waseem El-Rayes, whom I adore.

Black Autonomy

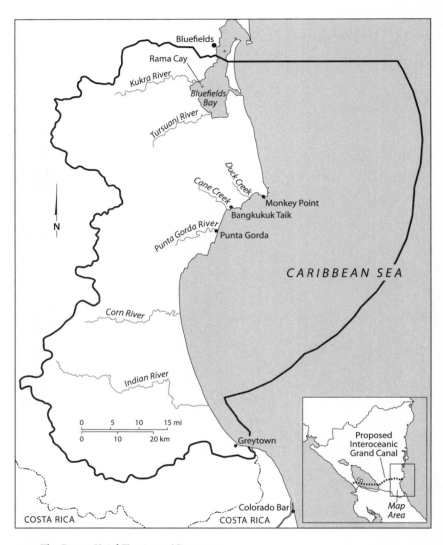

Map The Rama-Kriol Territory, Nicaragua.
SOURCE: The Rama-Kriol Territorial Government.

Introduction

A STOPPING POINT ALONG THE VAST STRETCH of shore between the Atlantic coast city of Bluefields and the Costa Rican border, Monkey Point is the easternmost rocky outcropping of land. Offshore cays with names like Frenchman, Three Sisters, and Silk Grass hug the shoreline, which is fringed with coconut groves. Just south of the community, the coast recedes inland to create a natural harbor protected from northerly winds and high seas. Small homesteads are situated along sandy beach inlets or on high bluffs overlooking the sea. The views from the bluffs are spectacular, the ocean breezes salubrious, and the surrounding hillsides verdant. One can imagine that Monkey Point offered an appealing haven to West Indian migrants who established the community in the nineteenth century. Just a generation or two removed from slavery, these migrants came to work in the bustling enclave economy that grew with the intensification of foreign capital in the region. But rather than depending exclusively on wage labor—a master of another sort—for their livelihoods, they settled lands in peripheral regions of the coast where they could fish, farm, and enjoy a rural lifestyle free from the conditions of racial servitude that structured the postemancipation Caribbean.

The freedom their Creole descendants found in Monkey Point was an attenuated one. Periodic upheaval and rapid change interrupted long stretches of rural quiescence and relative autonomy. Nicaragua's military annexation of the Mosquitia in 1894 followed by the construction of the Monkey Point–San Miguelito Railroad in 1904 brought foreign capital, white engineers and administrators, and black laborers to the community. When the railway project collapsed in 1909, community people went on with their lives surrounded by the detritus of a failed capitalist venture. Half a century later in 1963, they were introduced to Cold War militarism when the Somoza regime allowed an anti-Castro Cuban exile group to construct a commando training camp on their land after the failed invasion at the Bay of Pigs. The Cubans put up barbed wire around their encampment and knocked down the big Ibo trees in the back to build an airport. After the camp disbanded, the concrete landing strip grew a thick layer of grass, the commando barracks rotted away, and local families again resumed their lives amid the spent shell casings.

Monkey Point people stayed on the land, organizing community life around the subsistence economy, vernacular cultural practices, and intermittent labor migration until the outbreak of the Contra War in the early 1980s. As the conflict deepened, they joined the contras to fight the Sandinista state or fled north to Bluefields and south to Costa Rica. After the war, the Sandinistas established a new autonomy regime for the Atlantic coast, and community people began to return and mobilize for rights to territory and self-governance, drawing on their new status as multicultural citizens of the Nicaraguan nation. In the late 1990s and early 2000s, community leaders allied with their indigenous Rama neighbors and built a social movement for autonomous rights with the support of nongovernmental organizations (NGOs) and human rights advocates. In 2009, more than a decade of activism paid off when these communities secured title to a large swath of coastal lands, now officially recognized as the Rama-Kriol Territory.

As the process of recognition unfolded, the state remilitarized the region under the auspices of the hemispheric drug war and developed plans for an interoceanic dry canal or high-speed railway that would dispossess local people of their land. The homicide rate doubled after militarization, and the region became the most violent in the country (Policía Nacional de Nicaragua 2010). The Nicaraguan army established an outpost in Monkey Point to police the drug trade, and community people found themselves under military occupation for the third time in half a century. Already subject to color and class discrimination and living along an active coastal trafficking route, they became prime targets for counternarcotics policing and were depicted in the press and public discourse as racialized criminal threats.

Like elsewhere in Latin America, drug war militarization did not promote security. Mestizo soldiers stationed in the community used excessive force on local men and sexually harassed and assaulted local women and girls.

Meanwhile, communal land tenure grew increasingly insecure as mestizo colonists settled the territory and the state moved forward with plans for an interoceanic canal. Local people understood these processes to be interconnected: Drug war militarization secured capitalist intensification, while occupying forces permitted mestizos to colonize the territory. When community people rallied to confront this state of siege, women and men mobilized in distinct ways but both embraced a politics of black autonomy.

Black Autonomy tells the story of this gendered activism and its social and experiential roots by following a community-based movement for autonomous rights from its inception in the late 1990s to its realization as a self-governing territory in 2009 and beyond. Broadly speaking, this book examines what happens to multicultural activism under conditions of prolonged violence. Postconflict Central American nations are some of the most violent democracies on Earth with homicide rates that top the global charts (United Nations Office on Drugs and Crime 2013). Nicaragua has largely escaped this regional trend. The country has one of the lowest levels of violence and the most expansive multicultural rights regime in Central America. Yet these positive indicators belie the violence of everyday life for working-class Creoles and the failure of multicultural reforms to ensure the most basic forms of livelihood and security.

These conditions have led community activists to adopt a position of black autonomy based on race pride, territoriality, self-determination, and self-defense. For women and men grappling with systemic racism and postwar violence, black autonomy has its own gendered meanings as a way of crafting selfhood and solidarity. I theorize black autonomy as an expression of African diasporic identification and gendered political consciousness that cuts across the domains of sociality, livelihood, security, territory, and sexuality. The pages that follow describe the gendered strategies that women and men use to assert autonomy over their bodies, labor, and spaces and the forms of violent entrapment that they encounter along the way. Departing from traditional feminist ethnography, this book documents how racism and patriarchy interpenetrate the lives of both women and men and shape state-led processes such as multicultural governance, capitalist intensification, militarization, and policing. By interlacing analysis of gendered practices like storytelling, musical production, homosociality, and mutual aid with accounts of everyday and organized acts of political resistance, I show how black vernacular culture becomes a site for the production of oppositional consciousness and the basis for autonomous rights activism.

The argument I present is threefold. The first part of my argument concerns the social and experiential organization of politics. My ethnography reveals a porous boundary between everyday and organized politics, demonstrating how vernacular practices and subjective experiences drive collective challenges to the state and capital. For instance, sociality and shared labor are not simply survival strategies or sources of intimacy and pleasure; they promote political solidarity and activism among women. Everyday expressions of patriarchal privilege and masculine authority similarly shape men's mobilization for autonomous rights. Conversely, state and capitalist power are lived phenomena with subjective and relational effects. The coercive state is experienced in the dampness and despair of an overcrowded jail cell. Capitalist intensification is felt in the reorganization of intimate attachments between husband and wife or neighborhood friends. And patriarchal state power produces fear and familial strife, limiting women's and men's ability to institutionally confront sexual violence.

Second, when we take the social expression of power and the social origins of oppositional politics as starting points for understanding political action, we must centrally grapple with embodied social difference. Racism and patriarchy have deadly consequences for community people, yet women and men have distinct experiences of racial violence that are conditioned by their sexually differentiated bodies and gendered subject positions (Aretxaga 2001; Goett 2015). They also respond to violence and subordination in different ways, drawing on gendered practices to fashion complex racial selves and assert autonomy over their lives and social domains. Feminist anthropologists have cautioned that subaltern agency is not always liberatory and that resistance does not necessarily signal the ineffectiveness of power (Abu-Lughod 1990; Mahmood 2001). Similarly, I find that women and men are caught up in extraordinarily complex interpersonal and political dynamics that are textured by multiple forms of racial and gendered violence. Individual efforts to negotiate these dynamics vary widely and are not always emancipatory in nature.

Lastly, I argue that feminist activist ethnography attuned to socially differentiated politics can (in the best of circumstances) support political praxis in coalitional rights movements. Violence continues to plague Afrodescendant communities in Latin America even after they have gained multicultural recognition (Cárdenas 2012; Goett 2011, 2015; Loperena 2012). This case makes it clear that although rights to land and natural resources are a crucial step in the struggle for justice and equality, they do not resolve complex patterns of state, structural, and interpersonal violence. Situated experiences of violence and state power matter intensely to struggles for social justice today, but subaltern politics often remain fragmented in postwar Central America. Tracking the conditions that support and undermine collective resistance in the face of prolonged everyday violence provides critical political knowledge that can help build a more expansive politics of liberation.

Scholarship on ethnic autonomy in Latin America has focused on the political evolution and institutional design of autonomous regimes that devolve state power and accord special cultural and political rights to indigenous and Afrodescendant communities (see Van Cott 2001). Nicaragua represents one of the earliest and most expansive cases with the development of regional autonomy for the Atlantic coast during the Sandinista Revolution in the 1980s (Díaz Polanco and López y Rivas 1986; González 1997). Later scholarship has emphasized the limits of formal multicultural recognition, whether it be the compromised conditions of autonomous politics (Hale 2011), the failure to effect structural change (Hale 2002; Postero 2007), or the particular challenges that Afrodescendants face in rights regimes based on normative constructions of indigeneity (Anderson 2009; Hooker 2005b).

A few questions emerge from this body of work. Given the widely recognized shortcomings of territorial recognition in the neoliberal context, why does it continue to matter so much to movements for autonomy (Richards and Gardner 2013)? How can indigenous and Afrodescendant peoples move beyond the more limiting aspects of recognition to realize deeper aspirations for autonomy, breaking bonds of dependency on the state and capital altogether (Hale 2011)? And finally, to what degree is this kind of radical autonomy really possible, given how neoliberal states and economies depend on autonomous and flexible organization and participation (Böhm, Dinerstein, and Spicer 2010)?

This book grows out of these debates, even as it moves beyond to focus on the shared values and practices of daily life that support autonomous social and political forms. I am particularly concerned with how these values and practices persist over time despite the violent and disabling forces that besiege communities like Monkey Point in postwar Nicaragua. I start from the premise that autonomy, as a real and vital social practice, is far more expansive and robust than highly compromised multicultural autonomy regimes might indicate. Indeed, much of the radical potential behind autonomous politics stems from intimate spheres of social life, which remain peripheral in most studies of social movements. These values and practices drive oppositional politics in Monkey Point, taking shape in community-based mobilization against the state and capitalist interests. The obstacles to a more expansive politics of liberation are similarly evidenced by the violence of everyday life, which can at times hinder solidarities within the community and beyond.

Neoliberal Rights Activism

For the last three decades, the political fortunes of Nicaragua have tacked back and forth between the right and left with U.S. intervention often playing a decisive role. The country has transitioned from forty-two years of Somoza family dictatorship (1937–1979) to a leftist popular revolution led by the Sandinista National Liberation Front (FSLN, Frente Sandinista de Liberación Nacional) (1979–1990) to neoliberal democracy (1990–2007) to the return of the postrevolutionary Sandinista Party to power (2007–). After the Sandinista Revolution upended Somoza family rule in 1979, an illegal U.S. campaign of destabilization and a costly war with CIA-backed contra insurgents threw the country back into political turmoil. War weary and suffering from deep economic crisis, the Nicaraguan electorate brought a center-right coalition to power in 1990, beginning the country's transition from revolutionary socialism to neoliberal democracy.

I first traveled to Nicaragua in 1998 just eight years after the Sandinista electoral defeat. These years of center-right rule had chipped away at the socialist legacy with a "slow motion counterrevolution" that sought to "tie internal social order to transnational order" through neoliberal governance and economic policy (Robinson 2003: 75). Under the stewardship of the United States Agency for International Development (USAID) and the International Monetary Fund (IMF), the postrevolutionary state dutifully enacted neoliberal reforms (Spalding 2011: 219). Multilateral development banks had unprecedented influence over national policy making, and NGOs replaced popular revolutionary organizations as the primary vehicles for political participation.

When I lived and worked on the Atlantic coast between 2001 and 2004, the World Bank promoted expansive multicultural reforms, and international NGOs and European development agencies bankrolled civil society activism

Figure I.1 A multicultural banner sponsored by two World Bank programs in the Beholden neighborhood of Bluefields. The word *ethnic* refers to Afrodescendants.
SOURCE: Jennifer Goett, 2003.

for multicultural rights (see Figure I.1). Weeks after my arrival in August 2001, the indigenous Mayangna community of Awas Tingni won a precedent-setting case against the Republic of Nicaragua in the Inter-American Court of Human Rights. The Court ruled that the state had violated the community's right to property and mandated the demarcation and titling of their lands along with the claims of other Atlantic coast indigenous communities (Corte Interamericana de Derechos Humanos 2001). Afrodescendants were not included in the ruling, but the Court's decision applied to Creole and Garifuna communities, as they enjoy full multicultural rights to land and natural resources under Nicaraguan law.[1]

Just months after the decision, Enrique Bolaños won the presidency on an electoral platform that emphasized democratic reform and rule of law. In contrast to his notoriously corrupt predecessor Arnoldo Alemán, Bolaños made compliance with international law a new priority and sought to reconcile state policy on multicultural rights with reforms outlined by the Inter-American Court and World Bank. Less than a year into his presidency, the National Assembly approved Law 445, which provides the legal framework for the demarcation and titling of indigenous and Afrodescendant territories.[2] The law reflects years of negotiations between the Nicaraguan state and Atlantic coast communities that were largely funded by the World Bank. The final version of the law is expansive, granting indigenous and Afrodescendant communities the right to possess and govern communal lands under the authority of democratically elected territorial governments (Goett 2011: 364–365).

Organized civil society was a vibrant political space during these years, and I worked with communities, local and international NGOs, and regional universities to advance territorial demarcation and autonomous rights. I traveled up north to help carry out the participatory mapping of Awas Tingni's territory in 2002 and 2003. In the south, I collaborated with regional universities to develop the organizational capacities of indigenous and Afrodescendant communities in the Pearl Lagoon basin and the Rama-Kriol Territory. Most of my work was in Bluefields, where I joined lawyers from the Center for Legal Assistance to Indigenous Peoples (CALPI, Centro de Asistencia Legal a Pueblos Indígenas) and International Human Rights Law Group to provide support to Rama and Creole communities as they mobilized for territorial rights. I went to countless meetings and workshops on multicultural rights and did the mundane work of political organizing with community leaders and their NGO allies.

This was a period of intense mobilization that transformed ethnic politics on the coast as indigenous and Afrodescendant territorial governments became established institutional entities and international advocates lent increased legitimacy to multicultural rights. In a moment of pessimism years later, I asked an activist named Harley Clair from Monkey Point if Law 445 really changed anything for community people. This was in 2011—almost a decade after the law went into effect. The community had received its territorial title but was under military occupation and experiencing ongoing land incursions by mestizo settlers, and leaders were attempting to hold the Nicaraguan military accountable for the sexual abuse of local girls. The force of his response surprised me. "Yes girl," he insisted, "it have impact. Maybe the impact mightn't be big. But then you have more international coming to look on the community more serious, the territorial government more serious. And then the same government people them, them fighting hard for not to respect it, but openly they have to respect." From his point of view, multicultural reforms and civil society organizing had resulted in new political legitimacy and power vis-à-vis the mestizo state.

Still, my memories of these years are tinged with ambivalence. As I immersed myself in the daily work of multicultural rights activism, I found that institutional rationales often overshadowed community perspectives and needs, limiting the degree to which deeper forms of autonomous social action might take root in neoliberal civil society. A good deal (but not all) of this work was dominated by discrete project-driven agendas, obligations to international funders, bureaucratic procedures, the veneration of professional expertise, and the neoliberal ethics of citizen participation, rather than real citizen power. The most effective NGO advocates like CALPI and IBIS (a Danish organization for development cooperation) provided tangible services in the form of legal representation or logistical and technical assistance with the territorial demarcation request the community submitted to the government. But long-term support of this kind was the exception rather than the rule. Monkey Point activists often reminded me that NGO allies come and go, and it is best not to depend too deeply on their support. Even more telling was an intractable reality: Civil society organizing, statutory reform, multicultural recognition, and territorial demarcation did not seem to curb the violence of everyday life or the daily burden of structural inequality for most community people (also see Hale 2002, 2005; Postero 2007).

Outside of the institutional environment, I spent my time traveling to Monkey Point and socializing with the many families who maintain primary residences in Bluefields. As I developed relationships with community people, I became aware of the inner realms of sociality and conviviality that shape autonomous aspirations and activism. In these spaces of everyday intimacy, black cultural practices and vernacular ways of being in the world are powerful sources of oppositional agency. By the vernacular, I mean everyday ways of doing things, things that work well and make sense in their own context, cultural practices that encode valuable local knowledge about relationships, subsistence, and right ways of living that are not dictated by institutional, capitalist, or state-centric prescripts (Scott 2012). Ivan Illich used the term *vernacular* to denote "autonomous, non-market related actions through which people satisfy everyday needs—the actions that by their own true nature escape bureaucratic control, satisfying needs to which, in the very process, they give specific shape" (1981: 57–58). The vernacular includes "modes of being, doing, and making" like everyday subsistence practices, household activities, patterns of reciprocity, food preparation, linguistic conventions, sociality, pleasure, and play (Ibid.: 58–59). Hardt refers to these activities as "biopower from below" that produces intimate relationships, collective subjectivity, and community (1999: 89).

A focus on biopower from below might seem to eschew transnational modes of identification, but vernacular cultural practice grounds community people's everyday sense of themselves as black, diasporic, and autochthonous. Focusing on the African diaspora in Central America, Edmund Gordon and Mark Anderson argue for more ethnographic attention to actual processes of diasporic identification within communities, underscoring the importance of racial formation and cultural practice "in the making and remaking of diaspora" (1999: 284). Monkey Point people actively identify with distinctively black diasporic historical experiences. Social memories of slavery and racial servitude shape the stories they tell about migration from the Caribbean and resettlement in Central America. They brought with them vernacular cultural practices such as culinary and linguistic traditions, spiritual orientations, medicinal knowledge, and farming customs, which they then adapted to the local environment and economy. They formed close ties with indigenous people in the region as they underwent a process of becoming both Creole and autochthonous Mosquitians in the nineteenth century.

Community people continue to identify with other black people in the Caribbean today, consume West Indian *soca*, reggae, and dancehall, and embrace black diasporic modes of dress and stylistic self-presentation. They draw political inspiration from diasporic figures such as Malcolm X and Bob Marley. Moreover, they understand their own experiences of violence and political struggle to be connected to wider demands for racial justice in the African diaspora. Monkey Point people take pleasure and pride in black diasporic identity and vernacular cultural practice, the reproduction of which manifests as a self-conscious practice of freedom in the face of racism, structural inequality, and annihilating violence. Although tangential to NGO advocacy, these practices and related values are animating forces in community activism.

Over time, I also became acutely aware of how systemic inequality and violence curtail opportunity and cut short lives. By the end of the 1980s, the Nicaraguan economy was in shambles. The final years of the Sandinista Revolution were marred by armed conflict, a U.S. trade embargo, diminished social spending, massive external debt, hyperinflation, unemployment, and a hurricane that destroyed 80 percent of the structures in Bluefields (Arana 1997: 82–83; Stahler-Sholk 1990). After the transition to neoliberal democracy, the country's economic outlook remained grim. IMF-mandated austerity, privatization of state-run enterprises, and trade liberalization in the 1990s resulted in further cuts to social spending, rising unemployment, and the loss of national markets for rural producers. Poor Nicaraguans bore the brunt of neoliberal economic policies, which resulted in class restructuring and immiseration (Robinson 1997: 35–36). Despite steady economic growth after the initial years of structural adjustment, market-oriented reforms failed to resolve entrenched inequality, and poverty rates remained stagnant in the 1990s and 2000s (Spalding 2011: 220–221).

For Monkey Point people, armed conflict and postwar drug violence compounded these economic processes, accelerating land loss and cash dependency as families left their farms and joined a superexploited surplus labor force in Bluefields. From the 1990s onward, out-migration to work in the global service sector became one of the few viable earning strategies for cash-poor families struggling to get by in Bluefields. Prolonged violence, displacement, land loss, natural disaster, unemployment, scarcity, and institutional racism and sexism place a taxing emotional and physical burden on families, providing the material basis for substance abuse, ill health and early death, interpersonal and drug-related violence, and frequent conflicts with the police, military, and mestizo justice system (Farmer 2004). These diverse expressions of violence form webs of association and collusion, resulting in a "continuum of violence" with systemic roots and effects that exact a toll on community life (Scheper-Hughes and Bourgois 2004). In the absence of security, employment, and social services, local people grappled with postwar violence the best ways they knew how, relying on expansive social networks for support and turning to autonomous activism as an outlet for redress.

The Sandinista Revival

The neoliberal agenda that dominated politics when I lived in Nicaragua was interrupted with the return of the Sandinista Party to power in 2007, as the country joined the ranks of Venezuela, Ecuador, Bolivia, Argentina, and Brazil in Latin America's turn to the left (Goodale and Postero 2013). The left turn has resulted in a hybrid and confounding political condition in leftist countries that espouse a renewed commitment to social equality and the poor but show autocratic tendencies and embrace global capitalism as a path to national development. After I moved back to the United States in 2004, I returned to the coast almost annually for two or three months at a time between 2006 and 2013 and was able to witness Nicaragua's left turn.

On the eve of the Sandinista return to power, community activists and their allies expressed a guarded optimism that the new government would effect positive change. The Atlantic coast indigenous political party YATAMA (Yapti Tasba Masraka Nanih Aslatakanka, or Sons of Mother Earth), led by former contra commander Brooklyn Rivera, formed an alliance with the FSLN before the elections. Rivera's agreement with his onetime rival Daniel Ortega was based on the promise of land demarcation and titling, a process left unfilled by the Bolaños administration. Although Bolaños moved forward with the titling of five indigenous territories in the Bosawás Biosphere Reserve, his administration resisted granting indigenous and Afrodescendant communities full domain over their lands and natural resources, instead advocating for a truncated version of "co-ownership" and "co-management" with the state (González 2012: 436).

Not only did Ortega grant full ownership to communities, he made good on his promise to YATAMA by titling large swaths of contiguous territory to indigenous and Afrodescendant communities. The communities in the Rama-Kriol Territory began to document their claim in 2005 before Ortega's election with funding from the Danish Embassy and logistical and technical support from IBIS, one of Denmark's largest international development organizations (Jensen and Kjaerby 2010). As a result of these efforts, they were the second territory to be titled by the Sandinistas in the South Caribbean Coast Autonomous Region (RACCS, Región Autónoma de la Costa Caribe Sur) in December 2009. The Sandinista state demarcated most of the Atlantic coast by 2013, granting titles to twenty-one indigenous and Afrodescendant territories that encompassed 36,440 square kilometers or 28.14 percent of national territory, an area roughly the size of Portugal (Comisión Nacional de Demarcación y Titulación 2013). Only the Bluefields territory—the largest urban center on the Atlantic coast and home to the greatest concentration of Creole people in Nicaragua—remains untitled.

If the neoliberal period saw the expanding influence of transnational non-state entities in the areas of development, service provision, and citizen participation, Ortega has worked to reassert centralized state power. Rather than approaching NGOs "as mechanisms to promote democratic development," the Sandinista state has viewed them as potential "rivals" (Spalding 2011: 236). The effort to consolidate centralized state power has been aided by the Latin American turn to the left and a resulting realignment of political alliances in the region. For instance, between 2002 and 2011, development aid from the United States and Europe decreased from US$144.9 million to US$71.9 million. Still, the Nicaraguan economy continued to grow due to an influx of Venezuelan capital (Martí i Puig 2013: 270). Venezuelan aid has supported a range of redistribution programs that aim to reduce hunger, poverty, illiteracy, and infant mortality. The programs are administrated through Citizen Power Councils (CPCs, Consejos del Poder Ciudadano), which maintain a presence in communities throughout the country (Ibid.: 271). The CPCs represent a model of direct democracy based on citizen participation, which the FSLN refers to as *"el pueblo presidente"* or the presidency of the people (Perla and Cruz-Feliciano 2013: 87).

But critics suggest that state policies connecting redistributive benefits to participation in party-based organizations have resulted in clientelism and the politicization of social service provision (Martí i Puig 2013: 271; Spalding 2011: 232). Neumann argues that the antipoverty programs, which depend on the active and primary participation of women, increase women's gendered burden of labor while advancing a neoliberal logic that holds impoverished citizens responsible for their own development needs (2013: 814). And despite Ortega's populism and rhetorical critique of neoliberalism and Western imperialism, the Sandinista state continues to adhere to IMF oversight and the Central American Free Trade Agreement (CAFTA) and maintains an alliance with the powerful Sandinista business class that emerged in the 1990s (Martí i Puig 2013: 272; Perla and Cruz-Feliciano 2013: 97; Spalding 2011: 235).

Three and a half decades after the triumph of the revolution, some political analysts now suggest that the Sandinista state is a "hybrid regime," democratic and socialist in name but based in practice on soft authoritarianism and capitalism (Martí i Puig 2013). This authoritarian bent became evident after Ortega's reelection as he moved to consolidate "all sources of public power and coopt the private" to establish one party rule throughout the nation (Ibid.: 274). The consolidation of power has allowed Ortega to remove presidential term limits and rewrite Nicaragua's constitution with little political debate. The harshest critics of the Sandinista state—among them revolutionary figures from the 1970s and 1980s—assert that the FSLN has betrayed the revolution and become a corrupt and autocratic party based on a cult of Orteguismo (Belli 2002; Burbach 2009; Puente Sur 2012; Ramírez 2012).

For indigenous and Afrodescendant people from the Atlantic coast, territorial recognition and nine years of Sandinista rule have transformed multicultural politics. After the revolution, organized civil society in Bluefields was a space of political opposition to the state. The center-right administrations of Violeta Chamorro (1990–1997) and Arnoldo Alemán (1997–2002) were hostile to multicultural rights and treated the Atlantic coast as little more than a vehicle for national development. Enrique Bolaños (2002–2007) was the first neoliberal president to show deference to multicultural rights and international law, but his administration was reluctant to cede territorial control to Atlantic coast communities. Left-leaning mestizo and Creole professionals who were sympathetic to the revolution and fatigued with the abuses of the neoliberal right staffed most civil society organizations in Bluefields. Once the Sandinistas returned to power, oppositional stances to the state from these same actors were less overt and more ambivalent, in part because the Sandinistas were more committed to multiculturalism and rhetorically embraced egalitarian development models.

As Ortega's power grew and international funding became scarce after the 2007–2008 global recession, vocal opposition to the state became increasingly imprudent for many Bluefields professionals, as it could now result in political recrimination or the loss of a job. At the same time, the FSLN skillfully incorporated would-be detractors into state and party structures. Bluefields NGO professionals whom I worked with to defend multicultural rights and protest the interoceanic dry canal under the neoliberal right now work for the state and support the Sandinista-backed proposal for an interoceanic wet canal. Thus, when Monkey Point leaders denounced mestizo soldiers for the sexual abuse of local girls in 2010, they found few vocal advocates in Bluefields civil society and instead turned to Pacific-side organizations such as CALPI and the Nicaraguan Center for Human Rights (CENIDH, Centro Nicaragüense de Derechos Humanos) for support.

These shifts have occurred as territorial governance established under Law 445 solidified and grew in scope. The Rama-Kriol Territorial Government (GTR-K, Gobierno Territorial Rama-Kriol) is now the primary institutional space in which community people advocate for their interests in civil society. The GTR-K now receives its operating budget from the Sandinista state, which controls how the money is allocated, thus limiting administrative autonomy. The state has also improved service provision to Monkey Point and launched a fishing *acopio* (cooperative) that supplies pangas (skiffs with outboard motors) and ice to local fishermen. The growing power of the territorial government, expanded services, and development support bring some welcome changes. But the beneficent face of the state does little to assuage militarization, capitalist intensification, and human rights violations.

In recent years, the most vocal opposition to the Sandinista state has focused on the Interoceanic Grand Canal, a massive US$50 billion infrastructure project led by the Chinese-owned Hong Kong Nicaragua Canal Development Group (HKND Group). The National Assembly approved Law 840 in 2013, granting HKND rights to construct and operate an interoceanic waterway three times the length of the Panama Canal (HKND Group 2014: 4–7). This project is far more ambitious and controversial than previous dry canal proposals.[3] The law additionally authorizes the construction of subprojects such as vacation resorts, a free trade zone, an international airport, and a petroleum pipeline, which would transform the nation into a commercial hub for China (República de Nicaragua 2013: 4974).

Passed by the Sandinista majority in the National Assembly with little debate and no modifications, Law 840 grants HKND a concession to operate the canal for fifty years with the option to renew for an additional fifty years. The law privatizes the enterprise by allowing the state a one percent share that will increase just 10 percent with each decade of operation. The generous terms were established before finalizing the canal route and subproject locations, opening the country to Chinese capital with little regard for communities and the environment (López Baltodano 2014). Critics of the project say construction will displace tens of thousands of people and result in exploitative labor conditions, erosion of national sovereignty, environmental degradation, and the contamination of the country's largest drinking water reserve, Lake Nicaragua (Acevedo 2013, 2014; Gross 2014; Meyer and Huete-Pérez 2014; Salinas Maldonado and Olivares 2015). These impacts are potentially devastating for an impoverished and increasingly militarized population with significant vulnerability to climate change.

As the project advances, the state has used repression to stem dissent from communities along the projected route.[4] Since the government disclosed the canal route in 2014, a significant dissident block has formed that includes mestizo *campesino* communities, indigenous and Afrodescendant territories, environmentalists, human rights advocates, and influential public figures in Nicaragua. The state responded to anticanal protests in December 2014 with violence, beating demonstrators in the streets and imprisoning protest leaders without charge. Although people in the Rama-Kriol Territory have avoided direct confrontation with the state, community leaders have submitted complaints to the Inter-American Commission on Human Rights (IACHR), charging that the government has failed to follow national and international laws requiring free, prior, and informed consent for development projects in their territory.

The last nine years of Ortega's presidency have seen the evolution of a populist leftist project in Nicaragua that embraces socialist rhetoric and alternative political alliances to the neoliberal right but uses similar methods of promoting capitalist intensification and governing ethnic territories. Like neoliberal predecessors, the Sandinista state has courted transnational capital in a bid to develop a global transport sector to free the country from endemic poverty. Since taking office in 2007, Ortega has become a skillful autocrat, shoring up absolute power and securing capital with military might. The 2014 Constitutional Reforms attest to his efforts, as they give the presidency direct control over the armed forces, expand the role of the military in economic and civilian affairs, and allow for the use of soldiers in civilian policing (República de Nicaragua 2014).

For Monkey Point people, their experience of militarization has remained largely unchanged in the shift from the neoliberal right to the Sandinista left. The Bolaños administration established a military post in Monkey Point and militarized the south coast to police the drug trade in 2004 and 2005. Militarization in the region only intensified after Ortega took office in 2007. Early on, local people assumed the military occupation was tied to government-backed canal proposals, thus linking drug war militarism to the securitization of capital in the region. Dawn Paley calls this phenomenon "drug war capitalism" to emphasize the relationship between drug war militarism in Latin America and "the expansion of the capitalist system into new or previously inaccessible territories and social spaces" (2014: 15). In the vast ungoverned south Atlantic coast, mestizo soldiers from the Pacific now militarily secure capital and police the surplus labor force that maintains a claim to the land at Monkey Point.

Writing about Central America, Charles Hale observes that neoliberal states have given up claims to "national-territorial encompassment" and embraced new forms of "spatially differentiated rule," which include "nodes of dynamism that require active political-economic presence" as well as "large spaces that are rendered essentially redundant." The shift has occurred as economies become less dependent on agriculture and more focused on services, tourism, manufacturing, and remittances (2011: 194). So-called empty or ungoverned spaces coincide with indigenous and Afrodescendant regions where neoliberal states have shown some willingness to issue collective titles and devolve authority to local administration, as demonstrated by the well-documented trend toward territorial recognition in Latin America (Bryan 2012; Offen 2003). Hale views such developments as potentially disabling as they may focus political action on ethnically specific local affairs, promote the co-optation of community leaders in quasi-government roles, and limit participation in wider struggles for political and economic justice (2011: 195).

Some of these effects are evident in newly titled indigenous and Afrodescendant territories in Nicaragua. Yet countervailing processes are also at work. Postwar securitization has led some Central American states to militarize ungoverned spaces under the auspices of the U.S.-funded drug war. In the Rama-Kriol Territory, militarization undermines the devolution of authority, reasserts national-territorial encompassment, and provides the coercive force necessary to secure transnational capital. The trend is evident throughout Central America, where infrastructure development, hydroelectric projects, agribusiness, and extractive industries such as mining target indigenous and Afrodescendant regions for exploitation (see Finley-Brook and Thomas 2011; Imai, Mehranvar, and Sander 2007; Kerssen 2013).

Rather than viewing indigenous and Afrodescendant territories as peripheral and economically redundant spaces, I argue that the enclosure and release of these lands "into the privatized mainstream of capital accumulation" (Harvey 2003: 149) are violent processes that are hotly contested and well underway. For instance, if built, the Interoceanic Grand Canal would represent the largest land and water grab in Nicaraguan history. More creeping forms of dispossession, resulting from mestizo colonization and deforestation, signal how valuable indigenous and Afrodescendant lands and natural resources are to the lucrative shadow economies that support illegal logging and land trafficking. Given the violence that militarization and dispossession pose, territorial autonomy may turn out to be a crucial, albeit flawed, strategic asset for indigenous and Afrodescendant communities as they mobilize to confront this state of siege.

Feminist Activist Anthropology

My activist research has been set within the complex and evolving political environment that I describe here. I first traveled to Nicaragua to conduct predissertation research, having been trained in an activist anthropology graduate program in the United States. Although my colleagues would go on to do activist research that embraced a range of approaches, the predominant method the program advanced involved allying with an organized group engaged in political struggle and collaborating with this group in all stages of the research from formulation of the topic to data collection, sharing of initial written drafts, and revision and dissemination of the final product (Hale 2006: 97). This approach promised to yield empirically rich data and theoretically innovative analysis alive to the complexity of oppressive systems and subaltern political consciousness and agency (Ibid.: 98, 108). A central assertion here is that activist research methods produce better scholarship (Goldstein 2012: 35–36), in large part because activism reveals the "compromised conditions of the political process" (Hale 2006: 98). Activist scholarship is thus alive to contradictions that show how movements for social justice can become entangled in the same oppressive systems they challenge (Ibid.).

I have not always followed this model during my years of engagement with indigenous and Afrodescendant social movements in Nicaragua. If there is one organized group that I have consistently allied with over time it is the Monkey Point communal government, although I have worked with leaders from other territories as well as NGOs and regional universities. Many of my research goals have emerged from dialogue and collaboration with local activists, but I have pursued other goals because I found them to be urgent and relevant to the broader theme of autonomous rights and activism. For instance, as a feminist scholar, much of my research on gender and sexuality is of minimal interest to male leaders who are primarily concerned with cultural and race-based rights to territory and self-determination. Doing feminist activist research with groups that may not have woman-centered politics does not always lend itself to a seamless alignment of research goals. Similarly, many of the NGO advocates with whom I have collaborated over the years have not considered racialized policing or counternarcotics militarization to be a central problem for Afrodescendant communities in their struggle to secure territorial rights, despite the fact that I have found them to be violently destabilizing forces. Still, the broader political goals that drive my activist scholarship are shared goals born of long-term engagement and collaboration with indigenous and Afrodescendant communities. They include greater control over land and natural resources, greater ability to engage in consensus-based self-determination, and less violence of all kinds. And, finally, although I have sought feedback on my work from many local allies, not all of my scholarship has been vetted locally. Not everyone I have worked with has had the desire or ability to engage with my scholarship.

I entered into the work as a graduate student with a certain degree of youthful idealism and a sense of optimism that I could help create a more just and egalitarian world through activist research. Although my political commitments remain the same fifteen years later, my estimation of the impact of my activist scholarship is more circumspect. The struggle for social justice is an always-unfinished process that can produce the sensation of swimming against a stiff current for years on end. Monkey Point activists have seen their efforts rewarded with significant victories such as territorial demarcation even as violence and precarity continue to condition social life and the threat of total dispossession looms on the horizon. I have had the privilege to work alongside these committed individuals and have tried to make some tangible contributions that matter to them, but the compromised conditions of struggle are obvious. My own limitations have similarly quieted my youthful optimism and any overblown sense of personal agency that activist research might imply.

Over the years, I have produced scholarship and maps for use as evidentiary support in applications for territorial demarcation submitted to the Nicaraguan state. But I have also written *diagnósticos* or research reports for internationally funded projects that are now gathering dust in the corner of an office somewhere. In my efforts to share my work locally, I have translated my research into Spanish and published it in Nicaragua so that Atlantic coast people can have access to it. Still, my employment in the academy requires that I publish the bulk of my work in scholarly venues for English-speaking academic audiences. I have raised money for community legal defense and shared my labor, friendship, and solidarity with community activists. At my home institution and elsewhere, I give talks that advocate for community rights and critique the violence that plagues the region, emphasizing the U.S. role in provoking these conditions. I frame all my courses around social justice concerns both at home and abroad. Even so, most of my energy is focused on fulfilling the institutional requirements of my academic position. And, at the end of the day, I am infinitely more indebted to my community allies in Nicaragua than they are to me.

I owe the intellectual vitality of my work to Monkey Point people because it is based on the richness of their experience and their willingness to collaborate with me. As I have noted, my early activism led to fatigue with NGO

advocacy and a deepening concern with autonomous social forms and practices that so closely approximate traditional anarchist principles, such as self-
organization, mutual aid, and direct democracy (Graeber 2004: 2). I learned
about these social forms and their grounding in black vernacular culture from
Monkey Point people over time; indeed, it took me years to fully grasp their
relevance to autonomous politics. Only prolonged engagement gave me the
ability to benefit from and contribute to the praxis of social struggle. Praxis
involves "reflection and action directed at the structures to be transformed"
with subaltern peoples necessarily playing a "fundamental role in the transformation process" (Freire 2000: 126). I draw on Brazilian theorist and ed-
ucator Paulo Freire's definition because community leaders often describe
their activism as a process of action, reflection, and learning over time—
self-directed pedagogy born of social struggle—and because the analytical
framing and theoretical insights of this book emerged from my role as witness
to and participant in the process.

There is a good deal of emerging scholarship that focuses on engaged and
activist anthropology, which together encapsulate a range of methodological
approaches and theoretical insights that seem to have a growing audience in
the discipline (Craven and Davis 2013; Goldstein 2012, 2014; Hale 2006, 2008;
Juris and Khasnabish 2013; Low and Merry 2010; Reiter and Oslender 2015;
Sanford and Angel-Ajani 2006). And although the promise of activist anthropology is tinged with contradictions and limitations, this literature testifies
to its role in producing nuanced scholarship on subaltern politics, inequality, and violence. Within this scholarship, I find feminist activist approaches
to ethnographic research of particular value (Bickham Mendez 2008; Craven
and Davis 2013; Hernández Castillo 2006; Perry 2015; Speed 2006).

Craven and Davis define feminist ethnography as "a project committed
to documenting lived experience as it is impacted by gender, race, class, sexuality, and other aspects of participants' lives." Feminist theories, method-
ologies, and interpretive strategies that foreground power differentials, they
argue, provide an ideal framework for activist scholarship and interventions
(Craven and Davis 2013: 1). Others suggest that activist engagement itself
leads to "richer gender analysis" or better feminist ethnography (Speed 2006:
171), suggesting a mutually beneficial relationship between activism and feminist scholarship. Feminist activist ethnography is characterized by methodological and thematic diversity, addressing topics as varied as reproductive
rights (Craven 2013; López 2013); women's health (Anglin 2013); domestic and

interpersonal violence (Davis 2006; Goett 2015; Weis 2013); globalization and women's labor activism (Bickham Mendez 2005, 2008); racial and gendered state violence (Goett 2011, 2015; Hernández Castillo 2006; Perry 2013; Smith 2015); and indigenous and black women's subjectivity and resistance (Caldwell 2007; Perry 2013, 2015; Speed 2006). Although this is not an exhaustive survey of the existent scholarship, feminist activist ethnography has largely focused on women's experiences, which then provide an entry point for the analysis of wider social relations and political and economic processes.

Drawing on the insights produced by this innovative body of scholarship, I argue that feminist theory and methods provide vital tools for activist anthropology in general. Although women's experiences are critical to activist projects, feminist approaches have even wider resonance for activist scholarship. The melding of feminist and activist approaches nuances theory and ethnography on the state, capitalism, violence, conflict, inequality, and social relations. The political processes that activist ethnography examines are *always* socially differentiated; they are grounded in multiple intersecting forms of socially constituted and embodied difference and inequality. For instance, capitalism works through much broader and more complex expressions of social inequality than class (Federici 2012; Robinson 2000), as do political systems (Aretxaga 1997; Brown 1992; Nagel 1998). Attention to subjective and thus socially differentiated experiences of state power is crucial for teasing out state effects and affects in any given context (Aretxaga 2003; Stoler 2007; Trouillot 2001). Similarly, militarism and securitization are grounded in lived social experience and embodied difference (Cockburn 2004; Enloe 2014; Goldstein 2010), which also condition the nature and form of violence (Aretxaga 2001; Farmer 2004). And finally, subaltern consciousness and agency emerge from these same structures of inequality and "embodied politics" or "the intersubjective level of being and acting" (Mahmood 2001: 224).

My point is not that feminist analysis single-handedly reveals the deeper workings of social and political formations or that all ethnographic research should necessarily employ feminist methods but that there is an intimate relationship between the analytical strengths of feminist ethnography and the central concerns of activist anthropology. Feminist approaches lend greater nuance and depth to an analysis of the contradictions and compromised conditions that activist research promises to illuminate (Hale 2006). They may even reveal contradictions that are not readily apparent to the activist researcher and his or her allies in struggles for social justice. In my research, feminist ethnography brought to light the complex interpersonal and political dynamics that texture violence and oppositional politics in Monkey Point. It also gave insight into the fragility of coalitional alliances formed between power-differentiated groups with distinct repertoires of resistance and histories of struggle. And finally, when paired with long-term engagement, I have found that feminist activist ethnography can contribute to praxis or the process of reflection, reorientation, and recommitment that emerges from political struggle over time.

The chapters that follow are based on four years of research conducted between 1998 and 2013. Reflecting a collaborative methodology, the ethnographic narrative emphasizes local voices and dialogue. I try as much as possible to convey the rich oral tradition that shapes Creole culture and storytelling practices. Community people tend to be outspoken and gregarious on most topics, and no one ever declined to talk with me or provide an in-depth interview. In most interviews, the stories they shared are dialogue heavy. Rather than simply relaying what happened in their own voice, community people often recreate dialogues they had with other protagonists in their stories. Dialogues make for better stories. They communicate a structure of feeling, inviting the listener to imagine that they too are witnessing the unfolding of events. For this reason, I avoid social science conventions that present interview material in lengthy block quotes (except in Chapter 1 where they are impossible to avoid) and instead write dialogue exchanges as they might appear in a work of fiction. All quoted material, however, reflects the actual words of the speaker.

Community people speak Miskito Coast Creole English (MCC), which developed as a unique language in the seventeenth century Mosquitia. MCC is derived from the syntax and lexicon of English and African languages with additional loan words from Miskitu and Spanish (Holm 1983: 95–97). It is distinct from Standard English, although Creoles speak MCC along a continuum with the arcolect form closest to Standard English and the basilect form more representative of deep Creole. When speaking with me, community people usually lean toward the arcolect, even though they preference the basilect in everyday speech. Most adults are also bilingual but only use Spanish when speaking to native Spanish speakers. MCC is primarily a spoken language without a popularized standard orthography. I thus transcribe spoken MCC into Standard English, which makes the language more accessible to Standard

English speakers but unfortunately glosses some of its linguistic difference. I retain MCC's unique syntax and vocabulary to the best of my ability.

I should further note that, in the stories that populate the pages of this book, community people's recollections of dialogue exchanges are obviously not the same as what was said: They may or may not reflect the true words and intentions of all protagonists in the story. Individuals sometimes mis-remember events, and there are undoubtedly omissions and silences in each telling. Unsurprisingly, most people construct sympathetic narratives of their own actions. They also seek to protect their dignity in moments of vulner-ability or victimization. Even when they are involved in fraught or unflat-tering situations, the dialogues they relay humanize and contextualize their predicament and omit the worst of human folly. In many respects, the stories community people told me are politicized self-representations that challenge racist discourses, which cast them as delinquent, criminal, violent, deceptive, self-interested (rather than communally oriented), and having no legitimate rights to territory. They also communicate the subjective and experiential bases for political action. What community people say and how they say it convey particular kinds of political consciousness and agency. Rather than compromising the accounts, the subjective nature of stories provides a win-dow into a vernacular worldview shaped by oppositional values that might not otherwise be accessible to readers. I do my best to faithfully communicate that oppositional worldview without sacrificing critical analysis of contradic-tory or accommodative thought and action or the compromised political con-ditions of community activism.

I also figure in the ethnographic dialogue. Usually, I am asking prompt-ing or clarifying questions. There are instances where my recollection of events and the narrator's differ, and I express surprise or skepticism. Occa-sionally, the dialogues help position me in the research. As a white woman from a middle-class background in the United States, I formed relationships with community people that were not based on shared identity or experi-ence but on friendship and political solidarity that developed over time. This process was not seamless or without tensions. References to my racial and class privilege sometimes emerge in the ethnographic narrative, revealing the unequal relationship between researcher and research subject (Craven and Davis 2013). This happens mostly in my interactions with women with whom I had the closest friendships, underscoring what Visweswaran sug-gests is a potential strength of feminist ethnography—insight into "women's relationships to other women, and the power differentials between them" (1994: 20).

Like Monkey Point people, I leave out some experiences, intimate revelations, and contested incidents from the ethnographic narrative and do my best to preserve individual's dignity and anonymity in the retelling of painful or violent events. Interview respondents desired different degrees of anonymity. Some asked me to use their full names so that they are recognizable in the historical record of their community. Others asked to be identified by first names only, nicknames, or middle names. Still others desired complete anonymity.

The organization of the book is broadly chronological, beginning with oral accounts of community history as context for collective mobilization in the late 1990s and early 2000s and ending with territorial recognition and resistance to military occupation in the early 2010s. Chapter 1, "Women's Origin Stories," examines the community's past via the oral histories of three women elders who led the first wave of land rights activism in the late 1990s. It shows how diasporic subjectivities rooted in social memories of slavery, migration, and race-class-gender oppression drive activism for autonomous rights as do the vernacular cultural practices that characterized community life before the war. In their telling, women's stories of the past represent a form of political pedagogy that encourages young people to embrace similar kinds of historical consciousness and participate in autonomous activism.

Chapter 2, "'Bad Boys' and Direct Resistance," focuses on young men's cultural practices and armed resistance to the speculation of community lands by outside venture capitalists in the early 2000s. Many of the men involved in these events are known as "bad boys," a countercultural identity that the men embrace and reproduce in their oppositional politics, personal style, and investments in black diasporic popular culture. For these men, Monkey Point is an autonomous space where they can go to recover from drug abuse and escape the hardships of life in Bluefields. Although they are not often recognized as protagonists in multicultural activism, the men's resistance to land speculation signaled a deepening radicalism in autonomous politics and a new strategy for confronting some of the worst abuses of the state.

Chapter 3, "Life on the Edge of the Global Economy," examines women's sociality as an autonomous sphere of self-valorization that is resistant to capitalist and patriarchal social relations and values. It shows how livelihood politics are enmeshed in dense networks of gendered sociality and intimacy, where reciprocity and shared affective labor between women are central to survival under conditions of capitalist intensification. Creole women's sociality makes it possible to live independently of men should they choose to do so and undermines a racial and gender division of labor that promotes wageless women's subordination to male wage earners. But women's sociality is not a simple adaption to oppression because it produces pleasure, self-respect, and solidarity and therefore has autonomous social logics. As an affirmative practice rooted in working-class Creole culture, it drives women's activism for autonomous rights.

Chapter 4, "From Cold Wars to Drug Wars," tracks shifting security paradigms by drawing on narratives from community men who fought as contras during the 1980s and are now the targets of counternarcotics policing. Their accounts give intimate insight into how drug war violence and policing are historical outgrowths of Cold War conflict and U.S. intervention in Central America. Wartime stories show that coercion and physical violence were unavoidable for most Monkey Point men, as their age, gender, race, and class overdetermined their roles as Sandinista soldiers, contra fighters, draft evaders, deserters, and refugees. But rather than bringing peace and security, refuge in Costa Rica and repatriation to Nicaragua in the late 1980s and early 1990s signaled the demise of one securitized masculine subject (enemy combatant) and the rise of another (drug trafficker), producing new forms of securitized social control for community men.

Chapter 5, "Sexual Violence and Autonomous Politics," shows how ordinary life in the community was saturated and interrupted by military occupation and state sexual violence in the late 2000s. Drawing on racialized and sexualized fantasy, the occupation targeted local women and girls as objects of sexual domination, cast local men as masculine subordinates and racialized security threats, and promoted heteropatriarchal forms of mestizo territorial sovereignty. The soldier's abuse of girls initially followed preexisting patterns of gendered and sexual violence in the community before erupting into exceptional violence that provoked a public politics of opposition to the state. Diverse advocates for the girls struggled to fully decipher and politicize the racial, gendered, and sexual articulation of violence under military occupation, and state institutional power promoted impunity for mestizo state actors.

Finally, the epilogue reflects on more than a decade of community activism and assesses the political opportunities and potential entrapments that recognition offers as community people mobilize to confront systemic inequality and violence in their territory. I point to a reservoir of political knowledge and agency embedded in vernacular practice, gendered subjectivity, and black diasporic identification that challenges oppressive systems. I further suggest that territorial recognition holds the potential for both egalitarian change and deepening inequality: It can serve as a strategic asset that emboldens and radicalizes black autonomy and as a governance strategy that may facilitate the expansion of state and capitalist power. The tension between these two effects is likely to shape the contours of future struggle in the region.

1 Women's Origin Stories

ON A CLEAR DAY, ARRIVAL AT MONKEY POINT is a sublime experience. The intensity of the sun reflected on the seawater and the imposing physical beauty of the place mix with deep relief at having finally arrived. To reach the community, one must travel by boat on the open sea or, as in years past, walk for a day or two from Bluefields southward down the beach. Over the years, I have made many trips back and forth on wood or fiberglass pangas or on larger and much slower boats powered by inboard motors. Depending on the type of transport, the trip can take anywhere from one to ten hours, and in bad weather it can be a harrowing experience. My memories of that first year in Nicaragua are dominated by sea travel. There was no commercial transport to the community, and I quickly learned to tap into networks of community people in Bluefields to find out who was leaving for Monkey Point next. The result was that I rarely took the same source of transport more than once, I moved according to other people's schedules, and I never turned down a ride, not knowing when my next chance to travel would come.

Miss Pearl Marie Watson, then president of the communal government and the nurse in charge of the health clinic, accompanied me on my first trip to Monkey Point, just a few weeks after I arrived in Nicaragua to research Creole land rights. Many of the people who fill the pages of this book are her sisters, cousins, nieces, and nephews. As a point of clarification, after introducing me to a relative, she would say, "She's making an investigation about the history of the community." The understanding was that my research would support the community's efforts to document their territorial claim. Her explanation

Figure 1.1 Leaving Bluefields for Monkey Point.
SOURCE: Jennifer Goett, 2013.

seemed to satisfy any curiosity that people may have had about me, and I was received with an open and easy hospitality. Although I was one of the first to stay for any extended period of time, community people generally have positive associations with the (mostly white) international researchers and NGO workers who began to visit with more frequency in the 2000s. Other anthropologists have experienced this "privileged welcome" in Atlantic coast communities and associate it with the history of Anglo-American hegemony in the region (Hale 1994: 11). But, in the early 2000s, Monkey Point was a fairly isolated place that attracted few sympathetic outsiders, and the openness to international researchers was also motivated by a desire for political allies.

Although my rudimentary Creole sometimes made it hard to decipher what was going on around me, I soon settled into the rhythm of back and forth travel between Monkey Point and Bluefields (see Figure 1.1). Often, the time I spent with community people in Bluefields was just as generative as my visits to Monkey Point, as most extended families maintain residences in town, where they have access to churches, schools, health care, and consumer goods. A town–farm residency pattern has been around for generations, although it intensified after the war when families fled the community for the safety of the city. This wartime displacement has given rise to the impression that Monkey Point families are no longer connected to the land and the rural lifestyle they enjoyed in the 1970s.

For Monkey Point people, however, cultural constructions of belonging and ownership are based more on kinship and descent than on possession or use. A descendant of Herminia and José Presida has the right to a piece of land in Monkey Point, regardless of whether he or she was born in the community or maintains residence there. Although outsiders can live and farm in Monkey Point with permission, only kinship really confers "right" to the land. On one of my first days in the community, I sat on the veranda of the health clinic with Miss Pearl and asked for a list of Monkey Point families so that I could get a sense of who lived there. With the typically exhaustive kinship knowledge of women elders, she recited the names of over a hundred families. I later realized that only about a third of these families actually lived in the community with any regularity. The rest were in Bluefields, Costa Rica, and other more far-flung places. Still, they were "Monkey Point people" and integral parts of the community.

Family land is a widely documented tenure practice among rural people of African descent in the postemancipation Caribbean, where it is also known as "generation property," "children's property," or "succession ground" (Besson 2002: 141; also see Clarke 1953, 1957). I have never heard Monkey Point people refer to their own practices by any of these names, but their constructions of "right" closely approximate this form of tenure. A broadly egalitarian and inclusive system, family land accords inheritance rights based on unrestricted bilateral descent from mother or father to sons and daughters regardless of birth status or place of residence (Besson 2002: 14; Crichlow 1994: 77). Family land helps those who live far away to maintain a social attachment to the community despite their physical absence (Olwig 1995: 14). This form of tenure is also inalienable: No one has the right to sell the land to outsiders for personal gain. And as an informal or extralegal practice, use rights do not rely on state recognition or private title, and management follows locally defined norms (Ibid.: 2).

Most scholars recognize family land as a resistive practice that challenged racial and economic oppression in the postemancipation Caribbean, while promoting land ownership and maximizing kinship ties, both of which were denied to people of African descent under slavery (Besson 1984: 5; Besson 2002: 143; Olwig 1995: 1). For Monkey Point people, family land is an egalitarian vernacular practice that encourages collective identification and community cohesion even after labor migration, armed conflict, and displacement have led to a dwindling population base.

When I began my research, community people were building a nascent movement for territorial rights led by women elders. At this time, few people recognized that Creole land claims were grounded in any kind of cultural or historical experience unique to their communities. Most people outside of the Creole community viewed Afrodescendant land rights as suspect and secondary to indigenous rights. I often came across advocacy videos and articles that failed to identify a specifically Afrodescendant, Creole, or black presence within the land claim that later became the Rama-Kriol Territory. Even the addition of the word *Kriol* to the official title of the territory came only with significant protest from Monkey Point people, despite the fact that they were some of the most hard-line and committed activists to push for territorial recognition.

The community faced significant challenges in positioning blackness within normative constructions of indigenous land rights due to a series of factors (see Anderson 2007, 2009; Hooker 2005b). First, blacks had no primordial claims to the land, even though they were there before Nicaragua annexed the region and had clearly suffered a historical process of dispossession. Unless they could show significant admixture with indigenous people, they were deemed natives of Africa, not of the Mosquitia, and therefore had no legitimate claims. Second, communities had to demonstrate an unambiguous dependence on the land for their economic survival. As a community that self-identifies as black and has a significant population living elsewhere, Monkey Point people struggled to position themselves as deserving of communal rights. Moreover, they are racialized in the media and public discourse as delinquents and drug traffickers. These race and class stereotypes cast the community as a marginal and threatening space, rather than a legitimate beneficiary of rights.

Given this political environment, I spent a good deal of time early on producing scholarship that sought to historically vindicate Creole land rights. During my first few months in Monkey Point, I worked with women elders to produce an oral history of community settlement, focusing on experiences of enslavement, gendered racial servitude, and dispossession, as well as rural subsistence economies and vernacular lifeways. I tried to support these narratives with archival research in Bluefields, Managua, and London. Although I found a good deal of archival material on early land use and activism among Creoles in Bluefields, I found very little on Monkey Point, an absence that stood in stark contrast to the rich oral tradition and historical memories that shape community mobilization.

From my earliest days in the community, I was immersed in this oral tradition. Each night I sat on the veranda of the health clinic, resisting my urge to seek refuge from the sand flies indoors, and listened to Miss Pearl tell stories. She told intimate and often humorous family histories and even shared her experiences of working up north as a combat nurse in La Cruz de Río Grande when the war was "hot" on that part of the coast. Miss Pearl's niece Carla and I were a captive and compliant audience. There was no radio or television or even light to read by in those days, nothing to distract us or occupy our time on quiet nights, so we listened attentively and asked few questions. Storytelling is an art form, and I have yet to meet a group of people who do it as well as Monkey Point women. As I heard more of these stories, I began to see the pedagogic and political function of women's storytelling. When they relayed memories of the past, the women encouraged young people to embrace similar forms of historical consciousness and thus worked to mobilize intergenerational political activism.

Spanning some five generations, the stories circulated widely among Monkey Point people. Accounts of community origins and memories about "our old people" and what they once said or did became justifications for contemporary demands. Competing for recognition in a political field where mestizo nationalist and indigenous constructions of rights predominate, Monkey Point women used stories to make counterclaims grounded in a woman-centered black diasporic experience. As didactic accounts, the stories position women ancestors as political agents and show how intimate experiences of oppression shaped their lives. In doing so, they establish women's rightful place at the helm of community leadership and encourage young people to use historical experience to make sense of their own struggles for autonomy. Together the stories represent what Maria Cotera refers to as a "decolonizing imagination at work," harnessing the power of speech to "set the record straight" and promote liberatory forms of political consciousness (2004: 53).

This chapter features three women elders who led the first campaign for autonomous rights in the mid- to late 1990s. The three women were related to one another, were from the same generation, were heads of large extended families, and were among the most knowledgeable oral historians in the community. Not coincidentally, they were also the most authoritative voices in autonomous politics in the early 2000s, and they dominated community meetings with stirring appeals for resistance to the dry canal project and land dispossession. Although I had heard some of their stories in fragments before, I collected complete oral histories from the women in 2001 and 2002.

When I first met Miss Pearl, she was in her early sixties and sat as the president of the Monkey Point communal government. She received her high school education as an adult in the late 1970s and later studied to be a nurse in the 1980s. During the 1990s, Miss Pearl was an active participant in Sandinista electoral politics, running as a mayoral candidate for Bluefields and for councilwoman to the Autonomous Regional Council of the South Caribbean Coast. The mother of five grown children, she worked at the Bluefields hospital for many years. When the government built the health clinic in Monkey Point in the late 1990s, she asked the Nicaraguan Ministry of Health (MINSA) to transfer her there. She retired from her service with MINSA in the early 2000s. Miss Pearl long served as the community's formal representative to the government and outside organizations. The younger generation refers to her with respect and affection as Auntie Mar, and her fair-mindedness, education, Spanish fluency, and nursing skills accorded her considerable status as a leader. In recent years, her health has deteriorated, and she has passed on her leadership responsibilities to her nephew Allen Clair, who is the current president of the Monkey Point communal government.

Miss Bernicia Duncan Presida was Miss Pearl's older half-sister. She passed away in 2012 after a long battle with cancer. In my early years of work with the community, she held the title of *síndica*, a communal leadership position charged with the management of land and natural resources.[1] She became *síndica* after a group of women accused the standing *síndico*, a male relative from their extended family, of selling communal land to a speculator in anticipation of dry canal construction. I remember vividly when she told the former *síndico* in a community meeting that if he continued to challenge her authority, she would "flatten him like an iron." The domestic allusion stuck with me, as did his reaction: He furiously sputtered a response and then receded to the margins of the crowd. Her position as *síndica* was unique, as women rarely assume this leadership role in Atlantic coast communities.

Figure 1.2 Miss Helen Presida at the Monkey Point health clinic.
SOURCE: Jennifer Goett, 2001.

Miss Bernicia was the mother of eight adult children, including one son named Johnny who was killed by the Sandinistas when he was a contra combatant in the 1980s. Many of Miss Bernicia's children fled to Costa Rica during the war years, and two grown daughters remain there with their families. Two other daughters have served as the community's teacher and nurse. Her son Allen is the president of the communal government, and her younger son Harley has taken an active role in community politics. Miss Bernicia died at home in Bluefields but chose Monkey Point as her burial place. Perhaps her most important legacy is the political tutelage she gave her children, who are now central figures in community activism.

Miss Helen Presida Wilson, the third narrator, was in her mid-sixties at the time of the interviews and was the cousin of the other two women (see Figure 1.2). Of the three women, her historical memory was the most detailed. She passed away in 2010 after a decade-long illness that frequently landed her in the hospital. She had more than a dozen grown children. Miss Helen once had a central role in community politics and sat as secretary for the communal government. She had close ties to the indigenous Rama community of Bangkukuk Taik, located to the south of Monkey Point, because her mother was from there. Her aunt on her Creole father's side raised her in Bluefields from an early age in the same household where her cousin Miss Pearl grew up. Still, she spent a good deal of her childhood and young adulthood in the community, and her father was a Monkey Point farmer most of his life. Like Miss Pearl, she took an active role in regional politics, although she was politically aligned with the right and did not have a favorable analysis of the Sandinista Revolution. In the late 1990s, she was a candidate for regional councilwoman with the Indigenous Multiethnic Party (PIM, Partido Indígena Multiétnico), a regional party linked to Arnoldo Alemán's rightwing Liberal Constitutionalist Party (PLC, Partido Liberal Constitucionalista).

Competing Historical Narratives

Before engaging the women's stories, I situate their narratives within competing accounts of Atlantic coast history. Monkey Point people and their neighbors at other peripheral Creole communities on the south coast remain absent in conventional historical sources, despite the fact that the archives provide rich insight into the breadth of indigenous and Afrodescendant mobilization for rights after Nicaragua's military annexation of the region in 1894. References to Monkey Point focus almost exclusively on plans to build an interoceanic railway. The most prominent examples are an initiative promoted by British Royal Navy Captain Bedford Pim in the 1860s and a later project, during the presidency of José Santos Zelaya, known as the Atlantic Railroad or the Monkey Point–San Miguelito Railroad. Although Pim's early venture made little headway, laborers began construction on the Atlantic Railroad in 1904, laying twenty-two kilometers of rail before a U.S.-backed Conservative revolution toppled Zelaya and halted construction in 1909 (Comisión de Liquidación del Ferrocarril de Nicaragua 1997: 22; Pim 1863).[2]

In preparation for the construction of the Atlantic Railroad, Zelaya granted vast titles lining the route to relatives, political intimates, and a few European financiers.[3] The titles along the Punta Gorda River basin were slated for banana production, and the proposed railway would provide the infrastructure for their export via a new port at Monkey Point called Puerto Zelaya.[4] The railway would also create a transport corridor between the Caribbean littoral and the great Lake Nicaragua, uniting the geographic divide between Pacific Nicaragua and the newly annexed Atlantic coast. The Atlantic Railway was one of many initiatives in Zelaya's Liberal Revolution oriented toward capitalist intensification and national consolidation. Today General José Santos Zelaya is hailed as the father of the modern Nicaraguan nation or the leader who united a divided nation with the annexation of the Mosquito Reserve. On the eve of his removal from power, Zelaya described this act of incorporation as the most glorious and honorable moment of his presidency.[5]

Nationalist accounts of history refer to the military annexation of the Mosquitia as "the Reincorporation," but Creoles call the event "the Overthrow" (Gordon 1998: 107). Once a British protectorate, the Mosquito Reserve was controlled by Creoles at the time of annexation. The region's integration into the Nicaraguan nation marked the defeat of an autonomous state under their stewardship and the onset of a new colonial regime characterized by virulent racism toward indigenous and Afrodescendant people. The new regime promoted mestizo nationalism, which cast Nicaragua as an ethnically homogenous Indo-Hispanic nation by the end of the nineteenth century (Gould 1998: 9). Ideologies of *mestizaje* supported mestizo dominance during and after annexation and continue to legitimate the colonization and exploitation of indigenous and Afrodescendant lands today (Hooker 2005a: 15).

Although Monkey Point people do not appear in nationalist accounts of infrastructure development, Zelaya's railroad looms large in their oral histories because black labor was central to construction. The women's stories begin in the second half of the nineteenth century when emancipated migrants from the Caribbean began to settle the Central American coastline in search of agricultural lands and wage-earning opportunities. Their migration represents a secondary settlement of the coast well after the initial ancestors of the Creole population formed a Maroon community at Bluefields in the 1790s (Gordon 1998: 35–36). The mid- to late nineteenth century saw the influx of black laborers alongside colored planters and merchants to the Bluefields region, which was the center of a thriving enclave economy dominated by U.S. capital. Wealthier and lighter-skinned arrivals were absorbed into the upper echelons of Creole society, but poorer black migrants were labeled "Negroes." Their skin color, relative poverty, lack of education, and adherence to cultural practices associated with Africa like Obeah and Vodou made their assimilation into the Creole community at Bluefields more difficult (Ibid.: 66–67).

Edmund Gordon's ethnography of Creole identity and politics includes a chapter on oral history and social memory. The narratives he presents are in many respects distinct from the accounts I gathered from Monkey Point women. Gordon finds Creoles to be less than forthcoming about their history, describing the historical knowledge they relayed as limited in detail and often embedded in more authoritative scholarly accounts (Ibid.: 93–94). He highlights several recurring elements in Creole social memory. For instance, he finds that most Bluefields Creoles identified racially mixed people of color from Jamaica as the principal forebears of the community (Ibid.: 97). Some younger educated Creoles more readily claimed African origins for their ancestors, but most emphasized the European and indigenous components of their ancestry. European ancestors figured centrally in family genealogies, which tended to go back just two or three generations (Ibid.: 101).

Monkey Point women's stories depart from this pattern, lending insight into disparate processes of color and class differentiation within the Creole community. The women's histories are detailed and effusive narratives that are structured around ancestral female protagonists and family genealogies that go back as many as five generations. The women position their own accounts as authoritative because they are passed down from their great-grandmothers and grandmothers who experienced the events firsthand. They make little reference to white ancestors or European cultural antecedents and instead point to intermixing between Caribbean blacks and indigenous Mosquitians as evidence of their nineteenth-century Creole roots. The indigenous component of Creole identity, however, is secondary to a pointedly black identity grounded in African diasporic experiences of enslavement and migration in the Western Caribbean. The following stories chronicle this history of settlement and the vernacular lifestyle that community people enjoyed until the outbreak of armed conflict in the early 1980s.

Slavery and Migration: Charlotte and Hutchin (Mid-1800s)

Charlotte was a young indigenous woman enslaved by white people in the north near Sandy Bay Tara in the mid-nineteenth century, and her history always sets the stage for the women's origin stories. Indigenous slavery existed well into the nineteenth century, at least until 1841 when slavery was abolished in the Mosquitia.[6] Miss Helen shared with me Charlotte's experiences as an enslaved woman on the coast:

> Her mother had her for a white guy, and she was a very good-looking Indian girl. That's why the mistress son got in love with her. But well she was of low category, was a slave, she didn't have nothing in common then to say well that these people would accept her in their family through their son. She was known as a low-class person, but well, the boy didn't mind about that. He was really in love with her. So to get him to stop going around with her, his mother found a way to create a problem between he and the girl, and she end up by

hitting her on her nose bridge with a pot spoon to disfigure her appearance and her face. So after that, well, then the boy didn't worry too much with her.

Although the women trace their origins to a single indigenous female ancestor, her story is couched in the same kinds of racial and gender subordination that shape black women's historical experience of slavery. As an enslaved woman, Charlotte was subject to the sexual advances of her master's son and the physical violence of her mistress. It is not clear from Miss Helen's story if the feelings were mutual, but the son's advances replicate a pattern of white slaveholders treating enslaved women as sexual property. Harriet Jacobs writes in the narrative of her own enslavement in nineteenth-century North Carolina, "I would rather drudge out my life on a cotton plantation, till the grave opened to give me rest, than to live with an unprincipled master and a jealous mistress" (2001: 28–29). Jacobs describes the daily domestic torment she suffered under her white mistress and points out that it was only matched by the sexual predation of her master. But, like Jacobs, Charlotte eventually left the household. She then migrated to Grand Cayman Island.

Each woman's story of Charlotte's migration to Grand Cayman differs slightly. Miss Bernicia suggested that Charlotte was sent with her mother to Grand Cayman as a slave. "They went to Caymans," she told me. "A lot of Indians they catch and they carry them to Caymans." Miss Pearl said that Charlotte together with a group of slaves escaped from her mistress and left the coast for Grand Cayman, where she met her husband Hutchin Nixon. She explained, "This girl with the nose, she marry to an African in Cayman, so the children came out, you know, mulatto. Then she had these children, and they grow up in Caymans." A final version from Miss Helen suggests that Hutchin Nixon came to the Mosquitian mainland to work as a wage laborer. There he met Charlotte. She told me, "Well these black slaves came migrating all the way from the United States and ended up on the island them out there and on the main in Central America. So Hutchin Nixon came then and was working because the white people them open work on the coast here and the black slave them came and they get work then."

"They were working as free men?" I asked her.

"Yeah, they didn't have them like before working as slave," she replied. "They pay them then because well they had freedom. Somewhere around there they got freedom, and they came all about and settled themselves." When Hutchin met Charlotte, he was working for white people on the coast.

Miss Helen said, "He didn't mind about what did happen to her nose because well I believe she had a mark there but she was still good looking then. So he married her then, and they were here up in the north. Then afterward he took her to Grand Cayman."

While it is not clear if Hutchin was born in Africa or was once enslaved in the Caribbean, the women emphasize his identity as a black man with roots in a Caribbean slave society. Each woman's story focuses on what Monkey Point people refer to as "slavery times" and locates their origins in a history of resistance and migration during the emancipation era.[7] The social memory of "slavery times" remains strong in the community, and local people rhetorically contest any experience that reproduces a sense of race and class subordination with the statement, "This is not slavery times!"

Refuge in Monkey Point: Rachel and Hutchin Jr. (Late 1800s)

Back in Grand Cayman, Charlotte and Hutchin Nixon had a son named Hutchin Jr. who married a black woman from the island named Rachel Miles. Rachel and Hutchin Jr. returned to Nicaragua with their five young children in the 1880s and established themselves at Monkey Point, where they found black people already settled. "They was here in Bluefields," Miss Helen told me. "Because what my old people told me, they used to stay from the park go back. That time Bluefields wasn't even a village yet. Right where you see the park is now, right back there was big farm. Big plantation. So Rachel and Hutchin had farm back there too, plant and things. Then they went down to Monkey Point."

"Why did they go to Monkey Point then?" I asked her.

"Because this Bodden, Hafford Bodden, he and my [great-] grandmother they were friends from Grand Cayman, you would say well country people from Cayman. He told them that in Monkey Point they have plenty land and good place to work and no one there much, only Indians. And well they heard that and said they would go, and they went. That was before 1900." In an earlier conversation, Miss Helen described her ancestors' arrival more succinctly: "We black people was slaves. We came down to this place after we got our freedom, and we plant things—coco,[8] sweet potatoes—better than the Spaniards [mestizos] them. We got that from our ancestors that teach us to plant them things."

Miss Pearl suggested that Rachel and Hutchin Jr. bypassed Bluefields altogether because, although slavery had been abolished, "slavery was yet there."

That is to say racial inequality still structured labor and social relations in Bluefields, and Monkey Point provided a refuge for newly free black people in search of land and an independent livelihood. She explained:

> So when slavery time was free in Nicaragua, they wanted to come back. So they came back, but when they reach to Bluefields, slavery was yet there. It wasn't so much pressure, but a man by the name of Hodgson, that owned so many slave, he was like this, if you don't have money to buy food and your necessary, you'd have to go in to work with his group as a slave and they give you food. So when they reach here, they was so afraid of the slavery time again, they keep on. They came from Cayman in a big craft sailing boat and they keep on. They said they not going to stop Bluefields . . . So they land here . . . and they asked the Indian people them if they would let them be here because they were running from slavery.

All three women agree that when Rachel and Hutchin Jr. arrived at Monkey Point they found black people there along with Rama Indians. Miss Bernicia explained how black people became Creole after their arrival to the coast:

> Also the African them come and hide, hide into Monkey Point. They come all the way down, travel hiding years ago. They go to the islands, and from the islands they come across and all in sailing boats. So they come and hide in those places, like say in Orinoco, Monkey Point, and all the places hiding for years. So well the generation gone till well they don't even know they left a life to get back [to] or know anyone in them place to get back [to], the black people. So they just stay and mix up with the Indian. So that is why they are calling we the Creole. We are calling Creole through our Indian and African. Black people are mix up, so they call us Creole.

In each of the accounts, the women locate their origins in an African diaspora that brought black people to the Americas as enslaved laborers. The women describe their ancestors' settlement of Monkey Point as a form of resistance to racism and inequality in the postemancipation period. In an effort to extricate themselves from plantation economies and labor relations that too closely resembled their experience of slavery, new freedmen and women left home in search of fresh opportunities and autonomous livelihoods. They found these things in Monkey Point where they built an independent fishing and farming community.

The women associate the process of becoming Creole with this migratory strategy and subsequent mixing between Caribbean blacks and indigenous Mosquitians. European ancestors are absent in the stories, and the identity the women claim is a pointedly black Creole identity: "Black people are mix up, so they call us Creole." Although intermarriage with indigenous Mosquitians created a new Creole identity, blackness and the slavery experience remain central to their understanding of who they are and where they come from. As a testament to the strength of this historical identification, Sandra Morales, a younger woman who took a community leadership role in the late 2000s, spoke against the Sandinista canal project in a leading national newspaper in the following way: "We are not against progress; we know that our community surrounded by nature will change forever; what we cannot accept is that they violate our rights and deprive us of these lands and this sea that we inherited from our ancestors who were fugitive slaves and gave us rebellious blood" (Jarquín 2008).

The women say that Rachel and Hutchin Jr. were living at Monkey Point in the early 1900s when President Zelaya began railway construction. They associate the military annexation of the region with Zelaya's expropriation of Rama and Creole lands just before construction started. This moment represents the first time that their rights to land were violated by the Nicaraguan state. The women's accounts of the Zelaya land grants allude to disputes that resulted from the speculative sale of one of the grants to outsiders in the 1990s:

Miss Helen: So when Zelaya took over Monkey Point and share it up, black people was here already . . . They didn't ask no one anything, and President Zelaya didn't take into consideration too much the black people them either. Not even the Indians them because they didn't secure a piece of land for them with a document, "Okay, that for you there." Simply they went in and they started to work, and who was there work too. They didn't run the people them out, but they didn't give them no security with the land.

Miss Pearl: They come and when they had this revolution, the Conservative and the Red [Liberal Party]. And when the Red took over, Zelaya give to all his soldiers and those that he promote, he come and he measure up all this whole place here south of Bluefields right almost to Río Indio. This is their prize of fighting and win this Atlantic coast over, and then he name this whole department, "Departamento de Zelaya." Okay, all this while now they do this thing over the people them still living here in this land, my great-grandparents them.

Miss Bernicia: Okay, I say well so those documents is annul. Who the land belongs to is who maintain the position on the land, and we are not people yesterday who came here, nor today. I say we are the generation. We are generation [ancestral] people living on that land, and if they did want the land and want the use of the land and want it to live, they won't have a hundred and six years till the document had made.

Each woman describes land expropriation from a slightly different angle. Miss Helen suggests that, although black farmers were not considered owners of the land, their labor was necessary for railway construction, and they were allowed to stay. After annexation, state-managed tenure regimes usurped other forms of land tenure under the Mosquito Reserve. The British Foreign Office records for the coast chronicle the assault, harassment, and arrest of black landholders with quotidian frequency in the years following annexation. In response, West Indian and Creole landholders asserted their status as British subjects and wrote lengthy descriptions of the incidents to the British Foreign Office asking for protection from the crown. The complaints were logged in what one colonial official derisively referred to as the "nigger files."[9] Racialized state violence thus paved the way for the concentration of land in the hands of mestizo elites and foreign conglomerates such as the United Fruit Company. Miss Bernicia concludes that these forms of dispossession are illegitimate in comparison to her family's intergenerational use of the land.

During railroad construction, Rachel worked as a cook and Hutchin Jr. worked as a manual laborer. Domestic labor is a theme that runs throughout the stories, providing a narrative thread that links successive generations of Monkey Point women. The following account of Rachel's experience as a domestic worker evokes Charlotte's history of enslavement in the home of a white family a generation before. The anecdote demonstrates how an autonomous black social order was upset with the arrival of white foreigners during the railway years and positions the domestic sphere as the site where white women's racism toward black women was most keenly felt. According to Miss Helen, every morning the white mistress of the household where Rachel worked would take coffee and bread with butter. She gave Rachel access to most things from the kitchen, but Rachel was not to eat butter. It seems the mistress thought butter was too expensive for the cook to eat. So Rachel would go to the commissary to buy her own butter to carry to the mistress's house. Each morning she sat in the kitchen and took her coffee with bread and butter. One day the mistress saw that Rachel had bought her own butter and said, "I see you are taking your breakfast, Rachel." Rachel replied, "That's right," and got a great sense of satisfaction that the mistress couldn't say a word to her because she had bought the butter with her own money.

Miss Helen told me this story one day on her veranda as she recovered from one of her hospital stays. The story was filled with ironic humor and underscored Rachel's intelligence, sense of pride, and independence as a workingwoman. She described her ancestor as someone who found creative ways to assert her self-worth and autonomy despite the gendered racism she experienced as a domestic worker. Like the story about Charlotte's nose, the anecdote shows how Rachel's intimate experiences of racism and sexism inform the women's social memory, grounding their critiques of white supremacy and the racial organization of labor.

Throughout the twentieth century, women and men from Monkey Point sometimes used wage labor to provide the cash income necessary to buy clothing and send their children to school in Bluefields. Generations of women and men migrated to San Juan del Norte (Greytown), Costa Rica, and Panama in search of wage-earning opportunities. Lara Putnam documents these migratory routes in the late nineteenth and early twentieth centuries, noting, "Men and women moved back and forth . . . working for wages, buying and trading, washing and cooking, planting and reaping . . . creating a migratory field that expanded to include new sites of economic dynamism as the decades wore on" (2002: 10–11). In keeping with this trend, Rachel eventually left the community with her daughter Catherine to work in the Panama Canal Zone. Catherine worked as a seamstress.

I asked Miss Helen why Rachel left her community to travel to Panama. "I going to tell you now," she replied. "Rachel went to Panama because work did open up in Panama, a lot of work for women. Ench'ya know she was working for the white people them in Monkey Point and after that close down then her husband died and her children them was big and well she didn't have no one then to say keep her in Monkey Point then. She was a woman who used to like to have her own money. Then she decide that she would go to Panama too then." Catherine died in Panama from a blood infection that she acquired from a sewing needle, and Rachel eventually returned to Nicaragua on her own. She lived her final years between Bluefields and Monkey Point. Although the Nixon Mileses are Monkey Point's founding family, the surname has not survived in the community. "They are the first generation here," Miss Bernicia explained to me. "Then the Presida come after my grandmother married, the Presida start."

Vernacular Lifeways: Herminia and José (Early to Mid-1900s)

Before Hutchin Jr.'s death and Rachel's departure to Panama, their young daughter Herminia met and married a black man from Martinique named José Presida. José came to Monkey Point to work as a blacksmith when the foreigners were building the railroad there. He was thirty years older than Herminia, spoke French patois, and was known to be a skillful Obeahman. He came with a woman named Madame Valse who also practiced what Miss Helen referred to as the "black arts." When José took up with Herminia, Madame Valse became very jealous and worked Obeah on Herminia, who was still a young woman in her twenties. But as Miss Helen tells it, José was powerful enough to counteract the Obeah and protect his young bride. She told me how he used his power to initiate a love affair with her grandmother: "Because remember I told you he was very old to Herminia. He was over fifty years, and her parents didn't want she to marry him. But they both fall in love, and he did know his secrets [Obeah] so she just put her mind to him, and she couldn't get away from him then."

Herminia and José lived back and forth between Monkey Point and Bluefields and raised many children together. Monkey Point women and men express strong feelings of pride in venerable ancestors like Herminia and José. Men from the community remember José as a powerful and charismatic figure who could do things that seemed humanly impossible, such as walk the long journey between Monkey Point and Bluefields in just a few hours. They associate his spiritual power with a resistant political consciousness, drawing on the diasporic traditions of enslaved Africans in the Americas. In her study of the relationship between Vodou and Haitian history, Joan Dayan argues that Vodou was a response to slavery and "its peculiar brand of sensuous domination." In exile, enslaved Africans reconstituted "the shadowy and powerful magic gods of Africa as everyday responses to the white master's arbitrary power. Driven underground, they survived and constituted a counterworld to white suppression" (Dayan 1995: 36). Most memories of José emphasize how he used his extraordinary spiritual power to manipulate human will and shape material conditions in beneficial ways in spite of the racism and economic inequality he experienced as a black man born on the eve of emancipation in Martinique.

Women more often remember Herminia and her healing powers. She was known for her Christian morals, good character, hard work, leadership, and skill as a midwife and "bush doctor" who used traditional medicine and herbs to cure illness. Miss Helen described Herminia's work as a healer in the community:

> Herminia Presida was a first class midwife. She use to tend to people that was going to give birth, any sickness especially with the Indians them, she did. Well how Herminia was a good midwife, she was also a good, what the Spaniards [mestizos] here call *curandera* [healer]. She did know plenty medicine. That was a tradition in our family. [Her mother] Rachel also did know a lot. It seems to be in the old times the people them, our ancestors, did know a lot of medicine work to help themselves because doctor was scarce. So they learn the different herbs was good to help people with.

Herminia's lifetime coincided with the first Somoza regime (1937–1956). Her generation is remembered as the good years when rural communities were well-populated and bountiful places. Women describe diverse subsistence practices that shaped life in the small Creole settlements that dotted the coastline south of Bluefields. In places like Hound Sound, Red Bank, Devil's Creek, Monkey Point, Duck Creek, Long Beach, and Corn River, community economies were structured around crop production, horticulture or kitchen gardening, raising of livestock, hunting, gathering of resources, and fishing and turtling. These activities allowed for independent subsistence and sometimes provided black farmers a small cash income from the sale of goods in the regional market economy. Miss Helen described community life during these years:

> We had it good, very good. Because them time we had a lot of the older head that hadn't died yet. And we had what used to keep the people them up in their home, the agricultural work. Everybody had their farm, everybody used to plant, raise the chicken they had. Even goats we had then. When the old lady [Herminia] died we had goats there yet and we had the *breadkind*[10] and the coconut and used to sail and bring up to Bluefields and sell and things . . . And Sunday dinner everybody have a chicken cook in . . . The whole

week through could be fish, as well as it could be turtle. If it's turtle time, it turtle you get. If it guana [iguana] time, guana you get. If it's *wari*, they go and they hunt *wari* [wild pig].

The natural environment abundantly provided for community subsistence, and food consumption habits followed seasonal cycles.

Miss Helen emphasizes the pleasure community people took in their rural lifestyle and vernacular practices. She also notes how these practices supported an ethic of community sharing and cohesion. For instance, she described how sugarcane production and the use of wooden cane mashers or mills shaped such traditions in the community:

> When Friday come, everybody would, you would see people going into their farm. Because that was the day now that they are going to cut cane, and they are going to juice cane to bring the juice out to boil it to make pudding cake then Saturday. Sunday morning you could go to everybody home, and you would find where everybody had a cake. Maybe you make coco cake, I make coco cake too. The other one make a corn, the other one make a cassava. Even sweet potato cake we used to make and rice cake. All those thing we used to make from cane juice . . . It was a pleasure Sunday morning when you look over the whole community there, little village there, we see dish cover down, each home sending to the other home.

Writing in the late nineteenth century, Charles Napier Bell notes the use of "African mills" on the coast to extract juice from sugarcane ([1899]1989: 28). I saw a mill similar to the one he describes at a Creole homestead in 2001. The owner of the mill said that Creoles in rural communities still used mills to extract juice for cane syrup in the 1960s and 1970s. Conzemius speculates that this particular kind of sugarcane mill was a postconquest invention of enslaved Africans who worked on sugarcane plantations in the West Indies (1932: 38).

Farming life also provided an autonomous livelihood for poor families who had a difficult time making ends meet in Bluefields, where every meal required money to purchase ingredients. Miss Christina Cooper, who lives on a homestead just south of Monkey Point, explained the draw of farming life in this way:

> Well in the farm we hardly buy. That's why I tell you I like the farm because we eat without buy. Yes, we eat without buy. But Bluefields now everything is

money. Yes, everything is money. But down in the farm now, we eat plenty time and don't have to spend money. Yes, we hardly spend money in the farm. We plant corn, we beans, cassava, and we rice. We only go buy we matches and sometimes flour and sugar.

Women without partners often found it hard to get by on their own and migrated in search of wage-earning opportunities. Miss Pearl describes her aunt's migration to San Juan del Norte (Greytown) in the 1950s and 1960s to participate in the hawksbill turtle shell trade, an activity that had been central to the Creole trade economy since the first decades of the 1800s. The trade is usually associated with men, and generations of Miskitu and Creole men once left their communities to travel south each year to catch and trade turtles. Miss Pearl's story affirms women's participation in the trade. She remembered this migration in the context of her mother's death. "When she died," Miss Pearl told me, "I was in San Juan, there with my aunt, who went there was to, in those days they used to catch a lot of Oxbill turtle."[11] This was in September, and Miss Pearl described how her aunt would bring the turtle shell to Blue-fields to sell and then use the money to pay her school fees and buy her a new uniform and shoes.

The women's stories depict Herminia as a key player in community politics. One story relays how Herminia obtained a land title from President Anastasio Somoza García. This is the first time the women's ancestors petitioned the Nicaraguan state for collective land rights. Miss Bernicia described her childhood memories of Somoza's visits to Monkey Point. "When he come," she mused, "he come to all the whole coast and come and tie up his big hammock and right them time the mango tree them was plenty then and it was clean under there and everything. And dance and dance and have the hammock and lay down and rest, and he bring things to share for the children, all biscuit, all kind of things did bring and share and dance." Miss Bernicia relayed a dialogue between Somoza and her grandmother Herminia that affirms her family's historical rights to the land at Monkey Point:

And then he say to her, he say, "How long you are here?"

I remember it good by my granny was standing and she, "All my generation," she told him. "All these children is my grandchildren."

And he say, "Oh Miss Herminia, you have a big family here!" He say, yes and he say, "Okay, well then I have to say, how long you here?" She tell him how long from when her family come back to Monkey Point and bring her a girl from Cayman.

So he say, "Miss Herminia you come back with your parents who die, and you stay and keep up your community and all your big generation." Because my mother had plenty children. My aunts all have plenty children.

And he say, "Okay then, Monkey Point is for you!" He say to her, "Monkey Point is for you, and no one can move you from here."

And she say, "You will say that but maybe anyone who come and move me, the government."

He say, "Well, I give you a paper, a document and them don't move you."

So she say, "You just say that. When you go, you will not remember me. You're a big president."

He say, "You all see I going to remember you." And so he said, so he done!

Older Creoles often remember the Somoza years as a time of peace and relative prosperity, which was interrupted by the triumph of the Sandinista Revolution and the outbreak of counterrevolutionary warfare in the early 1980s. Both Hale and Gordon describe the decades before the revolution as one of political quiescence characterized by Miskitu and Creole accommodation to the Somoza regime (Gordon 1998: 80; Hale 1994: 116). Monkey Point people who are old enough to remember those years have largely positive memories of the Somoza dynasty, which showed a strong clientelism toward Atlantic coast communities. Miss Bernicia's account illustrates how this patron–client relationship was played out, shaping positive memories of the first Somoza and his seasonal visits to Monkey Point. Memories of the Somozas, however, are not uniform among Monkey Point people. The women's accounts of these years are varied, mirroring the complex, multiple, and often contradictory political subjectivity that Gordon describes in his ethnography of Creole identity politics (1998: x).

Miss Bernicia, who offered exuberant memories of the first Somoza's visits to the community, does not share the same feelings for subsequent Somoza presidencies, particularly that of Anastasio Somoza Debayle. She described the 1970s in a different light:

And the old Somoza died, cause he was good. The father of Somoza was good. The bad Somoza was the son. Not even Luis, but he son Tachito . . . Luis was like the father. But Tachito after him take over and after Luis died, cause [they] even say he is who poison his brother because he *mannish*. Because after he take over is when Somoza gone bad. Tachito was very bad. He was a fellow how you say warring and was maliant . . . World say they agree that Somoza them have to change because the children them was too bad.

Mannish usually means quarrelsome, cross, or obstinate. Here Miss Bernicia uses it to refer to aggressive or evil (maliant) behavior. Creoles call young people mannish or womanish when they take on the mannerism and prerogatives of older people without having earned the right to do so through age and maturity. Describing a son taking the position once held by his father, both definitions play into Miss Bernicia's description of Anastasio Somoza Debayle, also known by the nickname "Tachito."

Miss Bernicia alludes to the increasingly brutal political repression under the final Somoza presidency, but her younger sister Miss Pearl makes no distinctions between father and sons. She couched her critique of Somoza in an analysis of racism and cultural discrimination:

> We consider in Somoza time as the third class of society because you know we never speak Spanish and most of them has black skin, and what was the most problem was not speaking Spanish. You speak English them say you was American, and they make figure of you. When you go to Managua, they look on you like you look so strange. You look different from them. They ask you if you need passport to come to the Atlantic coast.

Miss Pearl suggested that racism toward indigenous people was even worse: "The Miskito, when was in the Somoza time, they did [not] want to be called Miskitos because the Miskito them did count like dogs, like nobody. The Rama the same, they have them like a mockery." She notes Creole's relative position of power vis-à-vis indigenous people. For instance, she told me, "The black people them was even a little more bigger" than the indigenous because "black people always could handle the two language." English and Spanish language skills and education enabled Creoles to better defend themselves from racial and economic exploitation during the Somoza years and even led some to discriminate against indigenous people. Black people from a poor farming community may have had a lower social standing than foreign whites, mestizos, and Bluefields Creoles, but, notwithstanding their skin color and poverty, their position in the social hierarchy in respect to indigenous people was higher.

Similarly, Miss Pearl associated the economic exploitation of indigenous and Afrodescendants with U.S. imperialism during the Somoza dictatorship:

> Central America is who used to keep up the United States most with all the *crudo* [raw materials]. They did sell them, they sell them the gold, they sell them the lumber, they sell them the banana, and they sell them the fish, they sell them the shrimps . . . And they had all of this freedom to do these things and nothing was coming back. So much ton and ton of gold was leaving from the different mines them and nothing. The people them was getting more sicker than anything else. You had something like almost a 60 percent of tuberculosis, that from the people them in the mines . . . The majority of these people used to die because these company, after you get sick, they used to throw you away.

Miss Pearl's analysis of U.S. imperialism represents a political stance most common among Creoles who supported the Sandinista Revolution. Monkey Point women who did not support the revolution tend to have more positive interpretations of foreign companies and the U.S. role in regional affairs.

The Cuban Exile Base

Herminia Presida lived until 1964. Her death marked the start of a slow transition from relative peace and community cohesion to political violence and community fragmentation. The Cuban base serves as a catalyst for this transition, marking the moment Monkey Point was first exposed to Cold War politics. Accounts of the Bay of Pigs acknowledge that the invasion was launched from Bilwi (Puerto Cabezas) on the north Atlantic coast, but the construction of a Cuban commando training camp at Monkey Point in 1963 after the defeat at Playa Girón has been relegated to historical obscurity. With unofficial U.S. backing, Luis Somoza Debayle gave an anti-Castro exile group called the Movement for Revolutionary Recovery (MRR, Movimiento Recuperación Revolucionaria) permission to train at Monkey Point in preparation for a renewed assault on Cuba. Somoza reportedly approached Costa Rican President Francisco J. Orlich for permission to build camps in neighboring Costa Rica. Orlich agreed, and camps were constructed at Sarapiqui and Tortuguero on the Costa Rican Atlantic coast. The MRR conducted only two minor raids on the Cuban Oriente in 1964 on a sugar warehouse and radar station. Soon after, the camps lost the support of the Costa Rican government and were disbanded (Burt 1965).

Although the covert nature of these operations and the secrecy surrounding the camps have made this moment an obscure detail in Cold War history, the Cuban base was unforgettable for the people of Monkey Point and serves as a precursor to a long period of Cold War conflict. In response to my question about why the Cubans came to Monkey Point, Miss Bernicia told me:

> Come to build a war business. Yes, to practice and to go fight too! To attack Fidel them now because Batista people they come to America aid and bring them down 600 men . . . And they come and they build up and they start to bam bam bam bam and they give us light, all over here big plants [generators]. They come with everything, and we didn't know them coming. They was the boss of we down to the very Guardia [Somoza's National Guard].[12] We had a Guardia. We had a Guardia them times in Monkey Point. Down to the very Guardia them did boss. These foreigners come and boss Nicaraguan government Guardia!

For two years, the Cuban exile base drew Rama and Creole people to Monkey Point from nearby farming settlements in search of wage labor. Miss Christina Cooper describes how she met her husband at Monkey Point when they both came to work for the Cubans. As in the past, Monkey Point women again provided domestic labor for the foreigners. Miss Christina remembered:

> Me and my mother and my father come Monkey Point. We come to cook and I come to wash clothes for the Cuban them, and same time my Alejandro him come from Cane Creek and he gone up an' gone work. And with that now, two of us take together, right in Monkey Point. Yes, I come and I start to get a little work there working for the Cuban washing cloths and my mama selling food. That was what we were doing, yes.

This period conjures both positive and negative memories for the women. They view the Cuban presence as another moment when the Nicaraguan state and powerful foreign interests infringed on their rights, but they also remember the time as the last years of peace and prosperity before the Contra War in the 1980s. Miss Helen describes these years: "In the '70s, we had the community going good, had a lot of people, had this church, we had a clinic, we had a school, and everything was going good till after the war started and everything was getting mashed up then and thing."

From Revolution to Counterrevolution

The violence and political repression that gripped the rest of Nicaragua during the late 1970s had little impact on Monkey Point. But the women agree that the eruption of counterrevolutionary armed conflict after the Sandinista triumph was devastating and signaled an abrupt end to rural life. The most obvious consequences of the war were the depopulation of the community and the destruction of its fishing and farming economy. Beginning in the early 1980s, Monkey Point families fled to Bluefields and to refugee camps in Costa Rica. Many more families left for Costa Rica in the mid-1980s, as the Sandinista government stepped up efforts to conscript young men into the army. If they did not flee the region, young men often joined the contras, and several families lost sons to combat violence.

Miss Bernicia, Miss Helen, and Miss Christina all had sons who fought as contras. Each woman shared memories of the Sandinista years. Miss Helen's memories focused on the dissolution of community life during the period:

> And always you find one of the Presida them there, no care even with the war, the family did mash up plenty in Monkey Point there through this war. Plenty had to run, plenty went Costa Rica, plenty came up this side and went all 'bout, but till finally in total some went in Punta Gorda bar were the military them was there. That was in 1984. Round there, they did have a big attack in Monkey Point, big shooting up one day there.

Miss Christina stayed in the community and described what it was like to flee her home with her husband and children in the midst of warfare:

> Ah yes, right here I tell you we stay. Right here. Sure when the war hit we did up in the Creek. Ah ha, Duck Creek. When we hear the lot of Sandinista bust out Monkey Point, thirty of them, yes, thirty of them bust out Monkey Point. When we hear the *rafa* them hit, they take over Monkey Point. Yeah, we up in the Creek yonder and we start to pick up. We leave animal, Jennifer! We leave hog, we left puss, we lose chicken, we left fowl, and we take [to] the bush! We gone way in the central up in Cane Creek head . . . Yes, it was five families of us, five families of us running from the Sandinista them. Because we all mix up with the contra them, you know. Yeah, so we had to run!

In contrast, Miss Pearl has positive memories of the revolution, which she associated with egalitarian social change for black and indigenous people:

They just, you know, it was just like the children of Israel. They never imagine they could get to be equal with Jennifer. Jennifer would come and sit with me and eat with me. And in Somoza time the white people, or the people with money, they would never look on you. As far as you can go to them is maybe through the back or if you be the maid of the house or things like that. You were not considered as nothing. But after the Sandinista took over, they is who begin to teach the people on the different qualities, the different rights. They teaching them self-esteem that who they are, teaching them to reclaim what is theirs and things like that.

Using a biblical reference to communicate her point, Miss Pearl drew me into the narrative to underscore how white supremacy structured social relations and economic power during the Somoza years. I listened and used the narrative to help make sense of my own relationship with community people and my role as their political ally. By implicating me in her history, she asked me to consider in a more visceral and personal way the impact of class hierarchy and white supremacy on the well-being of those who suffer marginalization.

Miss Bernicia, her older sister, had a less positive analysis of the Sandinista years. She did, however, find the Sandinistas preferable to the postrevolutionary right under Arnoldo Alemán, whom she held responsible for land speculation in the community:

But when we come to find out the Sandinista them, I will say it and I will say it over and over, the Sandinista did better than what the Liberal them, this Liberal doing. The old Liberal from Anastasio Somoza García him, they doing was good, righting our land. And they come in between, the Sandinista government, in between, they start do us bad. Then come back to this Liberal again, come back, he [Alemán] doing us more bad because they want to take us out from our land, our home, and everything.

Her stance defies Cold War polarization and instead expresses an alternative political consciousness grounded in "the social memory of struggle" to secure community land rights at Monkey Point (Gordon, Gurdián, and Hale 2003).

Regardless of their feelings about the Sandinista Revolution, the women's memories of these years are filled with hardship and loss resulting from the war and Hurricane Joan. Miss Pearl described how community people hoped to resume their lives on the farm after the war ended, but they were hampered by the hurricane. She said, "So after some of the people them went down in the '87, '88 you know they had the election and Daniel Ortega went on as president, and things get kind of a little cool and so people was going back home. Then just in that, the hurricane came in the '88 and it just mashed everything up again. Blew all the house down." Eventually families did return to the community, although not in the numbers from years past. Many remained in Costa Rica, making their lives in coastal cities like Limón where work opportunities were more plentiful and wages, social services, and education were better. Others stayed in Bluefields, where they had access to schools, churches, hospitals, and new houses under a posthurricane reconstruction program financed by the Cuban government.

Miss Helen remembered this postwar period of resettlement for the introduction of cocaine and the emergence of drug-related violence. "That stuff started come on in the [late] '80[s], after the war business," she said. "It started frequenting. And people getting adapted and in to it and know what it was and money was in it then. You see? But first they never know. Now you could die for it." Things weren't the same after the war, Miss Helen explained, "Monkey Point one time you didn't have to be scare of nothing." In the face of so much change, the women's memories testify to the richness of community life before the war and serve as a pedagogic guide for younger generations about vernacular practices and values. These values continue to shape political subjectivity and community responses to postwar violence and capitalist intensification.

I met the women who contributed to this chapter fifteen years ago, and their stories have lived in my head and my writing for just as long. I first interpreted their accounts more ambivalently, emphasizing Miss Bernicia's description of how autochthonous constructions of rights weaken Afrodescendant land claims (Goett 2006a,b). Early in my research, she told me, "Sometimes the people say that we are just black people. We are black people. They say that we have no rights here of this land, this community land, because we are from Africa. We are from Africa." This was a central political preoccupation at the time, and I saw the women's stories of their indigenous ancestor Charlotte as an effort to establish native Mosquitian ancestry. I understood the women's emphasis on mixing between blacks and Indians as a way to assert a more viable identity in the struggle for territorial recognition.

But time and experience have changed my interpretation. Today the language of political denial in Miss Bernicia's words impresses me less than her positive affirmations of blackness: "We are black people" and "We are from

Africa." I see how the women affirm and recenter black diasporic experience in the struggle for autonomous rights more clearly now, in part because this is a stance that subsequent generations of community activists have taken in their own activism. Together the women convey an intimate and historically deep critique of race-gender-class oppression as well as pride and pleasure in the rural lifestyle that their ancestors built for them. As counterrepresentations, the women's stories about the past challenge pernicious stereotypes that shape racism, class subordination, and state violence today. As I conclude the chapter, I am faced with the weight of finality. This represents my last chance to give an account that is true to the women's legacy. What stands out to me most now is the radical and expansive nature of the women's historical consciousness, their fine-grained analysis of power and inequality, and how much their stories matter to those who hear them.

2

"Bad Boys" and Direct Resistance

ON FEBRUARY 3, 2000, a group of some twenty young men from Monkey Point armed with guns, machetes, and sticks made their way to the Nica Holdings finca located on the southern reaches of the community. On their arrival, the men confronted the finca manager and mestizo workmen, making it clear that they would no longer tolerate their presence on communal lands. The employees put up little resistance. They fled Monkey Point for Bluefields and never returned. Over the course of the next day, the men sacked the finca, killing the livestock and destroying the nurseries. Afterward they distributed the remaining property. Miss Bernicia's son Allen recalled, "They mash up everything and share up to everybody. Everybody who did want, get." Looking back on the incident, Miss Pearl reflected on the efficacy of the men's actions. She told me, "Well the boys them get bad and some of the men get 'fraid and they say, well, they going, they going, they not going to fight." In a matter of hours, the men had achieved what more than a year of legal wrangling and political organizing had failed to resolve. Using the tactics of rural insurgency, they upended the capitalist order, engaged in a communal act of redistributive justice, and regained control of their territory. This was revolutionary action that reconstituted social relations if only within the communal domain (Graeber 2004: 45).

Once listed among the top foreign investors in Nicaragua, Nica Holdings was a U.S. corporation with subsidiaries in the Bluefields region specializing in seafood processing and export. The Nica Holdings finca stood on a stretch of land that two white North American executives purchased in 1998 from a descendant of John Bodden, a man from Grand Cayman who received one of the original Zelaya land grants at the end of the nineteenth century.[1] One of Bodden's descendants in Bluefields renewed the title in the 1990s and sold the land to the North Americans in anticipation of dry canal construction. The property was under the supervision of an executive named John Vogel, who occasionally visited Monkey Point and quickly became the principal target of community ire. Like the Zelaya railway project a century before, the dry canal proposal led to land speculation on both coasts. On the Pacific side, President Arnoldo Alemán had been linked to land purchases near a proposed port site in Rivas, and Monkey Point people widely assumed that the executives had acquired the title with his backing. Miss Pearl voiced a sentiment that was shared by most in the community when she and Miss Bernicia recounted the incident to me on the veranda of the health clinic one afternoon: "Who behind all of this is somebody bigger. This thing was fix up real neat and fine in Managua."

Many of the young men involved in the Nica Holdings incident were known as "bad boys," a countercultural identity that the men embraced and reproduced in their oppositional politics, expressive culture, and personal style. In the wider Creole community, bad boys are generally associated with the cocaine trade, drug use, and illegal activities ranging from petty theft to armed robbery and assault. And indeed, some of the men have had run-ins with the police, done jail time, struggled with drug abuse, and participated in the gleaning and sale of jettisoned cocaine from the drug interdiction wars that are waged along that stretch of coast. Most people in Monkey Point were accepting of this practice as a logical response to poverty and structural inequality, as whole families benefited from the proceeds. But a smaller group of men had violent histories and were known to "hijack" or steal things at gunpoint. These acts generated resentment and feelings of insecurity in the community. A local woman once warned me, "You see those boys them? Them is bad boys, you know. These Monkey Point boys are really bad. They get together with the bad one them and they thief things. They no work, you know. They only live that way. Them is nothing good, babe."

For many young men, Monkey Point is an autonomous space where they can go to recover from drug abuse and escape the violence of being poor, black, and heavily policed in Bluefields. Strongly identified with Rastafari and Jamaican popular culture, most of the young Creole men that I knew had a critical consciousness that was informed by their experiences of racism and class subordination. They also shared a disdain for authority, antipathy for the mestizo state, and a willingness to break the law and use physical force as a means of personal and collective empowerment. These men were vulnerable to interpersonal, drug-related, and state violence and sometimes engaged in peer and intimate partner violence within their own community. They were perhaps unlikely protagonists in the making of a social movement, but their direct resistance to land speculation signaled a deepening radicalism in community politics and an emergent strategy for dealing with some of the worst abuses of the neoliberal state.

In his study of peasant insurgency in colonial India, Ranajit Guha observes, "The outlaw has indeed some advantages over others in leading an insurrection: he is less bound by deference to the authorities with whom he has already been at war for some time; and of course he has already acquired a certain amount of expertise in the techniques of defiance" (1999: 94). Guha is careful to distinguish common crime and insurgency as inverse codes of violence (Ibid.: 79). If common crime is individualistic or characterized by small-group conspiracy, insurgency has a mass or communal character. Crime is conducted in the shadows, and secrecy is a central tactic of evasion, whereas insurgency is public and charged with discourses of moral legitimacy. Peasant insurgency seeks to upend a social order by targeting elite property for destruction. The resulting plunder is subject to redistribution through communal systems of reciprocity and exchange; in contrast, crime is appropriative and its spoils are not readily shared with others (Ibid.: 109, 115). But Guha points out that despite the inverse relation between the two codes of violence, insurgency may be awakened in acts of common crime, particularly those that are rooted in experiences of deprivation and inequality (Ibid.: 93, 109), suggesting that a resort to petty crime for survival produces a certain political awareness (Hall et al. 1978: 374). James Scott similarly suggests that rampant law breaking for survival under conditions of intense inequality is "a special subspecies of collective action" (2012: 13).

Frantz Fanon was perhaps the first to write about the potential for radical consciousness and militant action in the *lumpenproletariat* or, as he wrote, the jobless, juvenile delinquent, pimp, hooligan, petty criminal, vagrant, and prostitute. Departing from traditional Marxism, he believed this dispossessed class—"the wretched of the earth"—was the "urban spearhead" of insurrectionary struggle against colonial rule in French Algeria. As a group least likely to internalize European cultural norms and accommodate colonial rule, the lumpen were ripe for spontaneous rebellion (Fanon 1963: 81). Fanon believed anticolonial violence was a necessary catalyst for the transformation of colonial societies into new egalitarian decolonial nations. Insurrectionary violence at the hands of this unconventional vanguard had redemptive power that might deliver them to their rightful place in the independent nation (Ibid.: 82).

Fanon remains one of the few early theorists to see revolutionary potential in the *lumpenproletariat*, probing the relationship between violence, subaltern subjectivity, and oppositional politics. Young men from Monkey Point live under conditions of structural violence that resemble the colonial violence Fanon describes in French Algeria. Shot through with patriarchal power, this violence links the production of the state to the domination of subaltern black men under mestizo racial rule. Fanon thus provides a starting point for theorizing insurrectionary violence at the hands of the racialized and criminalized classes of the postwar security state in Nicaragua. His work offers a finely textured account of the social life of violence, emphasizing its deep structure, social differentiation, and interlocking effects in colonized societies as well as the emerging ties between militarism and capitalism in the postcolony.

Racial Violence in the Postcolony

In Fanon's Algeria, colonial rule was racial rule; thus, colonial violence was racial violence. The system of racial rule that he describes works on the basis of hard-and-fast exclusions between the colonizer and colonized, a Manichaean divide delineating good from evil (Fanon 1963: 5–6). A colonial-cum-racial violence is an all-encompassing violence for the native: "an ontological condition in which every social relation—economic, cultural, physical, and imaginary—is organized by violence" (Williams 2010: 98). The policeman and soldier are on the frontlines of this "regime of oppression" (Fanon 1963: 3), which regulates space and bodies through coercive tactics and entangles the mundane production of social difference and subjectivity in violent dynamics.

From the beginning, colonial occupation laid claim to native spaces and bodies. Fanon vividly describes the spatial expression of colonial violence and how it shapes the built environment, compartmentalizing lives into valued and abject categories of existence. He depicts a divided colonial city: One sector is clean, comfortable, abundant, and built to last, whereas the other is shabby, run down, overcrowded, and hungry (Ibid.: 4–5). The native city is "a disreputable place inhabited by disreputable people." Life is vulnerable and precarious in this sector. One can "die anywhere, from anything" (Ibid.: 4). In his imagery, we can recognize the concept of structural violence, which has become so central to anthropological analyses of inequality and social suffering in the postcolony (Farmer 2004). Fanon's emphasis on total structured violence may at times appear too complete, denying any possibilities for autonomous forms of identification, sociality, or cultural expression in native society. Still, it represents a rejection of reformist politics because total structured violence requires deep structural transformation, which can be realized only through the overthrow of the colonial order and the creation of a new decolonial nation.

For colonized peoples living in conditions of structured racial violence, subject formation and social relations are enmeshed in violent dynamics. Fanon describes how colonial violence in Algeria worked through social and sexual difference, producing it in new ways in the process. Saturated with patriarchal power, colonial rule had corporal effects that were socially differentiated for men and women living under occupation. For instance, the spatial segregation of the two sectors was deliberately planned to immobilize the native city and thus regulate where colonized people could go and for what ends. When Algerian women left the native city to enter the European city, they did so following socially prescriptive roles, to clean the homes of the colonizers (Fanon 1965: 52). During the war for independence, Algerian women raped by French security forces struggled with social shame and dishonor in their own communities (Fanon 1963: 186–187, 188, 193). Political terror infused pregnancy and the birth of a new child with anxious pain for refugee women who fled to Tunisia and Morocco (Ibid.: 206–207). Colonial violence thus shaped the gendered division of labor, affective relations within families, the social cohesion of communities, and even their biological regeneration.

In case studies of the psychological wounds wrought by the war, Fanon documents what contemporary theorists refer to as the continuum of violence or causal chains and interlocking effects that connect political, structural, and interpersonal violence in times of war and peace (Scheper-Hughes and Bourgois 2004). Feminist scholars argue that this continuum explains the heightened incidence of gender-based violence during and after armed conflicts (Boesten 2010; Cockburn 2004). Fanon describes how colonial authorities who tortured in the police barracks went home to abuse wives and children (1963: 194–197). Similarly, the structural violence of economic deprivation and exploitation promoted fratricide among colonized men and abuse within

Algerian homes (Ibid.: 231). Political terror had intergenerational effects as well: Children who lost parents to war violence suffered from adjustment disorders and acted out violently within their own peer groups (Ibid.: 199, 206). Fanon thought politically about these phenomena, suggesting that they were based on relationships among men, women, and the state, rather than cultural pathology or innate criminality as posited by colonial authorities (Ibid.: 228).

Although he wrote *The Wretched of the Earth* in the midst of Algeria's war for independence and died soon after, Fanon lived to see the formation of newly independent states across the African continent. Cuba and Haiti provided even deeper experiences of independence in his native Caribbean. A witness to history, he describes "the curse of independence" and presages the rise of a new world order based on neocolonial relations between the global north and south (Ibid.: 54). In this new world order, the global population is divided by gross overdevelopment and intractable poverty, and militarism secures capital in the perpetually insecure postcolony (Ibid.: 55, 60). The primitive Manichaeism of racial rule breaks down, and neocolonial elites begin to facilitate the extraction of wealth from the postcolony to global financial centers (Ibid.: 93–94). The solidarity and fervor of revolutionary struggle against the colonist is replaced with anomie, disaffection, even despair—"a penumbra which dislocates the consciousness"—as citizens of the postcolony discover that oppression and exploitation "can assume a black or Arab face" (Ibid.: 94). Revolutionary consciousness "stumbles upon partial, finite, and shifting truths" (Ibid.: 95).

Fanon was widely critiqued for his belief that colonized people could disarm the violence that governed the colonial world by redirecting it at the colonizer (Ibid.: 6). His most contentious idea was that anticolonial violence was cleansing for individuals (Ibid.: 51) and that life for the colonized would "only materialize from the rotting cadaver of the colonist" (Ibid.: 50). As a catalyst for structural transformation, he argued that anticolonial violence restored historical agency to colonized peoples, destroyed an old order premised on their subordination, and set the foundation for a new national society based on decolonial consciousness. Fanon was not naïve about the possibilities for a decolonial society, nor did he underestimate the emerging power of the neocolonial order. He did, however, hold out the possibility for a transcendent freedom that could be achieved through mass political education, redistributive justice, participatory citizenship, and solidarity among the formerly colonized.

But Elizabeth Frazer and Kimberly Hutchings suggest that in showing so compellingly how structured violence is at work in the production of manhood, womanhood, and political subjectivity under colonial rule, Fanon undermines his own theory of anticolonial violence as a liberating force (2008: 105). The suggestion that violence can liberate or be used for instrumental ends assumes that we can "detach violent doing from violent being, whether at the individual or the collective level." Frazer and Hutchings contend that this position "radically underestimates the levels of ideological and material investment needed to sustain violence as a repertoire for political action" (Ibid.: 107). For instance, Fanon does not theorize patriarchy as a source of unfreedom for colonized people or a form of ideological investment that sustains racial violence. He does not consider how anticolonial armed struggle can reproduce violent masculinity, further entrenching patriarchy, militarism, and authoritarianism in the political structure of the postcolony (White 2007: 880). Still, his ethnographically rich descriptions of violence illustrate how patriarchy and masculine aggression structure the nature and form of racial domination under colonial rule, giving strikingly intimate insight into how colonial power is exercised and experienced through embodied social and sexual difference.

Today Fanon's work on racial domination speaks to the persistent and annihilating violence that Monkey Point people experience as well as their resort to insurrectionary action when failed by the legal system and the reformist politics of multicultural rights. It also points to contradictions that arise from the use of violent tactics of resistance, suggesting that the "ethics of opposing power" is a crucial debate to be had in any revolutionary movement (Graeber 2004: 6). Young men's direct resistance is enabled by the mundane and normalized masculine violence that they grapple with in their everyday lives even as it emerges from a dynamic political field shaped by a much wider set of collective demands.

In the Nica Holdings incident, the men's direct resistance helped to radicalize community politics and support a collective movement for autonomy. Looking back, the event was a politicizing experience for many community members, reflecting a moment of solidarity and collective action that drew on kinship ties, vernacular cultural practice, and a shared moral economy. The cultural logics of direct resistance and autonomous activism provide a window into young men's political subjectivity that would otherwise be glossed in an analysis of the violent dynamics that shape their lives. The following sections of this chapter show why we must remain alive to how masculine violence entraps working-class Creole men while still continuing to think politically about the power and value of their cultural production, autonomous activism, and efforts to free themselves from the racial violence of postwar society.

Autonomy as Life over Death

The vast majority of young people with Monkey Point kinship ties spend their time in Bluefields, where their families have primary residences. Many families have sons and daughters who have shipped out to work on cruise ships or migrated to Panama, Grand Cayman, or Costa Rica in search of employment opportunities. A few have children who received an education and established themselves as middle-class professionals in Bluefields or abroad. The young men that I knew during my research in the community were a small subset who spent their time fishing and walking the beach in search of jettisoned cocaine. Some of these men were longtime residents, the sons of a core group of families that maintain a primary residence in Monkey Point. Others were nephews or cousins, part of the large extended family in Bluefields, who traveled back and forth, staying for short stretches of time before tiring of the rural isolation and returning to Bluefields. Still others were friends with no familial ties to Monkey Point who found the community a safe refuge from the hardships they experienced in Bluefields. The composition of the group was always in flux as new men arrived and others left.

Muche, however, was a constant during my years of fieldwork. Even today when I go back to visit, Muche is there. When we first met, he was in his late twenties. A native of Corn Island, he came to Monkey Point after meeting his brother's friend Fermín in jail in Bluefields. Fermín was one of three men arrested by the police after the attack on the Nica Holdings finca. Many years later, I asked Muche if he participated in the finca attack.

"No, I come after that," he said. "When Pito [Harley], when Fermín drop jail, I meet Fermín in jail."

Fermín instantly recognized Muche and said to him, "You supposed to have a brother that name Nino? That's my best friend." Fermín told him about the problem with a white man in Monkey Point named John Vogel. Eventually, Fermín brought Muche down to the community. He had been bouncing from place to place, doing various odd jobs in Bluefields. Mixed up with drugs and prone to trouble, Muche said he sometimes felt like killing himself because, as he put it, a dog's life was better than his.

Fermín told him, "Better you go in the bush."

Looking back on those times, Muche was glad he accepted the advice: "I really find it plenty better because maybe I'd be dead, you know?" Muche said that Monkey Point was a healthy place for young people struggling with drug abuse: no police and plenty to eat. These days in Bluefields the drugs business is everywhere, too much crime and delinquency, temptation and trouble around every corner.

He told me, "The onliest place that don't have those thing is down in the bush here. Now you get a little joint of marijuana, now and again you hit that, but we don't have no higher drugs than that."

"But sometimes people find drugs, no?" I said with some skepticism.

"Well yeah," he replied, "sometime, but what you find you don't bring it and consume it around your community . . . Because right now if I go and find something, I carry and I go, I go and I sell that. So what I'll bring down is a couple case of beer and, well, have a little drinking with the guys them. But well, we don't use say all that smoking rocks [crack], those things down in the community."

I looked a bit askance at him, remembering the early days before the military established the post in Monkey Point. Communal leaders had tried to outlaw the sale and consumption of alcohol and prohibit drug use with little success. When cocaine was in the community, young men rarely came by to visit the health clinic, petty theft increased, and clothing disappeared from the line. Fights broke out, and the rural tranquility took on a heavy and depressing air. In truth, these periods were intermittent, not a continuous state of affairs. And as much as I heard about drugs, I never actually saw any drugs ever, only the signs of drug use. Men were not proud of their crack use and concealed it from their family members and from me. Marijuana held fewer stigmas, and many men openly praised its salubrious qualities. But the figurative jump from "weed boy" to "rock man," a more abject and disempowered moniker used to identify men who suffer from severe crack addictions, was not one most were desirous of making.

Muche continued, "So down here for plenty of the young guys them, here is like a, like say a *reformatorio* [rehab]. You understand me? It very good for a lot of guys."

Remembering a young man who was killed in 2004, I asked Muche, "Is that why Breda came here?" Breda was family to Miss Pearl. Small of stature with short locks, he had a ready smile. He was alone and unarmed when a mestizo shot him on the beach north of the community. It wasn't the first time he was attacked and brutalized on the beach. Miss Bernicia's youngest son Harley found Breda's lifeless body and carried it back to Monkey Point.

Muche shifted uncomfortably in his seat and replied, "*Es que* [It's because], he used to do a lot of messing in the town. So well he come down here, and by here is a *reformatorio* for everyone, well."

"Too much trouble in Bluefields?"

"Yeah," he said, "so you'd rather be out. I bring some girls down here. I find a girl in Canal [a Bluefields neighborhood] and I say, 'Girl, you gonna die,' and I say, 'You don't want to go with me?' I say, 'Let's go and change life.' I bring her and she get big and she get fat again and a couple of days she gone. I have in a few months bring a next one again. The same thing. She come down here so small and in a couple of time she get so rosy. When she go back to town, they don't know she. But, well, she didn't want to stay. After a while she want to go back. She don't want to be good."

Drug treatment programs are hard to come by in Bluefields, as are economic opportunities for young men and women who struggle with drug abuse. Most men with serious drug problems end up in jail. According to data that I collected from Bluefields prison administrators in 2009, a third of sentenced inmates were convicted for nonviolent drug offenses, and as much as half of the male prison population was of African descent. This is disproportionate to their demographic presence in Bluefields, where Creoles are roughly a quarter to a third of the population (Goett 2011: 361). Prison is a largely masculine space. Only five women were serving sentences in the regional penitentiary system in 2009, although this number had risen to eighteen by 2013 due to more concerted policing of the drug trade and stiffer sentences for drug-related crimes under the Ortega administration. Although Nicaragua continues to have one of the lowest incarceration rates in Central America, since Ortega took power the rate has climbed from 119 prisoners per 100,000 people in 2007 to 171 in 2014. A move toward mass incarceration is hampered by the lack of prison facilities to house inmates with existing prisons at double capacity (International Centre for Prison Studies 2016). But rather than addressing the social and public health dimensions of the new drug economy, Ortega has expressed a desire to modernize and expand the national penitentiary system with confiscated assets from the drug war (Rodgers 2012).

In the men's wing of the Bluefields jail, conditions are so bad that inmates routinely stage what the press and prison administrators call "*motines*" (riots) and prisoners call "*huelgas*" (strikes) to protest. In the past, the state

has responded to the strikes by transferring prisoners to the national penitentiary on the outskirts of Managua. These transfers alienate the men from
their community and the daily care of their families, leaving them with only
meager prison rations to survive (Goett 2011: 361). Dylan Rodríguez refers to
incarceration as a kind of civil and social death, arguing that prison is "a point
of *massive human departure*—from civil society, the free world, and the mesh
of affective social bonds and relations that produce varieties of 'human' family
and community" (2007: 40). On any given day in Bluefields, female relatives
work to counter social death as they line the street in front of the jail with covered plates of food for prisoners inside. Families also bring mattresses, sheets,
towels, toothpaste, and toothbrushes, as the prison system does not provide
these basic necessities. This life-affirming affective labor, performed mostly
by women, maintains fragile social bonds for incarcerated men.

I visited the Bluefields jail in 2009. It is a truly horrifying place. Dimly
lit and rank-smelling cells overflow with two to three times their intended
capacity. Sheets and damp towels hang from strings that crisscross the barred
ceiling. Graffiti covers the cement walls. Some men hang hammocks from bar
to bar; others make do with improvised bedding on the ground. Plastic pans
dot the floors of cells to catch the steady drips of water from the sheets of rain
that thunder down on the corrugated zinc roof during the long rainy season.
The air is heavy with dampness and despair. Young black and brown men live
in these subhuman conditions for months at a time while awaiting trial or
release. Violence between prisoners is common, and violent and nonviolent
offenders of all ages sleep side-by-side in large overcrowded cells. Contrast
this scene with rural life in Monkey Point, and Muche's point comes alive.
The bush is a much better place to be.

A decade and a half of experience with young men who seek refuge in
Monkey Point indicates the extreme vulnerability and diminished life expectancy of this particular demographic. Of the sixteen men that I spent time
with in the early 2000s, two are dead, four are serving long-term prison sentences, one nearly lost his life after being shot in a Bluefields nightclub, several
others rotate in and out of jail, and many continue to struggle with drug abuse.
Another small group have made reasonably good lives for themselves fishing
and farming for subsistence and a bit of cash income. One man is working
for a cruise line. The factors that shape these divergent paths reside far more
in personal biography and circumstance than any real difference in the opportunity structures available to the men. The Bluefields Creole communal

government links narrow or nonexistent economic opportunities, little access to land and natural resources, and out-migration to other forms of structural violence that promote diminished life expectancy and insecurity such as family breakdown, traffic and consumption of drugs, high levels of HIV/AIDS infection, domestic and sexual violence, and a growing prison population (Comunidad Negra Creole Indígena de Bluefields 2012: 55). If postwar society and the global economy have little to offer the ranks of the Creole *lumpenproletariat*, the space of recovery that Muche describes promises, even if it does not always deliver, something transcendent and redemptive, a hopeful and healthful alternative to a grim lived reality in Bluefields.

I have seen the transformation more than once. One of my earliest memories of Miss Bernicia's eldest living son Rolando was of him lying crumpled like a sheet of paper on the tile flooring of the health center veranda. He was thirty-eight years old then and had been a contra up north in the 1980s. His mother brought him down from Bluefields just before a community assembly to discuss dry canal negotiations with the government. Rolando was rail thin and looked as though he had been on the streets for many days and nights. He slept for a full day in that spot. But as the weeks wore on, he came alive, regained his health, and rejoined community life.

Autonomy is life over death, freedom over coercion, and health over disease. It has become one of the ways that men like Muche and Rolando attempt to evade, with the help of their friends and family, "the powerful death grip" that state violence and economic inequality have historically produced for impoverished black men in the diaspora (Ellis 2011: 92). bell hooks writes, "Now more than ever before, the dark forces of addiction, of violence, of death, seem to have a more powerful grip on the black male soul than does the will to live, to love, to be healthy and whole" (2004: 149). Perhaps autonomy represents the loosening of this grip, a utopian aspiration and sometimes-real space, carved out of the bush and perched on the edge of the isthmus, where one can live, love, and be healthy and whole?

Dancehall Good to We

> *One good thing about music, when it hits, you feel no pain.*
> **Bob Marley, "Trenchtown Rock"**

Like the Creole men who formed the *cuartel* troop and were centrally involved in the armed uprisings against the Somoza regime in Bluefields at the triumph of the Sandinista Revolution (Gordon 1998: 215–216), the young men who led the Nica Holdings finca attack in Monkey Point some twenty years later were highly invested in black diasporic popular culture, particularly that of Jamaica. This earlier generation of men was of similar background and social standing as the men in Monkey Point. Deemed low-status *"vagos"* or "bad boys" by many in Bluefields, they embraced a newly popular dread culture from Jamaica that included listening to reggae, smoking marijuana, wearing dreadlocks, and "a growing pride in blackness and a strong rhetorical stance against racism" (Ibid.: 218–219). Dread culture and roots reggae remain popular today, although in the early 2000s young men in Monkey Point were most invested in Jamaican dancehall music. Outwardly, these men embrace many of the same modes of stylistic self-fashioning—dreadlocks, Rastafari colors and icons—yet they are living in very different political times in which social-democratic energies have faded, and they appear as little more than the racialized embodiment of apolitical criminality and violence to be contained by police and prisons (Scott 1999: 199, 212).

Young people from Monkey Point consumed a wide variety of dancehall, *soca*, reggaeton, roots reggae, and lover's rock, but more hard-core versions of Jamaican dancehall produced by artists like Elephant Man, Bounty Killer, Beenie Man, and Vybz Kartel had particular resonance for young men. This version of dancehall grew out of a Jamaican reggae tradition that embraced black pride and anti-imperialist politics and often depicts the harsh economic conditions, political disenfranchisement, police harassment, and everyday violence experienced by working-class Jamaicans. And much like hip-hop in the United States, dancehall lyrics have received considerable negative publicity for profanity, antigay and antilesbian themes, "slackness" or sexual explicitness, glorification of crime and gun violence, and the embrace of radical forms of conspicuous consumption—a shift away from the spirituality and consciousness-raising lyrics of 1970s roots reggae that Deborah Thomas suggests now foregrounds "the personal melodramas of making it in the market place" (2004: 81). Similarly, Dick Hebdige links this shift in popular Jamaican music not only to the death of roots reggae icon Bob Marley but to the onset of free market doctrine in the early 1980s, which promoted increasingly intense forms of structural violence in working-class Jamaican communities during the subsequent decades (1987: 122–125).

Hebdige is quick to dismiss early dancehall as representative of "Jamaica Inc. sex, money, flash, and nonsense" (Ibid.: 125), but others point to the ways diverse forms of Jamaican dancehall engage hegemonic formulations of capitalist consumerism, law and authority, morality and sexuality, gender, and class, becoming sites of contestation that can take both accommodative and oppositional stances to wider structures of oppression (Cooper 2004; Thomas 2004). As David Scott observes, "Dancehall is not to be thought of as a homogenous sphere but an internally contested one" (1999: 218). To illustrate this point, Thomas identifies "ghetto feminist" counternarratives in women DJs' lyrics that poke fun at male DJs and critique patriarchy and middle-class respectability in Jamaican society (2004: 251–257). Caribbean *soca* artists such as Alison Hinds or Terencia "TC" Coward convey similar forms of black feminist consciousness and enjoy popularity among Nicaraguan Creoles.

But, for young men in Monkey Point, Jamaican dancehall was embedded in a masculine aesthetics and politics that held tremendous appeal. A few even wrote and performed dancehall. My first exposure to DJ Macabi[2]— whom I later knew as Coybi, the cousin of my health clinic roommate and friend Carla—was on a promotional documentary entitled *Our Land, Our Future* made by the Coalition for Nicaragua shortly after the Nica Holdings incident. The documentary opens by asking viewers to "imagine a place where the people have lived in harmony with nature for thousands of years," stating that "the life of the indigenous people who live here is simple but full." Later the anonymous narrator warns, "Already, land speculators are laying claim to the land that rightfully belongs to the indigenous people" (Schehl and Knight 2000). Then the video cuts to a shot of Macabi rapping in hardcore DJ style to a song entitled "John Vogel." He has covered his thin chin-length dreadlocks with a white knit cap pulled down low over his brow and has red, gold, and green Rasta beads strung around his neck. Macabi's performance is arresting not only because of how a profoundly modern and pointedly black diasporic form of expressive culture is oddly glossed in a representation of timeless indigeneity but because of his clear vocal and lyrical talent, which like many Jamaican DJs he conveys in rich baritone and rapid-fire Creole. In a version of the song that I later recorded in the community, he sang with three other young men who took the stage names Original Selector, Fireflint, and Firemaker. Macabi sings:

> hear me now
> John Vogel wan come tek away me land
> tek away me land, where me born an grow up pon
>
> dis one man wan tek away we land
> dat not right
> we gone tek out dat man

Eager to claim a wider listening audience, Macabi asked me to record and transfer to CD thirty self-composed tracks, which together touch on a wide range of topics that affirm a bad boy aesthetic, flout authority and convention, and in one way or another critique the social conditions that young Creole men face in postwar Nicaragua. For instance, he pairs slack-style lyrics full of word play about explicit sexual topics in "1, 2, 3, 4 Gyal Wan It" with more reflective toasts in "Macabi Every Gyal Dem Wan," which chronicles his encounters with women in Bluefields and criticizes those who measure their affection based on appearances or the amount of money a young man has to offer:

> yesterday mornin' me bathe, change me clothes
> put on me tear up pants, tear up shirt, tear up cap, and me sandal latin
> two o'clock in the evening
> gone to the park
> gone to tek a walk
> see Suzy, I see Camilla
> shout, "hi me lassie"
> gyal look pon me and she dart her eye
> dat kinda gyal
> when me no got nutten
> the gyal *rechazar* [reject] me
> when me got something
> the gyal dem wan me
> dat's why me tongue keep yarnin'
> hey, dat's why me tongue keep yarnin'
> dem hot gyal you got to put the Macab pon

Although the song espouses a masculinist sexual politics, it also speaks to the particular kinds of racially indexed class marginality young people from the community face in Bluefields. The "park," or the central square in Bluefields, is an important meeting place to hang out and to see and be seen. To go to the park wearing "tear up" clothes would be cause for "shame" or embarrassment for most community youth. Macabi challenges this mode of class ascription and the notion that money is the true measure of manhood. He further critiques how capitalism structures social relations and intimacy when he sings about suffering rejection when broke and regaining popularity among women when he's got "something." "Something" is an oblique term that Creoles use to reference Obeah work, which some believe has the power to make a person fall in love with an individual whom they are not at first inclined to find attractive. Here Macabi suggests that money fetishism under capitalism has the same preternatural power to sway affection and intimacy with women as an Obeah talisman.

This critique of consumerism and class inequality has become pronounced in the Creole community as the region is fully integrated into the global marketplace. Men and women of modest class standing often point to the superficiality of a generation of Creole youth, described as "plastic boys" and "plastic girls," who are concerned with appearance, money, clothing, and nothing else. When directed at adolescent girls and young women, consumerist critiques take on sexual implications as girls are often described as willing to do just about anything for money and things. In Bluefields, gossip runs rampant about schoolgirls' sexual entanglements with taxi drivers in exchange for presents, rides, and small sums of cash. This preoccupation with adolescent female sexuality is so common that it inevitably crops up in everyday conversations about social change, consumerism, and morality. Ubiquitous in their bleached white button-down shirts, long pleated navy blue skirts, and knee socks, schoolgirls are rarely described as victims of the unwanted sexual advances of older men but as willing accomplices in a value exchange that gives them access to consumer goods they would be unable to purchase otherwise. Oppositional narratives about capitalist culture and consumerism tend to draw on gendered moral economies that associate material forms of corruption with sexual transgression, particularly in the case of adolescent girls and young women. Macabi engages in a contradictory critique of capitalist culture by challenging the impact of materialism and class inequality on social relations between men and women, even as he locates the source of moral corruption in female sexuality.

Other songs such as "Nicodemus" and "Work for God, Not for Satan" reference biblical verse and incorporate a strong moral message based in Christian tenets, which are so foundational to Creole moral economies. Macabi verbally samples tunes like the theme to *The Flintstones* and incorporates lyrical word play into songs like "Dig Out Your Yam from Your Plantation" and "Hold the *Givenot*,"[3] which reference Creole food ways and subsistence lifestyles. He delivers wry commentary on national politics in "Daniel and Violeta Wan Test Alemán," in which he references the war years when the Sandinistas forcibly conscripted young men from Creole communities and describes the political battles that take place between party *caudillos* in Managua. Other toasts flout generational norms of work and respectability ("Me No Wan No Boss Man") and the institutional authority of the state, particularly the police ("Good Breeze a-Blowin'"). The last song refers to the squalls that can carry jettisoned cocaine ashore and describes the feeling of blind luck or chance involved in walking the beach to find "white thing."

Although the songs sample rhythms from a wide range of Caribbean musical genres and borrow lyrical phrases and conventions from Jamaican dancehall, they reflect local experiences and vernacular sensibilities. The homophobic and sexist language that punctuates a good deal of the Jamaican music young men consume is absent from Macabi's lyrics. Instead, most of his songs narrate real events that unfolded in Monkey Point and thus serve as an oral record of community life. Some of these experiences are personal, humorously describing the unreasonable sexual demands of a lover, whereas others take on the work of the griot to recount community events, such as an incident when "bad men" from up the beach assaulted a group of local men. In these snippets of life, Macabi gives his listener a glimpse of alternative masculinities—sagacious, witty, moral, God-loving, communally oriented— to the bad man persona of some Jamaican DJs.

The songs also betray a vulnerability to violence, which Macabi confronts with the assertion that a bad boy commands masculine respect and fights fire with fire. Real men are never victims but handle injustices and violations between men as equal players, a stance that is conveyed in "John Vogel" as well as in the opening parable to the song "Minsa Man":

> now it was me and a boy got problem
> same time now my fadda come with him gun
> him breda come with him gun
> so I come with my machet
> and then he come out with he machet, you know
> and well, he say, he going to mince me
> so I say, no, it not you going to mince
> *we* going to mince
> so that just between family and friend,
> two'a we to solve the problem
> sing Macabi
> that's why me sing this song about minsa man

The lyrics celebrate an effort to recoup personal agency in a threatening environment through the medium of masculine solidarity and violence. Like most men everywhere, Monkey Point men know that demonstrating a capacity for aggression is the simplest way to claim the power that inheres in patriarchal manhood (hooks 2004: 46). Signaling the intergenerational nature of masculine solidarity, the song locates the socialization of boys and young men into the conventions of violent masculinity within families. Coybi himself suffered stiff physical punishment for his childish misdeeds when young. His father and uncle fought as contras during the 1980s and were exposed to wartime violence as young men. War also shaped Muche's adolescent experiences of violence. He described being terrorized in his early teens by a brother-in-law who was once a contra fighter in the bush and became violent when drinking. At the age of thirteen, Muche shot him in self-defense with a gun he kept hidden under his bed. For these men, histories of political, familial, and peer violence are intertwined.

"Minsa Man" also illustrates how patriarchy structures relationships between male peers as well as differentially positioned men within and outside the Creole community. Most young men from Monkey Point have very little access to patriarchal male respectability, which in Creole society is grounded in age, family, social status, profession, economic standing, and church affiliation. At the same time, they are subject to endemic violence. It is not surprising that they might seek empowerment in the face of this violence through masculine expressions of strength, physicality, and aggression. As an ode to agency and eye-for-an-eye justice, there is perhaps something individualistically redemptive in the song, but it does not address the shadow side of the equation: how personal histories of abuse can entrap men in violent social relations with their peers and with women and girls who become the objects of patriarchal social control or how violent masculinity paired with working-class Creole men's structural position in society obviate an ethic of self and social care for their health and well-being.

Creoles largely regard themselves as nonviolent in comparison to mestizos, but this is a class-based estimation that does not always follow through in discussions about Monkey Point. Bluefields Creoles describe Monkey Point people as quarrelsome, low-status country folk who are quick to fight. With limited access to middle-class respectability, professional prestige, and institutional power, many local men (and women) embrace a reputation for toughness or for being "hard," not "soft" like city people. One afternoon in 2009, Carla and I were sitting on her cousin's front porch in Bluefields passing time when her uncle Hombre stopped by to visit. Hombre had a badly infected wound on the sole of his foot. He had been to the health post for medical care days before and now asked for ibuprofen for pain. When he left, Carla mused that in truth her uncle must be in very serious pain. "Monkey Point men are hard, hard," she said. They don't ask for help or readily admit to feeling pain. Being hard, however, conceals a deep well of suffering for men who have lived through physical abuse, deprivation, combat, posttraumatic stress disorder, prison sentences, police violence, alcoholism, drug abuse, physical injury, and ill health. Coybi was not immune to these things. On April 15, 2005, he died from drug-related pulmonary disease at the age of twenty-eight in the Bluefields hospital.

But while he was still healthy and strong, dancehall was good to Coybi. It earned him the esteem of his community and provided him a creative outlet, a source of pleasure, self-affirmation, imaginative possibility, and political expression. For him, like his peers in other parts of the African diaspora, music was a sphere that represented a site of personal empowerment for young people who are denied access to quality education, living wages, and social respect. With so few representational spaces available to craft positive images of black masculinity, dancehall gave Coybi a vehicle to fashion a racial self that was complex, full of dignity, and representative of his community. It also provided a medium to engage and reformulate black diasporic identity through a vernacular sensibility with a powerful, oppositional, and at times contradictory message.

The Making of a Social Movement

The day following the finca attack, John Vogel wrote a petition to the Bluefields police demanding a prompt response to the men's violence. The petition elicited swift and decisive action. Not long after, the then Monkey Point *síndico* arrived with a police contingent to collect evidence, take statements, and detain those responsible for the attack. The police arrested Fermín, a young man from Bluefields named Sánchez, and Miss Bernicia's youngest son, Harley. When the three men got to jail, they found Rolando and Muche already there. In a 2001 interview, Harley told me, "Me was the only one first time gone jail in life, you know. Fermín already got a little antecedent. Sánchez did got a little antecedent." After being switched from cell to cell, he eventually landed in a cell with his older brother, Rolando. "Yeah, you know, him like smoke and thing," he explained. "Him all time get in conflict and get in jail." When I asked him why the police singled the three out for arrest, he replied, "Because they say we is the queen of the bee. So if they go with the queen of the bee, well, the bee them stay without leader, but there was many more what was leader. Everybody was leader for the community."

Harley explained that nonhierarchical organization and community consensus were the underlying conditions for insurrection. For the state, however, the men's resistance was unambiguously coded as criminal violence. As Harley put it, "They got us like bad one, number one criminal." In a later interview, more than a decade after the incident, he reflected, "Them did want to make it seem like it was three person gone to try to make it like a kidnapping or try to rob them, not like a communal movement then." But everyone I have talked with remembers the incident as a critical event in a community-based movement for autonomy. Secure in their autonomous rights, they waited for the police to arrive. Harley said, "We tell everyone we no have to be running like delinquent."

The finca attack came in the wake of more than a year of community activism in civil society and a series of failed attempts to challenge the Nica Holdings title in the Nicaraguan courts. A year prior to the attack, in the early part of 1999, Vogel visited the community with a delegation from Bluefields that included representatives from the Autonomous Regional Council and the Monkey Point *síndico*. He announced that Nica Holdings planned to extend its fishing operations to the community and promised a new era of prosperity and employment. Knowing the livelihood struggles that cash-poor communities like Monkey Point face, a proposal from the executive of one of the largest industrial fishing outfits in the country was received with a degree of anticipation. Shortly afterward, the *síndico* coordinated an effort to survey the finca property on the southern edge of the community where the dry canal wharf was slated for construction. Vogel brought a property manager from Managua to live in Monkey Point and transported livestock and seedlings to the finca in an effort to establish full possession of the property. With still no indication that he planned to initiate fishing operations, he paid a handful of mestizo families who were settled in the area to cede their claims to the land and then hired several of the men as finca workers. Harley told me, "Girl, them brought couple man from Bluefields and they give them gun, bridge-loader [shotgun], and .22 and .38 and them was guarding the place, the place that we used to pass years upon years walking." Vogel fenced the property and made it clear that trespassers would be shot. Harley added, "Anyway, during the time the people them get clide [fed up] and everybody start opening up them eyes waiting on this so-called fishining program that *nunca* reach [never came]."

On the few occasions that Vogel visited Monkey Point, he had contentious interactions with local people that they felt revealed his sense of racial superiority and privilege. These exchanges left community people with the understanding that his whiteness, wealth, and personal influence in Bluefields and Managua gave him a significant degree of impunity. Harley told me that they first tried to reason with Vogel, to engage him in dialogue so that he could understand that his land purchase violated their rights. He claims that Vogel dismissed them outright by saying, "I no have business with that. I business with no autonomous business nor no community business. I buy this land, and I going to do what I want with it."

"Before you spend on the land, buy anything," they said they pleaded with him to "consider this law, serious argument that we making here with you and something very personal for the community then. You have to respect it."

According to Harley, Vogel responded, "Naw, naw, I no have to respect nothing." He claims that Vogel told him, "These people them, I not even have time to sit down and speak with them because they are too ignorant. I can't talk with them because them is ignorant people. Them no understand nothing. They don't know they elbow from they ankle, and me no have nothing to talk with them."

Miss Bernicia relayed another exchange she had with Vogel in which she describes how she confronted his claim to impunity. She said she asked him, "What happen?"

"Well, you all don't have no money," she claims he replied.

Outraged, she said, "Money? So you abusing of us? Ah, money talk and bullshit walk! And what you think about Mr. John, so you're black you must stay in the back?"

Allen remembers similarly charged confrontations. After attempts at dialogue failed, he told me that Miss Helen's son Hanatoon struck John Vogel in the chest and warned him, "You white man, white-skinned man, we no playing with you. You don't know who you dealing with yet." Allen claims that Vogel ran to the judge in Bluefields to complain: "Yes, one of them black monkey boy, he hit me. Hit me up and beat me up. I want you put him to jail."

Whether or not Vogel actually said any of these things, community leaders draw on their "lived experience as a criterion for credibility" (Collins 2009: 257) in these dialogue-heavy narratives. bell hooks writes, "Dialogue implies talk between two subjects, not the speech of subject and object. It is a humanizing speech, one that challenges and resists domination" (1989: 131). Telling the story this way restores voice and agency in a dehumanizing situation and communicates a structure of feeling that textured the moment. The narratives make it clear that community people experience land speculation, class hierarchy, capitalist exploitation, political corruption, manipulation of the law, and the criminalization of community activism as racially structured forms of oppression. Experiences like these have led community activists to a position of black autonomy as one of the few viable responses to racial violence and inequality in postwar society.

As tensions rose, women leaders began to politically mobilize by appealing to politicians, the courts, and NGOs and airing their grievances on local radio stations in Bluefields. They found an early advocate in a regional councilman and party head of the FSLN and submitted their first claim in the civil court against Vogel and his business associates. At home, the women worked to have the *síndico* removed from his position. They informed him of his dismissal in a letter detailing his offences that was signed by nine members of the communal government, which now included Miss Bernicia as the new *síndica*. Miss Pearl even wrote a personal letter to President Alemán, appealing to him on the grounds of moral decency to recognize their rights to communal lands. The letter relayed an ancestral account passed down from her grandmother Herminia Presida that detailed abuses during the Zelaya era and linked them to land dispossession.

In response to the women's campaign, a group of local and international NGOs in Bluefields organized a support commission to advocate on their behalf and provided funds to hire human rights lawyer María Luisa Acosta to pursue the community's case in the legal system. With legal representation and institutional support from Bluefields NGOs, the women built coalitional ties with the indigenous Rama communities to the north and south of Monkey Point, constructing the basis for a new social movement, a form of grassroots politics emblematic of the postauthoritarian era in Latin America (see Escobar and Alvarez 1992). This was the women's first experience organizing in neoliberal civil society, which became a space for them to seize their statutory rights and become multicultural citizen-subjects after the war.

If the revolutionary project focused on dismantling preexisting state institutions to rebuild society from the ground up and inject new social investments in political life, the postrevolutionary 1990s represented a period of rapid neoliberal restructuring of the state and civil society. In the midst of this shift, Creole intellectuals, professionals, leaders, and activists refocused their political energies on the proliferating spaces of participation in "organized civil society" such as NGOs and regional universities, which now had ties to transnational funding agencies. Set free from the socialist state and its mechanisms for popular mobilization and collectivization, Creoles found a new space for the remaking of political subjectivity in civil society, becoming simultaneously autonomous and newly responsible for the welfare and development of their communities (Rose 1999: 174). Nikolas Rose observes that, "Advanced liberal forms of government thus rest, in new ways, upon the activation of the powers of the citizen" (Ibid.: 166). For Creoles, multicultural citizenship now inhered in and derived from their active participation in civil society and their moral commitment to their community (Ibid.: 171, 178).

Women elders from Monkey Point were, in many respects, ideal participatory citizens. In civil society, they found a community where their age, gender, and moral standing resonated with multicultural discourse about indigeneity, tradition, and ancestrality. The women's identities as mothers, aunts, and grandmothers fit well with the communitarian politics of multiculturalism, and they politically positioned themselves as pacifists and peacemakers, willing to sacrifice for the greater good of their families and community. The stories they told about the past reinforced this gendered investment in multiculturalism through references to spirituality, ancestors, and traditional practices such as herbal medicine and midwifery.

Feminist theorists of the nation describe women as the symbolic bearers of tradition. Figured as inert, conservative, and backward looking, women provide continuity with the past in nationalist ideology (McClintock 1993; Nagel 1998; Yuval-Davis and Anthias 1989). Latin American nationalisms similarly represent indigenous women as the bearers of culture and tradition or as "more Indian" than men, to quote Marisol de la Cadena (1995). Official multiculturalism as a new competing (and sometimes overlapping) political ideology reproduces some of the same gendered elements of mestizo nationalism, creating ambivalent openings for Afrodescendant women to claim a political voice in civil society as the representatives of communities, tradition, and the ancestral past. Women elders were adept at navigating these representational politics, and their efforts to mobilize resources and construct alliances were impressive. Before the community received its title and formal

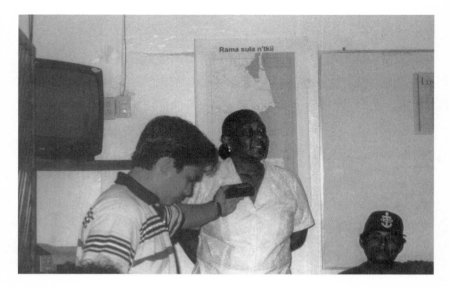

Figure 2.1 Miss Pearl Marie Watson speaking about territorial rights at a Bluefields meeting.
SOURCE: Jennifer Goett, 2002.

leadership positions in the territorial government began to hold prestige, the women did the hard political work that local men were unwilling to do (see Figure 2.1).

One day in 2011, I asked Allen to tell me how he first became involved with communal politics. He said that when he returned to Nicaragua in 1996 after a decade in Limón, Costa Rica, "Everything used to be the woman them. So when I come I used to drink every day. *Every day.* That is the same in Costa Rica. I used to drink every day, but it naw used to be the same. I used to have go work."

"Let's go. Walk with we," the women would tell him. "We need man to company we for make we can get this thing going, so let's go walk. We going today by the Casa de Gobierno [the seat of the regional government], so let's go."

"Aww, cho! I no got no time for that," he'd reply. But his attitude slowly shifted, and one day he said, "Okay, no problem. Let's go." From that time on, he accompanied them to meetings and entered into a sort of political apprenticeship with women elders.

"Why was it only women?" I asked him as I listened to his story. "Why weren't men involved?"

"The man never want to help them none," he told me. "Them all time saying, 'Working free is not the solution.' That's why only the women them used to work."

According to Allen, men were unwilling to engage in political labor that was not a direct benefit to them as individuals by offering greater access to institutional power and material resources. The gendered division of labor in patriarchal capitalist society and women's roles as unpaid reproductive laborers within households made women more likely to work without pay for the collective benefit of their community. Women elders head up dense networks of kin, in which mutual aid and shared affective labor between women are central to survival and community reproduction. Creole women also have a history of taking leadership roles in their neighborhoods, churches, and families and bring to the table organizing and community-building skills that are invaluable to the political work they do for autonomous rights. But Allen said the women desired a truly communal movement, one in which men and women contributed equal labor and had a shared commitment to community welfare. They believed they would be more powerful, carry more political force, if they all worked together. If the women couldn't sway the conscience of men of their generation, they could at least socialize their sons and daughters into the practice of community activism.

Still, in spite of all of this hard political work, little changed on the ground. Nica Holdings maintained its property rights, and relations between finca employees and community members continued to deteriorate. As the women mobilized to challenge land speculation, they found few legal avenues for redress. Instead, their encounters with state institutions, particularly the police and judicial system, left them with feelings of deep resentment and futility. They found that their multicultural rights to communal lands held little sway in a judicial system marred by corruption and grounded in more than a century of preexisting legal code that prioritizes mestizos, individual private property regimes, and state sovereignty.

Faced with Vogel's intransigence and a dead-end legal process, anger in the community reached a boiling point. Miss Pearl recalls the urgency of the time, "We went to the Dr. Acosta and told her that this place going to start in another revolution because everybody trying to defend their self. John Vogel was one side arms up and the boys them on this side arms up." She told me,

"Okay, we went and we complain, complain to our authorities in Bluefields and everybody give it a deaf ear. So afterward the boys them from here in Monkey Point, they group up together and they said, 'Nobody want to give us an ear? We going to do something.' So that's the way they pressure John Vogel and he not back here today. But if it wasn't for the action of these boys here, maybe he would be here yet." In short, they found that multicultural rights and civil society participation alone did little to change the material conditions of inequality in their community, leaving direct resistance as their only means of self-defense.

This dynamic indicates a reconfiguration of racial hegemonies and exclusionary tactics in the neoliberal era, resulting in an "uneasy fusion of enfranchisement and exclusion" (Comaroff and Comaroff 2001: 299; also see Winant 2009). In Central America, multicultural reforms have paved the way for the increased acceptance of a limited package of cultural rights but have done little to challenge systemic racism and class inequality, which only seem to deepen as neoliberal policy agendas advance (Hale 2002, 2005). The recognition and valuation of cultural difference over other forms of justice and equality have led to the emergence of what Silvia Rivera Cusicanqui calls the *indio permitido*—the token subject of official multiculturalism. The *indio permitido* or permitted Indian represents only "acceptable forms of ethnicity" that strengthen the alliance between multicultural policies, the neoliberal state, and transnational capital. As a token participant in the polity and valuable commodity in the capitalist marketplace, the permitted Indian is never fully modern, autonomous, or politically resistant (Farthing 2007: 7–8). Subaltern politics that challenge the underlying tenets of free market doctrine and seek redress from the state confront the limits of multicultural pluralism and often become subject to the coercive power of the state (Hale 2004). If civil society is the space (some say imagined and fetishized) in which participatory citizenship is created and experienced—a mediating space between transnational agencies, NGOs, the media, state institutions, new bodies of statutory rights, and society at large where disenfranchised people can find democratic inclusion—what happens when this space is incapable of delivering on its promise (Comaroff and Comaroff 2001: 331)?

Many years after the fact, Allen reflected on this moment when civil society and the courts failed them. He said, "So when we see the legal part take too long and we couldn't get it stop like we should, we decide to fight them then, our style-a-way, how we fight."

"Why do you call that 'our style'?" I asked.

"Because we no thinking," he explained, "no wait nobody tell us what to do. If I have to chop you, I'll chop you. If I have to shoot, I shoot you, and if we have to hang you, we hang you. Our style, we gone think it now, our way, how we wan do it. But out, them gonna get out."

It is worth noting that the community has never actually chopped, hanged, or shot anyone and that direct resistance is effective due to its self-defensive restraint. But Allen signals an intractable political condition that requires a different lexicon of struggle, the need to speak and act in the idiom of radical refusal when faced with dehumanizing conditions and the violation of autonomous rights. Belligerence has political force. When community people turn to direct resistance it is with the recognition that conditions of subordination are no longer tolerable and other lines of action are unlikely to produce desirable results. Direct resistance falls radically outside of neoliberal multicultural discourse and the permissible politics of civil society, but it has political force and value in the framework of autonomous struggle. In anarchist traditions of struggle, direct action involves acting in one's own interest and confronting a problem or injustice without soliciting the state or showing deference to politicians, bureaucrats, or laws (Graeber 2009: 201). Direct action thus entails "acting as if one is already free" or autonomous and "proceeding as if the state does not exist" (Ibid.: 203). It may be tempting to assume that direct resistance alone is a more effective response to land speculation than women's civil society organizing, but I suggest otherwise.

Direct resistance is most effective alongside a constellation of strategies that include collective mobilization, civil society organizing, the use of popular and alternative media, and litigation in national and international courts. As Harley pointed out in the introduction to the book, multicultural reforms and civil society participation have led to new forms of political legitimacy and recognition from the state and international actors. "Openly," he noted, "they have to respect." Recognition and legitimacy in civil society support direct resistance and limit violent backlash from the state. Multicultural recognition places this form of collective action into the recognizable legal and interpretive framework of autonomous rights. The police and military rarely distinguish between criminal violence and direct resistance as an insurgent code of violence in movements for autonomous rights. Nevertheless, multicultural reforms and civil society organizing have curbed the state's ability to respond to direct resistance with violence and legal sanction in the criminal justice system without being accused of grave human rights abuses against ethnic activists. Like a single node of a rhizome, direct resistance gains sustenance and support from other sites of political mobilization. It is one strategy in a repertoire of strategies that, when skillfully navigated, can produce political rewards. Here we can surely recognize "the contribution of lawbreaking to democratic political change" (Scott 2012: 17). Although much of the chapter focuses on young men's direct resistance, they are not autonomous political actors. Their political agency is embedded in a collective process in which women play a vital role. In the Nica Holdings affair, the men were released from prison after fifteen days and the charges against them were dropped due to the organizational efforts of women leaders and their allies in civil society.

Conclusion

After war, outmigration, return, and resettlement, community people slowly adapted themselves to new ways of doing politics in the postwar period. Looking back on the years of political organizing that began with the Nica Holdings incident, community activists stress that one learns through collective struggle, that developing political strategies of empowerment involves a hard-won, cumulative process of learning. Harley explained, "We do all kind of thing to get back the community in a normal, stable, how we expect to live then, you know, or at least, more or less then." Referring to the actions they have taken over the years to have a dignified social existence, he reflected, "You know, I say everything is experience so you could know how to run things maybe in the future or the present right now." Community people learned by doing, drawing on a widening reservoir of political experience to inform their activism.

For instance, women leaders—and later their children, who took up leadership roles as the women aged—learned to build and maintain relationships with national and transnational organizations in civil society, particularly those that publicize and litigate human rights abuses (CALPI and CENIDH) and European development agencies (IBIS from Denmark and KEPA, the Finnish Service Center for Development Cooperation) with access to enough capital to pay for legal support, purchase property for the territorial government, and fund and organize territorial demarcation. They learned to use popular media outlets such as local radio stations and the Creole cable news program to voice their complaints in the public sphere. They also began to videotape some of their more contentious encounters with state actors and to collect written and video testimony from local people about human rights abuses. "And when we make pressure," Harley explained, "we always try to have a camera so we can film to make people see the step we take is not say abusing of nobody. It just auto-defending our self and our own right like people and like family here then." The strategy thus anticipates and counteracts state efforts to criminalize community activism.

Monkey Point activists also began to appreciate the importance of statutory rights and international law. They became well versed in Nicaraguan law and adept at navigating the mestizo justice system, learning to engage in legal CYA ("cover your ass") tactics when challenging more powerful interests. Allen expressed his appreciation for legal CYA when he told me, "Because, look, when you working in the legal kinda way you all time got where to come out through. When you working it legal, you can get what you want. So anytime I do something, even from them time to now, I all time make sure I on the winning side." John and Jean Comaroff refer to this phenomenon as the "judicialization of politics" (2006: 26). They write, "People drawn together by social or material predicament, culture, race, sexual preference, residential proximity, faith, and habits of consumption become legal persons as their common plaints turn them into plaintiffs with communal identities—against antagonists who, allegedly, have acted *illegally* against them" (Ibid.: 27). In turn, state institutions engage in their own forms of "lawfare" against community people, more often coming "down on the side of bandit capital" (Ibid.: 29) and reducing young men to "bare life," excluded from the political realm and denied the protection of the law (Agamben 1998).

In the midst of this learning process, community people found new avenues to express old political sensibilities and desires that entail radical, even utopian visions of what black autonomy might promise. When men and women allied with one another in the face of shared oppression, direct resistance became a radicalizing force in autonomous politics. Alliances with women elders and the wider community helped to mold direct resistance into a more coherent expression of community solidarity and autonomous activism. Young men's contribution to the process demonstrates their desire to support and participate in their community in meaningful ways. Without romanticizing or unfairly condemning their difficult lives, we can recognize in their style, creativity, and collective resistance the justifiably political, showing the basis for oppositional consciousness and agency in the racially profiled and criminalized classes of the postwar security state. Learning to better parse youth violence and its relation to the political represents a first step in recognizing the humanity of men whose lives are so finely textured by multiple forms of annihilating violence. This involves recognizing them as political agents with a critical consciousness about inequality and oppression, while still holding them accountable for their acts of violence against peers and women and girls.

3 Life on the Edge of the Global Economy

Now this is a woman thing
And all man better listen
And listen good

Man! This is the last throw of the dice.
Because come the next century
A woman a gu run things . . .

Woman might be weaker than man, physically
But them tougher and stronger, mentally
Them independent and proud, just like we
Them only need a man to help out emotionally

Tek the average woman out there, she smarter than we
Brighter than we, more focused than we
If you think I'm chatting bull, just come with me
And le' wi count the female students in the universities

Yo! Women run most offices and women run the factories
Schools and hospitals and women run the homes
Now them stepping up in government, them stepping up in
*   parliament*
And in the corporate world, women a hold them own

Man! Believe! Believe!
This is the beginning of the end, yu hear? . . .

But there are some women out there, who don't have no head
Them sell them precious body, keep badman inna them bed
Some have a dozen pickney [children] and some of them tun
*   drug mule*
A few nuh have ambition and some of them, them fool

But man much worse than that, a them mek the country fail
Them perpetrate the violence, them full up all the jail
Them idle on the corner, them gamble at the race track
Them pack up all the run bar, them pushing the coke and
*   crack*

Most man not doing nothing, them only love to profile
*   [show off]*
Them depend on woman fi mind them, that is the latest style
For centuries man a run things, but now them finally flop
Woman used to be under them but now woman dey pon
*   top . . .*

I know some man mighta sey, that me sell out
But all o' unuh can stand there and run up unuh mouth
The writing is on the wall, big and bold for man to see
That the so-called weaker sex a gu run the country

It's not even a war, 'cause we lose already
The woman revolution, dey right on top of we . . .

Fab 5, "Woman's Anthem"[1]

IN MY EARLY YEARS IN BLUEFIELDS, one of my favorite songs to hear at Four Brothers, the local Creole dance hall, was a *soca* by Fab 5 from Jamaica called "Woman's Anthem." Released in 1999, it stuck around, as catchy and danceable songs tend to do in Bluefields long after they have faded from the charts. Women crowded the floor during *soca* sets at Four Brothers, dancing in groups of two or three as *soca* powerhouses like Alison Hinds flooded the sound system— "I'm looking for the ladies who know they're independent. It's your turn to riiiide. Let me see you ride it!" Her music conveys a message that sits well with most Creole women I know. Work hard. Make your own money. Take pride in yourself. Don't let a man abuse you. But "Woman's Anthem" was in a class of its own. Men sang it, and it heralded women's ascendancy, an end to the patriarchal order. The message was so subversive that an urban legend circulated in Bluefields that the lead singer was shot down and killed at a live concert in Jamaica for singing the song.

Years later, I finally got my hands on a copy of the lyrics and began to see in them a more complex message about gender and social mobility for working-class Creole women at the turn of the twenty-first century. "Woman's Anthem" resonated with Nicaraguan Creoles because it describes real gendered phenomena in the community alongside a series of commonly held stereotypes. Since the Sandinista Revolution, educated Creole women have broken barriers in the skilled professions. Many now have high-ranking leadership positions in government, NGOs, and regional universities. A recent unpublished survey conducted by the Bluefields Creole communal government found that young Creole women significantly outnumber their male counterparts in regional universities. They also have fewer substance abuse problems and are incarcerated at significantly lower rates than men. Women often point out that they are better administrators and manage money more wisely than men because they run households on slim budgets, saving for big purchases and making small sums of cash stretch each week to feed families. They criticize men who do not contribute to households because they are unemployed or waste their wages drinking rum with other men. Moreover, the negative stereotypes in the song about working-class women's sexuality and working-class men's violence and criminality are all too familiar.

But as popular as the song was in Bluefields, the picture it paints of male marginality and female ascendancy does not match the experiences of Monkey Point Creoles.[2] Economic autonomy is a valued ideal for women, but few are truly independent. They rely on dense social networks for daily survival. Men contribute in significant ways to household economies, sometimes as the sole breadwinner but more often not. Most women and men hustle, share, and survive without regular work, and few have prospects for long-term economic mobility without labor migration. Although underemployment is the norm for women and men, working-class men continue to have more lucrative job opportunities and ship out to work on tourist cruise lines in far greater numbers. Furthermore, the gender division of labor for working-class jobs is less flexible than in the professional sphere where upper- and middle-class women have made so many gains. Educated women have become doctors and lawyers, but there are no women taxi drivers or fishing boat captains. Most Monkey Point women still resort to low-paying and backbreaking domestic labor in the informal sector. When working-class Creole women do get an opportunity to migrate, regardless of where they go to work in the global economy, they are locked into an international division of labor as maids, cabin stewards, waitresses, nannies, cooks, and eldercare providers, repeating historical patterns of racial and gendered domestic work.

If this paints a bleak picture of structural immobility, chronic underemployment, and out-migration, it is because securing a livelihood in the twenty-first-century global economy is no mean feat. Community people lost much of their agricultural subsistence capacity due to armed conflict in the 1980s and the escalation of drug-related violence after the war. Today drug violence and mestizo land colonization make life in "the bush" too risky for most Monkey Point families. As community people retreat to Bluefields, lose control over land, and become dependent on cash for daily survival, they join a superexploited surplus labor force with few wage-earning opportunities. Rather than promising to rectify this dire economic condition, for most community people the Interoceanic Grand Canal signals the hastening of primitive accumulation or total dispossession and their transformation into a landless and wageless proletariat.

The fact that working-class families continue to be cohesive under these conditions is a testament to their ingenuity and the diverse livelihood strategies they use to get by. For women—the focus of the song and this chapter—livelihood politics are enmeshed in dense networks of gendered sociality, where reciprocity and shared affective labor between women are central to survival. Women's sociality and mutual aid make it possible for them to live relatively well on the edge of the global economy. Alongside flexibility in family form, household organization, and earning strategies, these gendered practices create a cultural space of self-valorization that is resistant to the logics of capitalist accumulation and value. They also mitigate the impact of a sexual division of labor that promotes wageless women's subordination to male wage earners. Many women have successful long-term domestic partnerships with men, but an equal number do not, often by choice. For these women, sharing and cooperation based on affective and familial bonds with other women make it possible for them to live independently of men, free from the social control and abuse that can sometimes structure intimate relationships. But as crucial as sociality and mutual aid are to survival, it would be a mistake to view them as mere adaptations to oppressive systems because they produce pleasure, laughter, and camaraderie between women and thus have autonomous social logics. Sociality provides a space for crafting selfhood and solidarity between women premised on autonomy from men, interdependence, and self-respect.

Sociality and mutual aid also shape women's activism for collective rights. The politics of livelihood are a rich site for the development of a critical consciousness about global capitalism and the place of working-class Creoles in the international division of labor. Previous chapters describe how women elders were able to politicize younger generations and establish legitimacy for their rights within civil society through communitarian politics, which are grounded in precisely these forms of gendered sociality and mutual aid. Creole women's work to ensure collective survival in the "unofficial, private, and seemingly invisible spheres of social life and organization" is a form of political work that drives community activism for autonomous rights (Collins 2009: 217). The first part of this chapter introduces women's sociality as an affirmative cultural practice that is central to the reproduction of community and promotes oppositional politics. The remainder of the chapter focuses on the history of one extended family from Monkey Point to illustrate how women's sociality as a vernacular practice operates in the context of political violence and postwar neoliberal restructuring.

Sociality and Self-Valorization

My time in Monkey Point was spent mostly in the company of women who are members of the vast network of extended kin descended from Herminia and José Presida. Life in a small rural settlement encourages social intimacy, and the days were filled with visits from Miss Bernicia, her daughters and granddaughters, and women from neighboring households. As they chatted about politics, community life, and the comings and goings of those who traveled back and forth to Bluefields, the vastness of their social networks and genealogical knowledge was readily apparent. But women's talk does more than convey knowledge; it represents a sphere for the socialization of values, the most important of which are relational. Relational values such as cooperation and reciprocity, behaving fairly toward others, not being "mean" (stingy or selfish), not being too "proud" (putting yourself above others), not being "brainsy" (calculating and manipulative), being clean and "brisky" (active and busy), and maintaining friendships and obligations to others, rather than "cutting style" by dropping friends or staying home are all imparted through everyday chat. Much of this talk is laced with humor and involves estimations of the relative justice or injustice of any range of actions or events. Everyday talk serves as a space for consensus building and social critique, as a vehicle to solidify and break alliances, and as an arena to air grievances, pass judgment, and seek vindication. Within these intimate spaces, women joke about men, criticize their behavior, and compare notes. They introduce irreverent laughter and pleasure into each other's lives, and they commiserate when they are depressed, anxious, or dealing with philandering, abusive, or controlling male partners.

Female sociality is organized around consanguineal kinship, and relationships among mothers, daughters, sisters, aunts, nieces, and cousins often matter most to women. But sociality is not bound by blood or any single kinship arrangement. Monkey Point women's networks are cast wide and include social ties developed from church activities, schooldays, work, and the Bluefields neighborhoods where many grew up. The households that participate in these networks are marked by diversity and flexibility. Community people live in male-headed and female-headed households. Some are organized around a nuclear family. Others incorporate large extended families and fictive kin. Some couples are legally married, whereas others are not. Partnerships between men and women can be short lived or last a lifetime. Legal marriage remains a marker of middle-class status for Creoles, but domestic partnerships are common and accepted in working-class families, and there is little stigma associated with single motherhood or having children with more than one partner.

Within these diverse and flexible arrangements, women-centered networks hold tremendous influence. This does not mean that men are absent or nonparticipatory or that women necessarily have more social or economic power but that relationships between women have considerable significance in the organization of household and community life in Monkey Point and Bluefields (Collins 2009: 192). A few common features of household organization attest to women's centrality in community life. First, subfamilies—or "the incorporation of young single mothers and their children" in larger extended family households (Safa 2005: 330)—are prevalent. Motherhood is deeply valued, and many women have their first child in their late teens or early twenties while living in their mother's household. They may remain with their mothers for much of their lives or eventually move out and begin a household of their own. Women also frequently inherit homes from their families or stay with the home after a marriage or domestic partnership ends.

Second, the fostering of other women's children is common. Gloria Wekker notes that "children are easily exchanged between households" in working-class Afro-Surinamese communities. This is especially the case for women without children, who might be "given" the children of female relatives to raise (Wekker 2006: 23). This practice occurs in Nicaraguan Creole communities, but other forms of fosterage are more common. For instance, women sometimes raise the children of their adult sons when young mothers are unable to manage their offspring on their own, women foster children from abusive or neglectful households, and they care for children whose mothers migrate for work. Like other working-class communities in the African diaspora, "othermothers"—or "women who assist bloodmothers by sharing mothering responsibilities" (Troester in Collins 2009: 192)—are vital to women-centered networks.

Third, domestic organization of households in Monkey Point and Bluefields can span multiple households that share economic resources and child-rearing responsibilities among them (Mintz and Price 1992: 65). Men also cooperate and share their labor with one another, but women are the central agents in interhousehold networks and their cooperation has a powerful community-building function. Cooperation is perhaps the most important way that solidarity is created and maintained between women. A friend or sister who washes for you when you are sick or minds your children when you cannot is the measure of a true ally. Women also give or lend money to one another when cash is scarce or emergencies arise. They shelter and feed women who have problems in their own homes or have nowhere to stay. They wash the dead and make ginger beer and soda cakes for the "set up" (wake). They recommend bush teas, attend births, and give advice on child rearing. Wekker describes similar forms of cooperation among Afro-Surinamese women, who, like Nicaraguan Creole women, use the West African proverb "the left hand washes the right" to valorize relationships of reciprocity (2006: 11). Hardt refers to this kind of work as "affective labor." As a form of bio-power from below, affective labor produces sociality and community (Hardt 1999: 89, 96–97).

Rather than rehash debates about Afro-Caribbean kinship and its origins in Africa and New World slave societies (Herskovits 1990; Mintz and Price 1992; Safa 2005; Smith 1996), I draw on an alterative analytical framework. This framework is attendant to historical forces and structural inequality but emphasizes self-valorizing vernacular practices. I argue that women's sociality and mutual aid are not simply strategies to cope with inequality but vernacular practices that build community and promote self-valorization. Coined by Italian Marxist Antonio Negri, the term *self-valorization* references "a self-defining, self-determining process which goes beyond the mere resistance to capitalist valorization to a positive project of self-constitution" (Cleaver 1992: 129). These noncapitalist cultural practices are "desirable in their own right" as "points of departure for the elaboration of autonomous ways of being" in the world (Ibid.: 123). Women-centered networks—and the deep sociality and reciprocity they promote—are not grounded in capitalist social values such as individualism, self-interest, competition, accumulation, and overconsumption. They do not conform to Christian and state-sanctioned models of marriage, family life, sexuality, and procreation, which promote patriarchal power and dependence on male wage earners. Nor do they aim to produce a particular type of worker, consumer, or citizen (Federici 2012: 97).[3] Instead, women's sociality and participation in community life are rooted in gendered vernacular practices, providing a broad basis for self-valorization in an environment saturated with structural violence.

But this realm of sociality is not without contradictions, nor are working-class Creole women impervious to the onslaught of global capitalism—"the most gigantic, totalizing, and all-encompassingly universal system of evaluation known to human history" (Graeber 2001: 89). Regular wage labor in the formal sector is a privileged position, and women who have obtained this kind of work often have more status than other women. The increasing reliance on money in a cash economy means that waged versus unwaged has become a more salient form of social distinction for Monkey Point people. Moreover, consumerist values are prevalent and growing. The desire for markers of modernity such as flat-screen televisions, computers, and smartphones is widespread, even if these products remain out of reach for many. Women's affective labor is also prone to incorporation in the capitalist labor market due to a social division of labor that naturalizes black women's work as caretaking, domestic work. When women find employment as domestics, cabin stewards, waitresses, nannies, cooks, and eldercare providers, their affective labor is removed from its vernacular social logics, subject to market valuation, and integrated into a social division of labor based on race-class-gender hierarchies.

Finally, not all women cooperate with each other. Some abuse other women's generosity, fail to reciprocate, and engage in malicious talk about the social lives of others, creating considerable strife among community women. Malicious talk can focus on other women's sexual behavior, mirroring the respectability politics that shape debates about sexuality in the wider Creole community. This chapter is not a meditation on universal sisterhood and social harmony. Having others intensely involved in one's life is not always easy or pleasurable. Sometimes women want peace and quiet, a bit of privacy, a space of their own where they can conduct their personal affairs free from the intervention of others. Women's social intimacy reflects the messiness of human relationships, which are imperfect by nature. Deep sociality can be trying when one is living on a shoestring budget in crowded and poorly constructed housing in Bluefields neighborhoods that lack clean water and sanitation services. Still, the benefits are considerable. Despite capitalist intensification, women's sociality remains a sphere of self-valorization that stresses interdependence and self-worth based on good character and strong affective relations with other women, rather than money, skin tone, or marital status. Within this intimate sphere, women still reject the idea that marriage or the market is the ultimate determinant of social value and that people with money and jobs are better than those without.

Friendship and Activist Research

The health clinic veranda was a very sociable place during my time in the community. I lodged there with Miss Pearl, her niece Carla, and Carla's two sons, Jarrel and Roy. During my first weeks at the clinic, I made what would become one of the most enduring friendships of my adult life. Although Miss Pearl welcomed me and actively promoted my participation in community life, relationships between women my age and older women are ones of deference. I quickly learned to reply "Ma'am?" when Miss Pearl called my name from her office, and in the early interviews I conducted with women elders from the community, I did very little asking and a whole lot of listening. Carla, however, was just four years my junior, and she and I became friends. She left Bluefields for Monkey Point to take a job as the community's radio operator after becoming pregnant with her second child. She also cooked, cleaned, washed, and occasionally attended to patients at the clinic as she had trained as a nurse's aide for a short time in her late teens.

Carla was on her feet most of the day, and I had little to do beyond listen, learn, write field notes, and do the odd interview here and there. In my desire to be useful and contribute to the domestic routine, I began to look after her newborn and help her with her daily tasks. The four of us shared a room at the health clinic and at nightfall, when the sand flies came out in full force, we retreated to our beds, safe under the mosquito netting, to talk. We quickly connected as friends and found that we shared similar sensibilities about the world around us. I cannot overemphasize how crucial Carla was to my early adjustment to life in Monkey Point and later Bluefields. In my loneliness, she provided friendship. She and her extended family gave me a sense of connection and belonging. As I struggled to understand Creole, she provided translation. When I misunderstood community dynamics, she set me straight and explained alternative ways of understanding.

But the relationship was reciprocal. After she gave birth to her third and fourth children in the Bluefields hospital, I kept her company. When she was feeling bored in Bluefields, she came by my little board house and passed the days with me and my next-door neighbor, also named Carla. We would listen to music, drink a beer or two, and laugh together as children toddled about the veranda. I loved to entertain my growing circle of Creole friends in Bluefields. As an avid cook, I gained great satisfaction from preparing local cuisine and showing off my newfound cultural competency in the kitchen. The three of us often prepared for those events together, grating coconut and peeling "breadkind" (starchy root vegetables) for "rundown," a coconut milk–based stew that is a staple of Creole cuisine. Once I returned to the United States, Carla and I maintained our friendship, and I helped her when I could by sending small sums of cash when times were tight.

For all of our mutual support and friendship, some fundamental asymmetries structure the relationship. My income and professional mobility create a central asymmetry. Economic inequalities are increasingly common among Creole women as they migrate for work and find themselves in better economic standing than women who stay at home. A redistributive ethic often structures their relationships with female family members. But my mobility is tied to my whiteness, citizenship status, and educational credentials, which exempt me from the racism and violence that so finely texture the lives of working-class Creoles.

There were many times during my research that these inequalities stood out in my relationships with community women. For instance, after I moved into my own house in Bluefields and work in other regions of the coast began to take me away from my social engagements with Monkey Point friends, more than one woman noted that I was "cutting style." One time during a chance meeting in Bluefields, a woman from the community confronted me with a half-joking remark: "Why haven't you been coming down to Monkey Point? Looks like you cut us off for good now." I heard that another woman thought I was too "proud" to go to Monkey Point these days. The implication was that I had smartened up and decided to associate with a different class of folks in Bluefields.

Despite early tensions, social and political solidarity has led to strong bonds of friendship and collaboration with community people over the years. Building strong friendships with political allies is in itself an act of solidarity. And, as I grew close to community people during my years in Nicaragua, I saw that I had something profound to learn from them, something that would deepen my moral fabric and broaden my human experience. I found it hard to explain at the time, but after returning to my atomized existence in the United States, I knew that Carla and other Creole women taught me a better way to be in the world with others. This way of being with others requires a different level of commitment and accountability than I was accustomed to in the States, but I have been loath to lose these relationships over the years.

I have avoided writing about my friendships in my ethnographic scholarship precisely because of the profound impact they have had on me. Writing felt like a breach of confidence. Ethnography is a representational form that, even when done well, can commit countless small betrayals in its making. But after a series of conversations about the terms of the research, Carla agreed to contribute her experiences to the book, even embracing our interviews as a collective endeavor. Together we sat down for three interviews in 2013, and she narrated her life to me. I interviewed five additional members of her extended family that summer. After completing a full draft of the chapter in 2015, I shared it with Carla, and she recommended changes to the text, which I then made.

The following sections of the chapter are devoted to these family narratives. They chronicle the most significant historical shifts of the twentieth century for Monkey Point people, from the prewar days of agrarian subsistence, to the violence and displacement of the war years, to neoliberal restructuring, postwar survival, and the rise of labor migration to work on Caribbean cruise lines. The narratives reveal how women's sociality and mutual aid produce community and oppositional subjectivity in the face of political and structural violence.

The Structural Break

Carla was born in Monkey Point in 1976 when the community was still a thriving rural outpost based on fishing and subsistence farming. Her birth mother was from the large clan of Presida descendants that form the core of the community, and her father was a Bluefields mestizo who had taken a temporary teaching job in Monkey Point. When Carla was still an infant, her birth mother gave her to Lucille Presida, an older relative who was a midwife with a large family of her own. Miss Lucille is married to a man named Limbert Sambola, known to most as Sammy (see Figure 3.1). He first came to Monkey Point from up north when he was a teenager. That was in 1952, and Sammy was working with a logging outfit that brought felled timber up from Colorado Bar, just south of the San Juan River in Costa Rica. When he and Miss Lucille got together, she had two girls of her own already. Together they moved up to Orinoco, a Garifuna community in the Pearl Lagoon basin, not far from La Fe, where Sammy grew up. They came back down to Monkey Point in the 1960s to work for the Cubans and stayed on until the outbreak of war in the 1980s.

Sammy's account of his work history demonstrates the diverse and flexible strategies that working-class men of his generation used to get by. In his life span, he has done almost every kind of physical labor imaginable. He discharged logs, husked coconuts at the old copra processing plant at the Cocal, cleared bush for the Cubans, did a stint as a stevedore up north in Bilwi, and worked on fishing boats all along the coast. All the while, he maintained his

Figure 3.1 Mr. Limbert Sambola and Miss Lucille Presida, Bluefields.
SOURCE: Darren Wilson, 2015. Reprinted with permission.

farm and subsistence lifestyle in Monkey Point. Miss Lucille was also on the move, attending births in the small rural settlements that hug the coastline south of the community. After each birth, she would stay with the new mother for a week or more and then travel back to her family in Monkey Point. She accepted no payment for her services. Midwifery was a skill that she shared with others freely in order to satisfy an essential human need within her community. Lucille and Sammy's work gave them social status among their peers, but the esteem was not based on market values. Carla explained to me that skill and hard work (rather than money and wage labor) were central to Sammy's core identity, his sense of himself as a man, and his reputation in the community. She said, "Sammy used to work hard from when he is young. He feel like he was, they call him, they have a name they call him, 'hard ass' and 'the iron man.' Because when him start work, him *work*. So in Monkey Point, he was the man who had *everything* from the farm. Food, plenty food and thing."

Wage labor was incidental to this identity, a complement to farming that allowed the family to buy clothing and other basic necessities that Sammy could not produce on the farm. When planting time was done, he'd leave the community to go look for work on the fishing boat at the Bluff, the barrier island across the bay from Bluefields. Sammy was a hard worker and an affable shipmate, so after a while fishing boat captains began to anchor at Monkey Point to look for him. The captain would come ashore and say, "Sam! Boy, I need you to work!"

When he was busy with his farm, he'd reply, "I can't make this trip, man. I have work here to do."

The captain would say, "Alright, next trip when I come back, I want you."

In ill health and too elderly to work on the farm at the time of our interview, Sammy sat in the living area of the family house in Bluefields, weaving a finely made fishing net for sale. Remembering the old days, he told me, "And when I ready, I no got no more work on the land, I get back out to sea again and work. I go to work. Bring my money, bringing my ration and everything. So I never meet no hard time down in that place."

"In Monkey Point?" I asked him.

"Yeah," he replied, "I no meet no hard time. One time, I count out three loving calendar year without holding one *córdoba*. I check it out, me myself. And why I check it out? I want to see if you can live without money or not." Not only did Sammy control when and for how long he participated in wage labor, he completely opted out when it suited his fancy.

Back then you could live without money. Sammy traded with Colombian boats that frequented the harbor at Monkey Point, exchanging the *chicha* he made from fermented corn and the juice of sugarcane for salt, sugar, diesel, and other goods. Men at sea were eager to barter for his *chicha*, as three good glasses were strong enough to make a man drunk. Sammy grew corn and sugarcane and just about every other kind of agricultural product that thrives on community lands. The bounty from the farm stayed in the community, as Monkey Point farmers had no local market for their surplus. Sammy shared his produce with others, and nobody in his household ever went hungry.

With the outbreak of war everything changed. Armed conflict in the early 1980s precipitated a structural break from a largely subsistence economy to a largely cash economy. The period saw a mass exodus of community people, the fragmentation of families, new dependencies on wage labor, intensified color and class discrimination in town, more precarious household economies, and less stable and nutritious food sources. In the space of a decade, community people lost food sovereignty or the right "to define their own food and agricultural systems," by putting their own "needs and aspirations . . . at the heart of food systems and policies rather than the demands of markets and corporations" (Forum for Food Sovereignty 2007). During the war, household economies and consumption were also tied to the Sandinista state. For Monkey Point families with members who joined the contras, the loss of food sovereignty and community fragmentation were enmeshed in an increasingly coercive relationship with the mestizo state.

When war broke out, Carla remembers, "Everybody scatter." Her own family left Monkey Point and settled up north in Haulover, a Miskitu community in the Pearl Lagoon basin. Sammy was able to procure a piece of land to build a house there for free due to Haulover's customary land tenure practices. Although he did not farm during the war, he joined a fishing cooperative made up of men from the surrounding communities and sold his catch for cash. But the family didn't stay together. Lucille and Sammy's older sons, Ricardo and Junior, joined the contras in the south with other Monkey Point men. Three elder daughters went to Bluefields and took work as domestics. The younger siblings and a few grandchildren stayed with Lucille and Sammy. Coybi was the grandchild closest in age to Carla. Not long after Miss Lucille adopted Carla, she brought Coybi into her household due to his birth mother's neglect. Carla explained, "She used to like go on the street, come next day, and leave Coybi abandoned. Then he had a lot of sore over him whole skin. One day Junior [his father] gone visit, gone carry things for him. And when he gone, he find him nasty, sorey, crying, alone. Him take him and carry him. That is why me and Coybi was like this, like brother and sister."

Up in Haulover, Lucille and Sammy lost two more members of the household when their teenage son Leonardo and a grandson joined the contras north of Tasbapauni. Carla told me that they went to fight with the contras due to the Sandinista policy of forced conscription that began in 1983 as the war escalated. She explained, "Say them young man about the place then, them go in your house, them take you and they carry you. *Have to*, you can't tell them you no want to go. So long as you have the size and you have age, them go and take you and carry you. So them prefer was to go in the bush with the contra them and go fight."

With her sons in the bush and her grown daughters working, Miss Lucille suffered during the war. Carla said, "She used to fret plenty, and Sammy was like, 'Old lady, be strong, don't cry,' because she was always crying and crying." The anxiety and stress were compounded by the violence unfolding around the family. Carla describes how it felt to live in the midst of armed conflict as a child. She told me, "When them big bomb drop, it shake the house, Jennifer, and it make you so frighten, so you was like, 'Lord, I wish I was dead.'" The family's association with the contras also led to problems with Sandinista officials. After a friend from the fishing cooperative was arrested and taken to Managua, Sammy told me, "I get to understand that the government was after me too," and the family decided to relocate to Bluefields. The couple had no money to buy land or rent a house in town, so they stayed with Sammy's sister in the Creole neighborhood Pointeen.

Years earlier, the couple's daughter Dafny had gone to stay with an older sister in another Creole neighborhood called Old Bank. Dafny had her first child at seventeen and soon after began domestic work. When her first job offer came, she told me, "I say, okay. I have a baby, and I'm a single mom, so I willing." The child's father was a neighborhood boy who left for the United States to avoid military conscription. Their son eventually followed his father to the States. Dafny's third job was with a mestizo family that had political ties to the Sandinista Party. When their daughter left to study medicine in Managua in 1983, Dafny went with her to keep house. Dafny's two older sisters also did stints as domestics on the Pacific side of the country, as work was hard to come by in Bluefields. All three sent money home for their mother and the children she was minding for them. But Dafny didn't care for Managua and returned home after a year. Alone all day in the house, she was beset with anxiety for her family. Dafny told me, "And then I hear about this war and they shooting up and this one dead and the next one, and I say, 'Oh my gosh, my baby down there.' I said, 'I think I better go home and be together with them.'"

After she returned to Bluefields, Dafny secured a job in the formal sector, working at the Sandinista Workers' Supply Center (CAT, Centro de Abastecimiento de los Trabajadores). In the mid-1980s, the Sandinistas established CATs to respond to a drop in real wages in the formal sector and skyrocketing prices for consumer goods. Plummeting wages and hyperinflation were matched with significant trade and fiscal deficits and negative GDP growth between 1985 and 1990 (Stahler-Sholk 1990: 59). The CAT offered products like cloth diapers, clothing, and shoes at a fraction of the unofficial market price to government, health care, and education sector workers as well as retirees, families of drafted soldiers, and veterans. Shopping at the CAT was time consuming, as large numbers of beneficiaries and irregular supply resulted in multiple visits each month and long waits in line (Ryan 1995: 179, 181–182). Dafny was the only member of the family with the right to shop there, which she did weekly, helping to clothe many members of her extended family.

Carla told me that, in those days, "Bluefields was *pésimo* [awful], very, very bad." Although the Nicaraguan economy grew in the first few years of the revolution and social welfare significantly expanded under Sandinista leadership (Walker 1997: 9), by 1985, the economy began to suffer from mismanagement and an intense destabilization campaign waged by the U.S. government that would inflict more than a billion dollars in material damages and approximately five billion in direct economic costs by 1988. On top of this, the civil war was consuming some 40 percent of state spending in the final years of the conflict (Stahler-Sholk 1990: 57). Defense spending was needed to counter direct U.S. aid to the contras, which totaled more than US$400 million by the end of the war (Booth, Wade, and Walker 2010: 91). To make matters worse, many local merchants fled Bluefields after the triumph of the Sandinista Revolution, and the intensification of armed conflict in the early 1980s brought agricultural production to a near standstill in the region. These factors, along with Reagan's 1985 trade embargo, reduced consumer access to imported goods and local staples, requiring state provision of goods and rationing of foodstuffs (Gordon 1998: 244–245). The growing economic crisis limited further investments in education, social security, and health care, as the state reoriented spending priorities to military defense (Stahler-Sholk 1990: 62, 70).

By the mid-1980s, the work of feeding and clothing a family in Bluefields was a time-consuming and dispiriting chore that fell largely on the shoulders of women. Basic consumer goods such as sanitary napkins, lightbulbs, toilet paper, meat, and clothing were scarce or unavailable, and women spent a good deal of time searching for these items and waiting in lines at state-run supply centers (Gordon 1998: 245). Carla told me, "In each barrio, you have these building that have this food then. You have to make one big line. And if you is a way to the end, you going to eat say like one or two o'clock. And you have to keep, because what you going to eat? And you have to economize whatsoever you getting." At the CAT, she said, "They give you a ticket and if you don't have that ticket, you don't have rights of buying nothing. Not everyone was to get a ticket neither, you know. You have to be *cien por ciento* [100 percent] Sandinista." Creole families that defied the military draft and had little access to salaried jobs found themselves on the margins of the political community, struggling to make ends meet in an informal economy that was increasingly targeted for containment by Sandinista economic policy (Ryan 1995: 169–170).[4]

Out of all of her jobs, Dafny remembers the CAT most fondly. As formal sector work with compensatory benefits like CAT consumer goods, the job held prestige and allowed Dafny access to other institutional resources, such as the low-interest bank loan the family used to buy land in Bluefields. When I asked Dafny why she liked the CAT, she compared it favorably to the isolation and low pay of domestic work. "I don't know," she said, "I do my home work, but I just really need to get out and do something. Because the first time when I start working and I receive my money, it's so nice, you know?" Dafny met her former partner and the father of three of her children at work. He had a job at the bodega (warehouse) behind the CAT. After the relationship got serious, he asked her to quit her job, but she told him, "I used to making my money, and I have two kids what is not for you." So he didn't insist. Dafny told me, "I really love to work for my own money. I love to be independent. You have some man just stingy and if you need something, you have to go and asking them for that. I don't like that. I'd rather have work and have my money." She said that when the man has the money in a relationship, he has "a power, domination over you."

Women-centered networks were crucial to the family's adjustment to city life in the mid-1980s. After their relocation to Bluefields, Miss Lucille asked her cousin, Rosita Monroe, to help her find a plot of land. As a new arrival to the city, she didn't know many mestizo families or how to get things done there. Miss Rosita introduced her to a man who had land for sale in the Canal neighborhood. With her good job at the CAT, Dafny got a loan from the bank to pay for the land. Dafny's partner served as the loan guarantor, and, although they had established their own household in Old Bank, they paid off the principal in just three years. Dafny put the land in her mother's name, and Mr. Sammy bought some third-class lumber to build a three-room house on the property. Carla told me, "But that land was one big swamp, Jennifer! When you walk, you go down to this [gestures to her knee] in the mud." The children spent their first years there carrying dirt, rocks, and oyster shells to fill in the swampy land, which after all of these years still becomes soggy and fetid during the rainy season. Not fond of city living, Sammy went back down to the farm after the war, but Carla, Coybi, Dafny's children, Junior, and many other members of the family have stayed in the Bluefields house over the years.

Women's Networks and Postwar Survival

After the war, Miss Lucille joined Sammy on the farm to escape the hardships of life in Bluefields. Carla stayed in Bluefields to attend secondary school, but she felt lonely and began to slip into a depression. "Most of the time, I used to pass alone," she told me, "and I never like that. So I gone back to Monkey Point, and that was the *fin* [end] of my study." Within a year, she was back in Bluefields. When Carla was in her late teens, a neighborhood boy named Clayton began to court her. Later, she began to see an older man who was a teacher. After a falling out with him, she got together for a brief time with Clayton. When her first child, Jarrel, was born, she was twenty years old. As an upright Christian lady, Miss Lucille did not approve of her daughter's choices, but Carla suffered no long-term stigma for her pregnancy. Families police the sexuality of adolescent girls and young women, partly due to respectability politics and partly out of fear for their safety, but this belies the commonality and general acceptance of youthful pregnancies outside of marriage. Carla said, "You know, I didn't give my mother a hard time when I was in my teenage." And by the age of twenty, she was ready for a child of her own.

Jarrel had Clayton's face, and Carla's best friend Hermita went to Clayton's mother to tell her about the baby. From that moment on, Jarrel was the apple of his grandmother's eye. She doted on him, and the family provided Carla with child care and economic help. Although their relationship was short lived, Clayton bought Jarrel what he needed in those early years with his wages from construction work. Carla also got support from Hermita, who was older and owned a house in Canal. Hermita's husband was working on a ship, and she traveled to Managua frequently. Carla minded the house when she was gone, and Hermita paid her fifty dollars a month for her services. When Jarrel was a few years old, Carla met the father of her second son at Hermita's house. After she got pregnant, she learned that he had another woman who was also pregnant. Angry and in no mood to bear the indiscretion, she and Jarrel went down to Monkey Point, where she took the job as radio operator. Miss Pearl welcomed her and attended to the baby's birth at the clinic. Carla and I met two months after Roy was born.

Economic dependence on her children's fathers was not a problem for Carla because she found support in an extensive social network of women that included the men's female kin. For women who want children but do not want to deal with infidelity, controlling behavior, or abuse, women-centered networks provide an alternative to marriage and domestic partnerships. After Roy's birth, Carla took the baby up to Bluefields to see his father's family. They offered to mind him while Carla was down in Monkey Point, and she agreed. With time, he got used to his father's family and began to fret for his grandmother and aunt when he spent nights away from them. Carla relented, and the baby's aunt, who had no children, began to raise Roy as her own.

That same year, Carla met a young mestizo who was the captain of a Gulf King fishing boat. He often anchored in the Monkey Point harbor and visited the clinic when Miss Pearl was away. Carla was "controlling" with injections but still became pregnant. She struggled to accept the pregnancy, as the relationship was troubled due to his infidelity. Carla confronted the father of her unborn child. She says that he told her, "I is man, and I can't live without woman." His response reflects a pervasive mind-set among mestizo and Creole men that sexual desire is a powerful natural drive, a physical urge that men cannot control. This construction of masculine sexuality naturalizes male infidelity and promotes sexual violence by suggesting that men have a right to sex with women and girls based on innate and uncontrollable physical desires.

Aware of the double standard, Carla told me, "Him want it and nothing else wasn't there. You know, the man them is *machista* so them always say what they feel like, they could do. But we woman, if we do that, they cut off our head." She added, "And I don't know if him protecting himself or what." Women who worry about infidelity may not feel they can ask men to wear condoms, as it suggests that at least one of the partners is unclean and un-trustworthy. Men also resist using condoms because they say it dulls sensa-tion. Thus, for most women, sex with an unfaithful male partner is a dan-gerous prospect. Carla dealt with this reality by cutting off the relationship and moving back to Bluefields. During her pregnancy, he would come by the house in Canal after a night of drinking. "When he drinking," she recalled, "he like make scandal, fighting, making noise." She said he told her, "If you want your son to raise up good, take me back and we go rent one place and live together." If she didn't take him back, he wouldn't help her when the baby came. Carla remembers telling him, "No, I not going nowhere with you."

This was a stressful and unhappy time. Carla would come by my house and rest on the sofa, looking pallid and queasy from morning sickness. The house in Canal was hot, noisy, and full of people, and she was emotionally spent and exhausted most of the time. The hardship intensified after her third son Jamal was born with clubfeet. Unlike her experiences with the pater-nal relatives of her older children, her relationship with the mestizo side of Jamal's family was more distant, and full responsibility for his care fell on Carla's shoulders. Gathering her strength, she told herself, "We grow up in a poor life and we survive. I'm going to survive with Jamal."

Jamal had multiple surgeries during his first year of life. Carla sought eco-nomic support from an advocacy NGO for physically disabled people in Ni-caragua. She also began to work as a domestic to make ends meet. Her first job was for a Bluefields mestiza who promised to pay her C$600 (less than US$50) per month, a pittance for long days of hard labor. The woman paid Carla the first month, but for her second month, she received half pay, and for the third month, she got no pay at all. Soon after she left the job, she met another mestiza who worked as a money changer. She wanted Carla to mind her house and children while she was working. The woman offered her a fair wage (C$2,800 per month) and a contract through the Labor Ministry; Carla stayed with her for more than a year.

After I left Nicaragua in 2004, Carla experienced two personal tragedies that were rooted in the structural and drug-related violence of the postwar years. She lost her beloved cousin Coybi to drug-induced pulmonary disease, and her oldest son Jarrel was hit by a car in Bluefields. One Sunday in 2005, as Jarrel and his grandmother headed home from church, a passenger bus bar-reled down a steep hill by the Bluefields Indian and Caribbean University. The bus collided with a taxi, and the taxi jumped the curb and struck Jarrel. His legs were crushed, and the doctors were forced to amputate below the knee. Bluefields lacks safe and effective traffic control, and pedestrians are at the mercy of the taxis that congest city streets. With few jobs in the formal sector, taxi service has become a booming informal economy. The number of taxis on city streets has vastly multiplied in the last decade, making walking from one end of the city to the other a treacherous journey. For those with physical disabilities, the city is profoundly inaccessible.

The bus owner denied culpability, forcing Carla to sue the owner's Managua-based insurance company. The lawyer won a C$50,000 settlement (about US$3,500 in the mid-2000s), paltry compensation for a lifetime of prosthetics and disability. With no social security benefits for the disabled and insufficient compensation for injury resulting from the negligence of others, the family faced a daunting challenge in managing Jarrel's care. Carla let the boy's grandmother keep the settlement and asked her to look after him. She told the family, "I can't handle this me alone. I don't have my own house. You all have to give me a hand." Others from the community also lent support. For instance, a local mestiza who worked by the *Lotería* (Lottery) heard about the case and wrote to Enrique Bolaños, the Nicaraguan president at the time. The first lady was moved by the letter and arranged lifetime prosthetics for Jarrel from the Center for Different Capacities (CAPADIFE, Centro de Capacidades Diferentes), the government disability agency in Managua. The family suffered another loss in 2009 when Clayton traveled down south to Corn River and never returned. The circumstances of his death remain murky but are indicative of the violence and precarity of life that working-class Creole families face these days.

After the accident, Carla took Jarrel to Managua for regular fittings as he frequently outgrew his prostheses. She met the father of her fourth and final child during one of these early trips. Aaron was a mestizo economist who worked with the Independent Liberal Party (PLI, Partido Liberal Independiente). He was much older than Carla and had grown children of his own. The two maintained a long-distance relationship for seven years that resulted in the birth of Carla's daughter in 2009. I was in Bluefields when she was born and remember Carla's joy at finally having a daughter. She told me, "Jennifer, I always wanted a girl. I wanted something in my image. So we plan it." Aaron asked Carla to stay in Managua and get married, but he could be jealous and controlling, and she was loath to lose her freedom. Far away from her family and community, Carla felt a sense of boredom and isolation in

Managua, where mestizo racism is more overt than in Bluefields. The coast held more appeal than marriage and economic security in Managua because her life there was steeped in social intimacy, mutual aid, and relative autonomy from men. Still, Aaron remained a supportive presence in Carla's life, encouraging her to return to school and helping her to pay for her passport and training when she applied to work on a cruise ship. When he died from a heart attack in 2013, Carla was stricken by the loss. Before his death, Aaron had made their young daughter the beneficiary of his life insurance policy. Carla began receiving monthly installments of C$2,842 (just over US$100 at today's exchange rates) shortly after his death. The monthly installment would have been twice the dollar amount when I lived in Bluefields in 2003. Inflation, the devaluation of the *córdoba*, and the creeping dollarization of the economy have hit working-class families hard in the last decade, as unemployment remains the norm.

Although the economy stabilized by the mid-1990s, there are few earning opportunities for working-class Creoles outside the usual *chamba* in the informal sector. Stuart Hall quotes the Trinidadian-British writer and activist Darcus Howe's description of what Creoles call *chamba*, which literally translates from Spanish as "work" or more accurately the hustle of moving from one earning strategy to the next in the informal sector. Howe writes, "In the Caribbean it is not simply that you are unemployed and you drift in hunger and total demoralization from day to day. That is absolutely untrue . . . the unemployed that I talk about in the Caribbean, that has not got a wage, an official wage of any kind, no wealth, is a vibrant powerful section of the society" (Howe in Hall et al. 1978: 373). This section of society survives by "hustling," or *chamba* for Creoles, "eking out" a survival without generally resorting to crime. The vibrancy Howe describes "emerges in the positive stress on avoiding the humiliation of work" and the myriad ways that the wage and social division of labor reproduce race-class-gender subordination for working class Caribbean people (Hall et al. 1978: 373).

One can still survive and sometimes live well with *chamba* and the mutual aid of others, but true intergenerational security requires a home in Bluefields and schooling. Carla's greatest desire is to have a house on land of her own, somewhere she can grow old with her children and future grandchildren. Land and construction materials in Bluefields, however, are prohibitively expensive these days. A decent-sized lot with a modern cement-block house can cost as much as US$30,000—a sum of money that requires years of hard labor on Caribbean cruise lines for most Creole families. With this long-term security in mind, Carla followed the example of her aunt Dafny and cousin Vianka and began to prepare her application to ship out.

Navigating the Global Labor Market

For Creole women, labor migration is fraught with hardships and sacrifices that can exact a great price on their personal well-being, relationships, and social lives. Under these conditions, the decision to stay makes as much sense as the decision to go. There are no precise figures for Creole participation in the cruise industry, but roughly 10 percent of the Creole population in Bluefields worked on ships when the labor market peaked in the late 1990s and early 2000s. As many as 40 percent of Creole families still had members on ships in the late 2000s, according to Bluefields crewing agent Wade Hawkins. English-language skills and access to a Creole-owned crewing agency in Bluefields gave the community a clear advantage over mestizos in this global service sector. Although shipping out is more common among Bluefields Creoles than Monkey Point Creoles, about a dozen men and two women from the community have worked on cruise ships in the last three decades, a gender ratio that reflects men's dominance in the sector.

Creole men worked on cruise lines in small numbers in the 1980s, long before cruising grew into a US$36 billion industry serving more than 21 million passengers each year.[5] Christine Chin writes that this global service sector epitomizes the flexibility and hypermobility of twenty-first-century capital (2008: 6). Three lines owned by multinational conglomerates monopolize the cruising industry, together controlling more than 80 percent of the global market (Chin 2008: 11; Wood 2004: 159). The largest of the three, Carnival Cruise Lines, has not recruited in Bluefields since the early 1990s, but the smaller Royal Caribbean and Norwegian Cruise Lines continued to contract Creole seafarers throughout the 1990s and 2000s. The companies are headquartered in Miami-Dade County, Florida, but each is incorporated in a second country and has ships flagged by third countries. Most crucially for workers, flag states oversee labor, health, and safety protocols on ships and are used to circumvent more restrictive regulations in the United States and Europe (Chin 2008: 8–9; Wood 2000: 35; Wood 2004: 160).

Cruise ship labor reflects the deterritorialized and denationalized character of the industry with seafarers hailing from as many as eighty different countries on some of the largest ships (Chin 2008: 2). Distinct from other forms of landed labor migration, shipping out involves extended contracts for six to ten months on a ship, with usually two to three months of home leave per year. Creoles who ship out do not migrate to another country, and their travel is legally secured with U.S.-issued C1D visas (nonimmigrant crew member transit visas), which give them, *as laboring bodies only*, the ability to cross national borders with few legal obstacles. Shipping out is preferential to landed labor migration because Creole seafarers earn tax-free wages without taking on First World expenses for housing, transportation, and food, thus allowing them to save and repatriate most of their earnings. Moreover, they are not criminalized by host country immigration laws and may return to visit their families every year without the dangers of unauthorized border crossings.

Despite these benefits, Creole seafarers are subject to long periods of spatial confinement, surveillance, and segregation based on a division of labor that separates crew from staff and officers—or unskilled workers from the global south from higher wage workers who mostly come from the global north. North American and Western European seafarers enjoy better positions, higher wages, shorter contracts and workdays, paid vacations, superior cabin accommodations, and greater access to ship amenities than seafarers from the global south (Chin 2008: 21; Wood 2000: 353). Cruise lines recruit Creole applicants into the most menial entry-level positions in the utility galley, which pay US$600 to $800 per month. Hawkins told me that galley jobs taking out garbage, washing dishes, and stocking groceries require "manpower," resulting in an overwhelming preference for male applicants. He said that just 10 to 15 percent of new hires are Creole women, although they apply in far greater numbers. Women who do get contracts often take positions as restaurant stewards, refilling water glasses and tending buffet tables. Once onboard, men and women have opportunities to cross-train for promotions to other departments. Even as they work long shifts seven days a week, most Creole seafarers pursue extra hours of training for cabin steward or waiter because these positions have higher monthly earnings (US$1,500 to US$2,000) due to gratuities from passengers who are overwhelmingly from the United States and Europe.[6] Even as the cruise industry promotes economic globalization and corporate profit, the social division of labor and the server–consumer relationship on board ships recreate and naturalize colonial hierarchies on these "floating chunks of capital" (Chin 2008: 143). The all-inclusive resort at sea creates a contained space of hyperconsumption that channels profits to transnational corporations and segregates U.S. and European passengers from actual landed communities in the Caribbean.

The flexibility and hypermobility of global capital feeds on neoliberal economic restructuring in the global south. After the Sandinista electoral defeat, Creole participation in the cruise industry intensified as Nicaragua underwent neoliberal restructuring.[7] Hurricane Joan destroyed some 80 percent of structures in Bluefields in 1988; by 1990, the country faced an unemployment rate that was five times higher than before the economic crisis of the mid-1980s (Arana 1997: 82). Nicaragua was additionally saddled with the highest per capita foreign debt in the world (Ibid.: 83). IMF-mandated structural adjustment under Violeta Chamorro's administration only increased the pain for popular sectors, as the social cost of adjustment fell on their shoulders. Privatization and public sector layoffs doubled the unemployment rate from 1990 to 1995, and trade liberalization and an import boom deprived rural producers of their market (Robinson 1997: 35). Cutbacks on social spending hit women who manage household resources particularly hard (Metoyer 2000: 5). The Chamorro administration's uncritical embrace of free-market doctrine injected bias into economic policy, which consistently "favored large business and strengthened the positions of monopolies, oligopolies, and the business elite close to the government" (Arana 1997: 84). Robinson argues that this neoliberal program led to a "far-reaching process of class restructuring," creating a massive reserve army of under- and unemployed Nicaraguans by the mid-1990s (1997: 36).

Latin America's neoliberal debacle rendered people from the region more "flexible" or more desperate in relation to capital, allowing cruise lines to recruit workers with low wages, punishing work schedules, no overtime, ten-month contracts, and no job security (Chin 2008: 18). But by the time the global recession hit in the late 2000s, Creole seafarers had fallen out of favor with companies like Royal Caribbean, as aging employees began to file compensation claims for on-the-job injuries and exhausted workers were fired for misconduct or poor customer evaluations. When Latin American and Caribbean seafarers began to challenge management on the terms and conditions of their employment, companies looked to Asia for a more flexible labor pool (Ibid.: 130). Hawkins told a Nicaraguan newspaper in 2013, "It seems that the companies have realized that Indonesians and Filipinos are more humble [desperate and compliant] than Caribbeans and Central Americans" (*El Nuevo Diario* 2013).

The exploitation and insecurity of the cruise industry is reflected in Dafny and Carla's efforts to secure employment on ships. After she separated from her long-term partner, Dafny decided to apply to ship out. She had *chamba*, ironing for a lawyer, a judge, and a local business owner and cleaning a hardware store after hours. But her children were growing up, and she was eager to replace the decaying board house in Canal with a larger, sturdier cement structure. After passing all of the preliminary application hurdles, Dafny went to the U.S. Embassy in Managua to get a C1D visa and was inexplicably denied. Heartbroken and back in Bluefields, she shared her experience with a friend who told her, "Don't worry, when one door close, many are open." The friend contacted her niece in Grand Cayman, and she helped Dafny find employment as a nanny for wages comparable to those on cruise ships. Dafny spent the next seven years in Grand Cayman, faithfully sending money home to rebuild the house in Canal bit by bit.

One day, Dafny and Carla were chatting long-distance when Dafny said to her, "Why you don't look how to get one chance to ship out?" Carla replied, "Me? I don't see myself going ship." She didn't have the money necessary to apply. But Dafny said she would help and encouraged her to give it a try. Carla soon started to train at a local hotel for the position of cabin steward. The training cost US$50 and consisted of unpaid work cleaning hotel rooms. After successfully completing her training, she took an English test and went to Managua for her medical exam. Applicants submit to a host of invasive procedures that include a pelvic exam (for women), colonoscopy, and blood and urine tests for drugs and sexually transmitted infections. The tests cost several hundred dollars, which Dafny and I split between us. After meeting these requirements, the crewing agency informed Carla that she would need to raise US$1,200 to cover the travel expenses for her first contract, a sum the company would later reimburse. International Labor Organization (ILO) conventions forbid agencies from charging applicant fees for placement, and cruise companies must pay for seafarer travel and lodging up front after issuing a contract. Chin, however, found that applicants from the global south often pay between US$250 to several thousand dollars to secure a job on ship (2008: 116). As Carla devised a plan to raise the funds, the crewing agency announced that they were no longer issuing contracts. Floored by the news, she and her large cohort of applicants turned to a less-reputable agent who required a fee to initiate a new application. Carla paid US$200 to secure a place in the queue. Not long after, the agent disappeared and stopped answering her phone. Carla told me that desperation drove the risky investment. By the early 2010s, getting a contract to work on a ship was like winning the lottery.

Solidarity and Sexuality in the Marketplace

Labor migration is not new for the Creole community, which has its roots in a fluid history of mobility and travel in the postemancipation Caribbean. Monkey Point is the product of a dynamic nineteenth-century Western Caribbean migratory field that was driven by export agriculture and infrastructure development on the Central American coastline. Men's labor fueled commodity production and infrastructure construction, but the indispensible work of social reproduction belonged to women (Putnam 2002: 6–7). Earlier generations of community women, like Rachel and Catherine, followed these migratory circuits and exchanged their reproductive labor for a wage. Because migrant men outnumbered migrant women two to one, Caribbean women labored in a seller's market as cooks, washerwomen, housekeepers, seamstresses, barwomen, and sex workers, giving them ample economic "alternatives to an exclusive relationship with any given partner" (Ibid.: 7).

Sexual relations between women and men continue to be enmeshed in market relations today, and labor migration is a central site of contestation over sexuality and social solidarity within the Creole community. Kamala Kempadoo argues that Caribbean sexuality represents a diverse set of socially constructed discourses and embodied practices that are embedded in colonial history and the global economy, having multiple meanings "not all of which have to do with reciprocity of sexual desire or feelings of love" (2004: 39, 43). As part of a vernacular worldview, many working-class Creoles embrace the idea that the values and social hierarchies produced by capitalism are immoral and corrupting. The critique extends to those working on cruise lines who come home with money to spend, new consumerist styles, and a different set of friends from the ship. Their incorporation into a global capitalist labor regime places migrants in an ambivalent position between exploitation on board and social mobility at home. Heteropatriarchal discourse about sexuality peppers critiques of capitalist intensification and the social transformations that accompany labor migration, and rumors frequently circulate in Bluefields about the sexual promiscuity of men and women on ships who are no longer subject to the moderating influence of their families and community. Scrutiny of the sexual lives of Creole women on ships is particularly intense.

Carla's cousin Vianka was one of the lucky few to ship out before Blue-fields recruitment stopped in 2012. Young, slim, attractive, and personable, she was a desirable recruit for the company, which, Hawkins told me, looks for workers who outwardly display mental acuity, energy, enthusiasm, and happy dispositions during the interview. Ideal candidates must perform "a flexible bundle of skills" and reflexively manage their personal affect and in-terpersonal communication in ways that conform to the global hospitality industry. Most applicants are physically capable and willing to do unskilled entry-level labor on cruise ships, but not everyone successfully performs the disposition to labor in this space of hypercapitalist consumption. Nor do they outwardly demonstrate the potential for self-improvement and acquisition of new skill sets—or what Ilana Gershon calls "neoliberal agency" (2011: 542).

Vianka had considerable success her first year on ship, working her way up from restaurant steward to waiter in little time. As she listed off the countries she had visited, she told me, "That's the best part of working on ship because you get the opportunity to know different part of the world." Men and women who ship out gain social prestige at home due to the urbanity that comes with money and international travel. Vianka admitted, "Plenty people, whenever you go on ship and you come back home, them believe that because you go on ship, you change. At least, certain people them change a lot when them go on ship."

"Like how?" I asked her.

"But I mean because them is not the same," she said. "Them don't match up with the people what they used to match before them ever go on ship."

"Like they start hanging out with new friends?"

"Yeah, hanging out with new friends, with people what working on ship," Vianka replied. Taking on a more reflective tone, she added, "Actually, when you working on ship, you don't got to change because you never know when you can get fired. That's not your company. You're just working for them. You don't know when you could get fired. So for me, I would always be the same."

For most working-class Creoles I know, the change Vianka describes is not simply a problem of class differentiation and the social tensions that result from increasing stratification. They describe it as a deeper phenomenologi-cal shift in values, consciousness, and subjectivity. Creoles who ship out be-come different *kinds* of people who interpret and experience the world in new ways. What used to bring you pleasure no longer does. The people you once relied on for friendship and mutual aid now want more from you than you are willing to offer. Your behavior and relational values change. Your sense of self-worth is more tied to work, money, and consumerism. The shift offends a vernacular worldview premised on egalitarianism and reciprocity.

Carla mirrored these sentiments when she told me, "Like I see a lot of people what I know, when them go ship out and they come back, them no talk to you anymore. I don't know why." She thought for a minute and said, "Money change them, I would say."

I pressed her further, "How does it change them?"

"Becausing, like say, when them was here before them gone to ship out, all of we be together," she replied. "We make *chamba* sometimes. We make *chamba*, get some money, and buy our use for around the house, and whatsoever stay, we go and take some beer or rum or whatsoever. We was always unite in that aspect. Alright, so say they go ship and when them come back, them forget all of those thing them."

This description of the change that seafarers undergo is embedded in vernacular practice and the social solidarity it creates among working-class Creoles. Although a resort to *chamba* is driven by economic lack, Carla also associates it with self-valorizing practices in the community that promote unity, sociality, and pleasure. From her perspective, integration into the global labor market disrupts sociality and thus changes one's subjectivity and relationship to community. Vianka suggests that it is foolhardy for seafarers, who are expendable in relation to capital, to allow themselves to change. Bluefields has a large population of middle-aged Creole men who spent the most productive years of their lives working on ships. These men bought land and built houses, but they often return home embittered with no access to future earning opportunities that would allow them to continue to provide for their families. They also return to independent wives who have spent years raising families, running households, and living full social lives on their own.

The intensification of capitalist values and social relations that comes with shipping out provokes debates within families and the wider community about women's sexual behavior, social autonomy, and economic independence from men. Vianka told me, "Actually, a lot of guys have the mentality that ship don't make for a woman." This perception is based partly on patriarchal values and the myth of the male breadwinner (Safa 1995) but also on the organization of labor at sea. Chin notes that "the social construction and use of commercialized oceanic space remains distinctly masculinized" because seafaring has been dominated historically by men, and today the vast majority of seafarers are men, outnumbering women crew members four to one (2008: 21). When Creole women ship out, they do not just strengthen their social and economic autonomy in relation to men at home, but they do so by entering a masculinized space organized around neocolonial hierarchies and capitalist values.

In Bluefields, this masculine space is thought to be a sexually permissive space where anything goes. Men on ships are assumed to have multiple casual partners or temporary girlfriends for the length of their contract or to pay for sex at port. Male cabin stewards are also said to have sex with single female passengers, although employee–guest interactions are tightly surveilled by cameras and supervisors and infractions can result in termination. Moreover, labor migration is associated with HIV/AIDS as some of the first cases in the Creole community came from return migrants who worked on ships. The association between shipping out and HIV infection has continued despite the fact that it now occurs independently of labor migration throughout Nicaragua. Thus, for many Creoles, the ship represents a masculinized space of labor exploitation, neocolonial hierarchy, surveillance, sexual promiscuity, adventure, and infection.

Vianka told me that Creole men "feel like because you are a woman, you going on ship, you going to do the same thing what them do out there." Women are assumed to take on men's sexual prerogatives with their new employment and earning power. This supposition ignores how racism and patriarchy continue to structure Creole women's labor experiences on ships. Regardless of their new earning potential, women seafarers are still subject to sexual harassment in their jobs and a double standard that naturalizes male sexual freedom while stigmatizing their own. Moreover, the social disciplining of women's sexual behavior does not stop once they board ships. Most women work on ships that employ many other Creole seafarers, and third parties often report on their behavior to family and friends at home.

Perhaps the most intense gendered debates about shipping out focus on heteropatriarchal economies that merge marriage and sex between women and men with market relations. The expectation that men and women who lose their partners for ten months of the year, sometimes for a decade or more, will remain faithful may be unrealistic. Many marriages do not survive multiple repeat contracts on ship, not simply due to infidelity but because couples find it difficult to maintain a long-distance relationship for years on end. But most men still expect their wives at home to remain faithful when they provide monthly remittances. Nevertheless, the power that a male wage earner has in a relationship shifts when men remit wages to women who stay at home. Men control how much they send home, but women have the freedom to decide how to spend the money and with whom they spend their time. The anxiety that this arrangement produces for men is captured in the "soft hand" phenomenon. A "soft hand" is a man at home who has sex with the wife of a man on a ship. He is not working, hence the soft hands, but is benefiting from the seafarer's wages and sexual privileges. Carla told me, "Soft hand is who doing the job for the husband. Help spend him money, keep his wife happy, and handling everything until when him come back home." Although I have never met anyone with this arrangement, I have heard men express this concern.

I asked Carla if the reverse was true. Do wives with husbands on ships expect them to be faithful? She told me that if the man is maintaining them, most women pardon their husbands for extramarital sex. Other women have told me that they want husbands to remain faithful but recognize that they cannot control men's sexual behavior. Some women ask men to wear condoms on ship, even if they do not feel they can ask them to wear condoms at home. Men also say that they are careful to protect themselves on board. A positive test for a sexually transmitted infection will keep a seafarer from renewing a contract with the company. Most Bluefields Creoles also remember the case of a man who shipped out in the late 1980s and infected his wife with HIV. The couple and their child later died.[8]

Still, many Creoles believe that remittances should guarantee fidelity for female partners only. When I asked if women on ships expect their husbands at home to remain faithful, Carla replied, "No, him can't. It's hard, Jennifer, for one man." Women recognize that heterosexual sex and marriage are in some respects akin to market exchange and that women "sell" rather than "buy." Men are seen as individuals who can and should provide for themselves, and no self-respecting woman is desperate enough to pay for a man's company. Most women I know, however, are not opposed to a collaborative and egalitarian relationship in which the man and woman both contribute equally. Dafny and Vianka agreed on this point. Vianka explained, "It's good, too, to make man and woman working, so you can get ahead better, because both of you are working, you can see the future better."

What the future holds for Monkey Point people remains unclear. A decline in seafarer recruitment has forced many working-class Creoles to migrate to

Managua to work in international call centers or leave Nicaragua for hotel work, domestic labor, and construction jobs in places like Grand Cayman and Panama. The United States is a less viable destination due to the difficulties in obtaining a work visa and the dangers associated with undocumented status, but Creoles still migrate to southern Florida, New York, and Los Angeles for work when they can. After returning from Grand Cayman, Dafny left Bluefields in 2013 to reunite with her son in Miami, who was able to help his mother come to the United States through the family reunification program. But out-migration, along with the cumulative impact of violent conflict, neoliberal restructuring, capitalist intensification, land loss, and the war on drugs, is another line of assault on working-class Creole communities in Nicaragua. Monkey Point activism for autonomous rights represents an effort to ensure collective survival, stave off dispossession, and craft a meaningful future in the face of prolonged structural and physical violence. Women's sociality is foundational to this "positive project of self-constitution" (Cleaver 1992: 129). When Fab 5 heralds the women's revolution, perhaps they are signaling other sources of resilience and revolutionary action that make working-class Creole women in Nicaragua powerful social and political agents in their own right.

4 From Cold Wars to Drug Wars

PERHAPS THE NADIR OF THE WAR YEARS came in May 1985. In the midst of economic deprivation and warfare, a small contra detachment from the south landed at the Bluefields police headquarters in the predawn hours. A second group of contras followed, attacking a Sandinista military base to the south of the Bluefields airport. Some of these men retreated with casualties. The Frente captured others. The first group had nowhere to go but the sea, and Sandinista forces quickly overpowered them. Miss Bernicia's eldest son Johnny was among the twenty-four men captured alive and killed by the Frente Sandinista. Their bodies were displayed in the Bluefields central park and then buried in a mass grave. John's story mirrors the experiences of many community men born in the 1950s and 1960s. After the triumph, he voluntarily joined the Sandinista People's Army (EPS, Ejército Popular Sandinista). Johnny identified with Rastafari culture and eventually got in trouble with the law for selling weed. He had frequent conflicts with mestizos in the military and later fled to Costa Rica to join the contras. On the southern front, he fought with other Creole and Rama men who were affiliated with Edén Pastora's ARDE (Alianza Revolucionaria Democrática, or Democratic Revolutionary Alliance) and Brooklyn Rivera's MISURASATA (Miskitu, Sumu, Rama, and Sandinista Asia Takanka, or Miskitu, Sumu, Rama, and Sandinista Working Together). By the time of his death, most community men were looking for a way out, walking away from contra encampments, laying down their arms, and turning to the Costa Rican authorities for refugee status.

John's capture and the violent spectacle of bodies in the park encircle most community accounts of armed conflict during the 1980s. Among men, wartime memories reveal the inevitability of coercion and violence as they cycled between state security forces, counterrevolutionary forces, and oftentimes incarceration. The men's age, gender, race, and class appear to overdetermine their roles in Cold War securitization as Sandinista soldiers, contra fighters, draft evaders, deserters, refugees, and ex-combatants. Rather than focusing on the ideological battles of the era, community men narrate an embodied and intensely personal politics of security in which encounters with state security forces and the Sandinista policy of mandatory conscription became central sites of politicization in the 1980s. These experiences in the early years of the Sandinista Revolution dovetailed with an aggressive U.S. campaign of destabilization and military aid to the contras, drawing community men into a bloody and protracted conflict with the Sandinista state. After the war, these same men became racialized threats in the hemispheric drug war, which continues to target them as objects of securitization. For two generations of men who have lived through the Cold War and the drug war, security has become a central "mode of social reproduction" (Cowen and Siciliano 2011) that connects their intimate experiences of racism and state violence to wider geopolitical forces that emerge from militarism and U.S. intervention in Central America.

This chapter focuses on what Cowen and Siciliano (2011) call "securitized social reproduction" or ways of producing, disciplining, and curtailing human life and subjectivity that bring marginalized men into frequent contact with security apparatuses through a range of violent institutional practices and regulatory processes in times of war and peace. For two generations of community men, racially charged encounters with mestizo security forces have become so routinized and embedded in daily life that they are now a form of social reproduction underpinning subject formation and political agency. During the war years, these security practices included enlistment into civilian militias, forced conscription, military training and service, policing of draft evaders, incarceration of suspected contras or contra deserters, coerced recruitment into contra groups, profiling at border crossings, institutional control and policing in Costa Rican refugee camps, and deportation to Nicaragua. Postwar security now focuses on counternarcotics policing and includes search and surveillance checkpoints, racial profiling, incarceration, and military occupation.

Men are particularly vulnerable to these forms of regulation as they are the central agents and objects of securitization—both violence workers for the state (Huggins et al. 2002) and anticitizen security threats (Inda 2006: 53).[1] As agents and objects of securitization, they represent "surplus masculinity" or reserve armies of young and often racialized men who are locked out of labor markets due to uneven economic growth and neoliberal restructuring. Economic crisis during the civil war followed by postwar neoliberal restructuring tethered this disenfranchised male labor force ever more "tightly to the risks and response of the security state" (Cowen and Siciliano 2011: 1516, 1535). In the vast areas of the south Atlantic coast that remained ungoverned by the state after the Contra War, marginalized mestizo men from communities outside of the region now militarily secure capitalist intensification and police the surplus labor force that maintains a claim to the land at Monkey Point.

At the same time that the state began to remilitarize the coast, the neoliberal right under Enrique Bolaños began to tentatively accept (at the behest of the World Bank) multicultural citizenship as a positive departure from the conflict-driven ethnic politics of the Sandinista era. This version of neoliberal multiculturalism was based on two limiting precepts: multicultural rights must not challenge the neoliberal economic regime, and legitimate subjects of rights must conform to narrow models of ethnic identity and activism (Hale 2002, 2004, 2005). Community men did not conform, nor did their encounters with security forces change for the better, suggesting that the policing of their community picked up where this narrow model of multicultural inclusion fell short. From their point of view, policing betrayed the egalitarian promise of state multiculturalism, reasserting mestizo state power through militarized force. One effect of these contradictions has been the radicalization of community activism and the embrace of an autonomous politics of security and self-defense.

Broadly considered over the span of three decades, the demise of one securitized masculine subject (enemy combatant) and the rise of another (drug trafficker) reveals both continuities and permutations in state and imperial power during the transition from ethnic conflict and Cold War securitization to multicultural rights and drug war militarization (Zilberg 2013). This chapter tracks these continuities and permutations through the experiences of six men who fought as contra combatants in the 1980s. Born between 1950 and 1966, the men are close relatives from four Monkey Point families. Together they have been exposed to a range of violent security practices that target community men and entrap them in securitized social reproduction.

Each of the following sections of the chapter uncovers the geopolitical and experiential roots of autonomous self-defense in Monkey Point by examining the men's participation in wartime violence, their reinterpellation from enemy combatants to criminal threats, and their responses to racial profiling and postwar militarization. The chapter ends with an account of a paramilitary incursion in 2002 that community people successfully deterred through an act of self-defense. The men's wartime experiences set the foundation for this act of direct resistance to the postwar security state.

The Gathering Storm

The 1980s represented a period of convergence in U.S. policy for Latin America between a waning anticommunist agenda and a new hemispheric drug war. Reagan-era support for counterrevolutionary forces in Nicaragua reveals a cynical manipulation of growing anxieties about illegal drugs in the service of military intervention, even as this support allowed contra forces involved in cocaine smuggling to develop the drug trade with little interference during the war (Bagley 1988; Bullington and Block 1990; Johnston 2010; Morales 1989; Scott and Marshall 1991). As anticommunist interventions grew politically passé in the late 1980s, the drug war provided an alternative "laboratory to project US power, train local militaries in the new strategic doctrine, transfer military hardware, and gather intelligence" (Morales 1989: 155). In hindsight, U.S. military intervention along with a protracted campaign to destabilize the revolutionary state appears to have been an influential force in promoting postwar drug violence in the region.

The political discourses of injury that frame the men's accounts of the war years, however, focus on the Sandinista state rather than the U.S. government. Gordon locates this political sensibility in experiences of racial conflict and exclusion during the initial years of the Sandinista Revolution. At the time of the triumph, he writes, most Creoles were happy to see the collapse of the Somoza regime as they saw in the revolutionary process an opportunity to empower their own community (Gordon 1998: 205, 213). But contests for local power between Creole and mestizo factions in the weeks following the triumph quickly devolved into racial enmity and strife (Ibid.: 216–217). As the FSLN consolidated regional power, the revolutionary government favored the mestizo community, granting the majority of leadership positions in state institutions and mass organizations to mestizos (Ibid.: 226–227).

Creole resentment toward the Sandinista state culminated in September 1980 with a large protest for better representation in government, unrestricted markets for consumer goods, and regional separation from the Nicaraguan nation, for a radical faction of the crowd (Ibid,: 234). Managua responded by sending Internal Order Police (POI, Policía de Orden Interno) to restore calm to the city. Once in Bluefields, the POI used force to subdue Creole protest. Outfitted in battle gear, they set up barricades, discharged guns to disband protesters, searched Creole neighborhoods, arrested suspected agitators, and according to witnesses used excessive force and racial epithets against members of the community (Ibid.: 235–236, 238). Gordon describes the protest as a watershed moment in Creole resistance to the revolution, marking the end of open political dissent and the intensification of anticommunist sentiments (Ibid.: 238–239).

Monkey Point people witnessed the events Gordon describes. Hubert Duncan, who goes by the nickname Cow, remembered, "I was a young guy. I have around seventeen years. But well, we used to watch the movement of what them [the Sandinistas] want to do with the coast, Bluefields, and things. So they [the Creoles] had a manifestation [protest] in Bluefields, fighting against the changing of the way, the system." The changes in the system that men remember most include curtailed access to consumer goods, private property confiscations, and the state's use of force to quell dissent. Nevertheless, almost all of the men who fought as contras describe a willingness to participate in popular mobilization after the triumph, reflecting the initial support for the revolution that Gordon describes. Several community men voluntarily trained with Sandinista forces in Bluefields in the early days of the revolution. Armed and in uniform, they returned to their community to serve as civilian militia after basic training. Cow's older brother, Edward Duncan, known by the nickname Jumbo, was among the group. Jumbo told me, "Them tell we was just to mind the community and defend our people in the community."

But the men began to grow uneasy as conflict with the Sandinista state intensified after 1980. As civilian militia, they were concerned that they would be forced to fight against the armed groups that were forming in opposition to the revolution. Jumbo told me that a small group of men decided to "run to Costa Rica, looking for refuge, for no fight." Sullivan Quinn was the eldest member of the group that left for Costa Rica. Born in Corn Island, Quinn grew up in Monkey Point, married a local woman, and eventually had a large family of his own there. In those days, Quinn built lobster traps for a man named Charles Notice. Notice had a fishing boat, and local men said that he worked as a contra liaison along the south coast. Quinn told me that one day Notice's "wife send a letter down from Bluefields telling him directly that them [the Sandinistas] was coming to pick him up with all the man them working with him, and them was going to kill us." Quinn thought to himself, "You know what, if that be the case, I don't want to dead crazy like that, so I got to go."

About five Monkey Point men left for Costa Rica with Notice and another group from Tasbapauni. Jumbo said that the Costa Rican authorities received them and delivered them to Edén Pastora, a dissident Sandinista commander and revolutionary hero who broke with the FSLN to organize resistance from the border. The CIA recruited Pastora and began to fund training camps in Costa Rica in 1982 (Kornbluh and Byrne 1993: 1). Pastora, along with another former Sandinista, Alfonso Robelo, formed ARDE and later allied with Brooklyn Rivera, the Miskitu leader of MISURASATA, a popular revolutionary organization that formed after the triumph and grew into an influential advocate for indigenous empowerment and autonomy (Hale 1994: 133). MISURASATA was alienated from the Sandinista state by 1982 and split into two armed factions: MISURA, led by Steadman Fagoth in the north; and MISURASATA, led by Brooklyn Rivera in the south (Ibid.: 153). The southern front contras that community men joined distinguished themselves from the Nicaraguan Democratic Forces (FDN, Fuerzas Democráticas Nicaragüenses), the main contra group in Honduras made up of right-wing former Somoza National Guards. ARDE was, instead, "dedicated to restoring the original goals of the Nicaraguan revolution" (Fritz 1995: 11, 45), whereas MISURASATA primarily sought indigenous self-determination.

With money and arms from the United States, contra forces on the southern front began to attack Nicaraguan targets in mid-1983, and the region descended into violence. Philippe Bourgois suggests that U.S. intervention more than any other factor was responsible for protracted warfare between Sandinista forces and indigenous and Afrodescendant combatants. Without U.S. funding, training, and military hardware, he writes, "There may have been some bloodshed, but it would not have degenerated into a prolonged, bloody, fratricidal civil war; it probably would have been resolved through a tensely charged—but largely non-violent—process of dialogue, confrontation and compromise" (Bourgois 1986: 8). The insight is supported by community men's initial reluctance to take up arms against the Sandinista state and their efforts to extricate themselves from combat once they joined the contras. Almost all of the ex-contras from Monkey Point whom I interviewed said they had had little desire to go to war. Jumbo even told me that community men were "not no fighters."

Despite their reluctance to fight, the men were unified in their condemnation of Sandinista conscription policies. The Sandinista government passed the Patriotic Military Service Law in 1983 in response to escalating conflict. Conscription focused on men eighteen to twenty-five, but the law mandated that all men between twenty-five and forty must serve in reserve forces. Military service was voluntary for women. Draft evasion was punishable by up to four years in prison (Internacional de Resistentes a la Guerra 1998). After two years of service, veterans would join the Reserve Military Service (SMR, Servicio Militar de Reserva), which would serve as a vital defensive force for the Pacific side of the country in the advent of a direct U.S. invasion (*Envío* Team 1985a). On the south coast, members of civilian militias included workers for state enterprises and institutions concentrated in Bluefields as well as people who were independently employed.

Gordon writes that Creoles considered mandatory conscription "the ultimate invasion of individual rights and further proof of the nefarious and communistic nature of the government" (1998: 249). Monkey Point people shared this perspective. Most of the men reported that the draft was their principal reason for armed resistance to the Sandinista state:

Cow: I decide because I no like that way of living and catching up the young boy and come forcing them for go. In combat, the contra them, them ask you if you want to go to the war or you want to go Costa Rica refuge [refugee camp]. So them give you opportunity, anything you want. If you want go refuge, well them send you. But the Sandinista no, them take you one time and give you a gun and thing and say you going.

Rolando: [The people were fighting] to free Nicaragua from the military service and from the actual Daniel Ortega. They didn't like him through the same system, taking the young peoples them and carry them to the service to fight. So that was the biggest problem what we did have on the Atlantic coast here. Cause he go into your house and take you. Hardly anybody escape it . . . It was violating. They destroy a lot of life.

Junior: In almost the whole Atlantic coast, or the country, people didn't like how these people abusing of the kids. Young people in military service them go and lose they life innocently . . . Abusing, they abusing. So, you know, any time people abusing, you try to cool, but later on you get rebellious. And that is what was taking place.

These accounts indicate that Sandinista militarism and forced conscription of young men led to Creole opposition, further repression, and ultimately armed resistance to the state.

Gordon, however, notes that recruitment for Patriotic Military Service (SMP, Servicio Militar Patriótico) did not begin in Atlantic coast communities until 1984, when most men from Monkey Point had already taken up arms against the Sandinista state (Ibid.: 249). Despite the fact that community men remember forced conscription as the most serious violation of their rights, their testimony indicates that they joined contra forces at different moments in the conflict for a range of reasons. Most people in their community had begun to reject mestizo revolutionary nationalism by the early 1980s and were living in an environment of escalating violence, uncertainty, and state repression. Moreover, there was a limited range of options open to working-class Creole men for nonviolent dissent or safe exile abroad between 1982 and 1984. Hastened by political violence and the threat of state repression, the majority of community men left for contra camps in three principal waves. Only the final group joined to avoid forced conscription into the Sandinista army.

The first group left for Costa Rican training camps with Notice in 1982. Once in Costa Rica, the men found they had few options. They could train with the contras or return to Nicaragua and face the Sandinistas because, as Jumbo said, "We no have no document to be in the country and if the immigration catch we here, them gon put we to jail. So we run from danger and gone straight in danger back." The Costa Rican government established reception centers and camps for refugees in May 1983 to serve the surge of Nicaraguans crossing the border to flee violence (Basok 1990: 730–731). But in the early days of the conflict, Jumbo explained, there were no camps to receive refugees. By the time the camps opened, he said, "We'd a done sign up as fighter, and they receiving no fighter. They receive civilian at refuge."

The men decided to stay and train with the contras. After many months, a group returned to fight in Nicaragua, where they recruited a second wave of men from their community, mostly close relatives who were now living in a combat zone and wanted to support their family members in the fight. Jumbo's father and younger brother Cow were among this group. Sammy and Miss Lucille's son Junior also took up arms to fight alongside his cousins. Cow described how his brother and other men from the community returned to Monkey Point and began to fight the Sandinistas. "So them start to visit we," he said, "and the people them start to running, running 'bout in the bush. Them come with them coast guard and plane and push and pull [military aircraft] and thing and throwing bomb in the town. So everybody just start taking bush, and well I decided for go on the contra side."

A final group of teenage boys joined contra forces up north near Tasbapauni to avoid conscription a year or two later. Sammy and Lucille's youngest son Leonardo and their grandson Alan were among this group. The two fled the school they attended in Haulover with nearly thirty other boys, some as young as fifteen years of age. Contra forces from a neighboring community took them to the bush where they began to train as fighters. Recalling those difficult times, Leonardo told me, "My mind was worried, because I say, I leaving my education and going. Now I going to learn maybe about killing people, instead of learning, getting good things in my head. Now is about murdering people. That's the next trade that I'm going to get. So I was worried." He had hoped to go to Costa Rica to join relatives in the refugee camp and continue his studies. But, when Leonardo arrived at the contra camp, a few of the fighters recognized him and said, "I know you. Your dad is Mr. Limbert. You're welcome to us." Leonardo thought, "I green green. I don't have no trainment [combat training] at all. I'd rather to have some, that I could defend myself at least." So he stayed and trained for six months before joining combat forces to fight.

Johnny's younger brother Rolando fled to Tasbapauni with a large group from Bluefields around the same time. Rolando grew up in Beholden, a Creole barrio in Bluefields, and left with a group of young men from his neighborhood to avoid mandatory conscription. By the mid-1980s in Bluefields, Gordon notes, "Young men of draft age were picked up at school, off the street, in the movie theaters, at parties, and the like. A decision was made not to invade homes in search of draft evaders, but young men in public spaces were fair game" (1998: 249). This group from Bluefields had heard that they could catch transport to Costa Rica or the Colombian island of San Andrés from Tasbapauni, but, when they got to the community, the contras forced them to go to a training camp in the bush. Rolando told me that one morning the contra commander roused the young men from their sleep. "Move," he said, "because them going to take unu and unu [you all] to the bush." The Bluefields boys protested, "We all don't want to go nowhere." But Rolando said the contras were "firing bullet all around by we, the whole hundred of all of us there," and they were compelled to go. He and the other young men from Bluefields spent a year deep in the bush where, he said, they were so isolated that "everything was silence."

War Stories

Sullivan Quinn said that the first group of Monkey Point men to fight came up to Nicaragua in a small combat detachment in 1983. They crossed the San Juan River and continued north on foot. While he was still in the training camp, Quinn had made up his mind to desert the contras and rejoin his family in Bluefields, where his wife was preparing to give birth to their first son. He told me, "And well after I get Monkey Point here, I say, this is it. I just take my arms, take off my clothes, and I bury it, and I went to Bluefields bareback, naked like, just pants. So me run right up the beach." Quinn didn't stay long in Bluefields. "Sandinista looking me," he recalled, "and when the contra get to find out that I come in also they was looking me." So he went to Corn Island and then left for the Pacific side of the country where his uncle had a cattle ranch. But he was unhappy there and decided to take his chances and return home. "I was want to get free outta this moving and going and pushing," he explained. Back in Bluefields, Quinn was detained by the Sandinistas and jailed for two months. After his release, he reintegrated into civilian life and eventually took a job piloting a boat on the Escondido River for the government.

The other men in his group stayed with the contras and saw the worst of the south coast combat between 1983 and 1985. Jumbo had the longest involvement with the contras on the southern front, even serving as a bodyguard for Edén Pastora in the early 1980s. His understanding of contra logistics and organizational schisms is detailed in comparison to other ex-combatants from the community. Jumbo told me that the men fought all along the south coast in places like San Juan (Greytown), San Francisco, Kukra River, and Wiring Cay in a detachment made up of mostly Creole and Rama contras from the region. The detachment was stationed at a base camp along the Tursuani, a small river that feeds into the southern part of the Bluefields Bay. The Creole men in the unit were mostly family, cousins and brothers who had grown up in the same community and felt a high degree of solidarity toward one another.

The most memorable battles for the men were at Rama Cay, Pearl Lagoon, and Bluefields. In July 1984, MISURASATA fighters took Rama Cay, a small island in the Bluefields Bay where the indigenous Rama population is concentrated. The men arrived in the evening and warned local residents to take shelter on the mainland. The contras held the cay for several days until they ran out of ammunition and the Sandinistas began aerial bombing. "We no had no more bullet," Jumbo remembered, "so we there just waiting on death." Cow told me, "Some of the boy them get shoot up, get wounded, so we come, we reach on the land back, on the mainland." While they were waiting for the *piraña* (speedboat) to come up from Costa Rica to evacuate the wounded, the group was ambushed. Cow was shot in the throat, and his father, Jumbo, Johnny, and Junior took him down to Duck Creek to shelter before heading back to Tursuani. Cow spent months in the bush with no treatment for his wound beyond the natural bush remedies his family members administered.

The attack on Bluefields in May 1985 remains the most significant wartime memory for many community men. Contras from the south conducted a two-pronged assault on Bluefields in the early hours of the morning. The assault was meant to be coordinated with an offensive in the north against the town of Pearl Lagoon, but community men who were on both fronts describe the attacks as ill conceived and disorganized missions. Rolando served as a member of the reserve forces for the contra units that fought in Pearl Lagoon. The men had been drinking and smoking marijuana, and he explained, "Them get out they head, and they make the attack first. They smoke and feel like them got more ability to do anything." But the Sandinista forces at Pearl Lagoon were waiting for them. "Some of them [contras] no even get up onto the land," Rolando said. "They just start to shoot them down in the water and well, who survive and get on the land start to fight." The contras suffered heavy casualties, and Rolando, who helped evacuate the fighters, remembers seeing the dead and wounded that day.

Two days later, Rolando's older brother Johnny was among the forces that led the Bluefields offensive. Jumbo told me that a commander called Mano Negra came up from Costa Rica to inform them of the planned assault. The man told the contras at Tursuani, "What unu doing here? Unu go take the *posta* [post] in Bluefields." But the idea was met with resistance. According to Jumbo, the men responded, "No, we can't go to Bluefields. What we going do there? Go dead?" But John and another group of men were willing. "The next guy them, they start smoke the same marijuana," Jumbo said, "and them must'a get them brains high and them gone. So they went in a little boat, and they gone straight to the *comando*, to the police them, soon in the morning." Junior recalls a similar chain of events: "He [Mano Negra] the one take out some man to go and fight. That time we never prepare yet. We didn't ready because we was to coordinate with the north and the south to go attack Bluefields."

After the first group left for Bluefields, the commander in charge of Jumbo's group said, "We can't make the boy them, them is brothers then, we can't make them dead so neither. So let's go reforce them." This group headed to the Sandinista base near Kukra Point on the southern border of Bluefields. Jumbo said they held the base for several hours before retreating. The next morning they heard on the radio that the Sandinistas had captured the contras who attacked the police headquarters in Bluefields. Most community people who are old enough to remember the event have told me that the Sandinistas captured the men alive and then tortured and killed them. Jumbo said that his bother Felix was jailed there and witnessed what happened to Johnny. The description of his death in custody is gruesome. Many of Johnny's family members were living in Bluefields at the time. His younger brother Allen said that the government laid the men's bodies out in the park, "For make example, for nobody no try to do what them do." When the families went to ask for the bodies, he said they were told, "Them no due to get a Christianity burial cause them is Nicaragua enemy."

Not long after the assault on Pearl Lagoon, Rolando and a few other Creole contras deserted the camp for Costa Rica. Leonardo followed with another group of combatants a few months later. Rolando recalled the journey, "I pick up myself one evening around five o'clock, and I start to walk. I tell the next five guy what come with me, I say, 'Well, we going, we have these gun them in we hand, but if we carry these gun, we can lose we life.' Because at that time, the fight just happen in Lagoon, and they running crazy round into the Lagoon and out to sea with panga." The men walked the whole night from Tasbapauni to Set Net and down to False Bluff before reaching Bluefields. The following day, they left for Costa Rica. Rolando said, "That time my brother done die here, but I don't know."

Rolando describes the contra camp up north as a violent environment shaped by physical hardship and substance abuse. During his time there, he learned of the murder of deserters and suspected Sandinista informants as well as the massacre of two-dozen captured *cachorros* (cubs) or young draftees to the Sandinista's Irregular Fighting Battalions, which led EPS forces in combat against the contras (*Envío* Team 1988). Both Rolando and Leonardo told me how hard it is to understand wartime violence and its corporal and psychic effects without living it firsthand. "I used to like watch war picture on television," Leonardo explained, "but when I get into the war now, my personal body is in war, then I says, this is not nothing good. This is real, very dangerous and serious. It really cruel to see human killing other human."

By the time most of the men left for Costa Rica, the worst of the fighting was over. The ARDE alliance in the south had crumbled with the withdrawal of U.S. support for Pastora, while an extended Sandinista offensive along the San Juan River forced the remaining ARDE forces to retreat into Costa Rica (*Envío* Team 1985b,c). Poor leadership, tactical blunders, and what increasingly came to seem like a senseless loss of life alienated community men who were still fighting for ARDE. Jumbo has particularly bitter memories of Pastora. He told me, "Edén Pastora is a *traicionado* [traitor]. Him is a man, him send you go fight, and when him done, him send next guy behind us to kill us . . . Him wasn't enemy with no Sandinista. Him was friend." Jumbo's observations likely reflect the intense factionalism among contra forces stationed along the Costa Rican border. U.S. intermediaries were eager to replace Pastora with a more compliant right-wing ally in the south, as the Reagan administration sought to represent the contras as "freedom fighters" who were ideologically unified in their struggle against the revolution (Cockburn 1987: 23, 37). But Pastora continued to portray himself as a "true Sandinista" and refused to cooperate with the FDN, which was made up of the same Somocistas he had fought before the triumph of the revolution (Ibid.: 78). Brooklyn Rivera also refused to align with the MISURA–FDN coalition and defer his group's political goals to U.S. strategic objectives (Honey 1994: 233).

Soon after an assassination attempt against Pastora at the La Penca camp, several ARDE commanders broke ranks to join FDN factions (Cockburn 1987: 23). One of these commanders was Fernando "El Negro" Chamorro, who was deeply involved in the drug trade (Honey 1994: 227; Scott and Marshall 1991: 105). Despite his dealings in cocaine, the CIA reportedly chose Chamorro to succeed Pastora when he fell out of favor with the agency (Johnston 2010: 52). After the unsuccessful attack on Bluefields in 1985, most of the men from Jumbo's detachment returned to Costa Rica. There, he said, they were taken from a contra border camp and delivered to "El Negro" Chamorro at Upala in north central Costa Rica. Chamorro had assumed leadership of the newly formed United Nicaraguan Opposition (UNO, Unidad Nicaragüense Opositora), which was made up of largely FDN fighters (Ibid.). But the men from Jumbo's detachment refused to join the UNO forces. He remembers that they decided together, "Dead or live, we going back to the town, but no want fight no more." The men were weary of war and had developed a distrust of mestizo contra groups, which Jumbo describes as corrupt organizations involved in drug trafficking.

As Creole and Rama contras, they were aligned with and fought under the leadership of Brooklyn Rivera. Although MISURASATA was an indigenous group representing largely Miskitu interests, Jumbo said that Miss Jenelee Hodgson, an influential Creole leader from Bluefields who was in exile in Costa Rica, helped advocate for Creole fighters. Hodgson was the president of SICC (Southern Indigenous Creole Community), an organization that promoted racial pride and empowerment among Bluefields Creoles before its leaders were jailed and forced into exile (Gordon 1998: 188, 238–239). Both MISURASATA and SICC had close ties to the Moravian Church and were allied for a time in the mid-1980s (Envío Team 1985d). But beyond the group solidarity that held the men together in combat and their political identification with MISURASATA and SICC, many said they no longer knew what they were fighting for by the mid-1980s. "We pass a very bad sufferment," Jumbo said, "because they did had it that, well, them had we fool up say we was to defend we land. So we was fighting in a way defending our land, but that time wasn't no land we defending. There was no land we defending them time." Instead, he said, the war had become a lucrative business for ARDE and FDN leaders.

This was also a time of growing rapprochement between black and indigenous combatants and the Sandinista government. MISURASATA had begun to negotiate with the state in late 1984 and 1985, and, although talks broke down, the period marked a slow shift from open hostility to negotiation and eventual peace (Hale 1994: 174). The battles at Pearl Lagoon and Bluefields represent some of the last major combat experiences for community men. By 1986, Hale writes, "It was not uncommon to see former Miskitu commanders, who months earlier had been in fierce combat with the government, strolling through the streets of Bluefields and staying in hotels at government expense" (Ibid.: 176). After the losses at Pearl Lagoon and Bluefields, most Monkey Point men permanently abandoned their combat units and fled to Costa Rica, where they began the process of transitioning to civilian life.

Refuge in Costa Rica

Both Junior and Leonardo left for Costa Rican refugee camps in late 1985. Junior had been stationed at the San Juan River on the Nicaraguan side of the border, where the Sandinistas were conducting intense aerial bombing. He remembers bombs dropping so close that the impact lifted him off his feet and slammed him back into the ground, leaving his body bruised and his ears ringing for days. Suffering from a badly infected tooth, he decided to head to Costa Rica to seek medical treatment. So he turned in his weapon and put on civilian clothing to make the trek across the border. Junior first went to a refugee intake center at Santa Rosa de Pocosol in north central Costa Rica. There he describes insufficient food and bad treatment from camp officials. After local police jailed one of his travel companions, he left Santa Rosa and made his way to the Pueblo Nuevo camp near Limón on the Atlantic coast of the country.

Pueblo Nuevo was the first refugee camp to open in 1983. The barracks once housed workers who built the Atlantic coast road that passes through Pueblo Nuevo, a largely working-class Afro–Costa Rican neighborhood on the outskirts of Limón (Pacheco 1989: 39, 43). The camp received the initial wave of indigenous and Creole refugees who left their communities in mid-1983. Most Creoles fleeing violence went to Pueblo Nuevo to be with friends and relatives. In 1985, the camp had a population of more than a thousand refugees; 45 percent were Creole (Diaz and Achi 1989: 15). Creole residents also had a strong affinity with the Afro–Costa Rican population at Limón, an Anglophone community with historical ties to Nicaraguan Creoles. Refugees staying at the camp had significant contact with this larger community, as camp officials allowed them to visit relatives living in Limón and to participate in sporting and cultural events there. Children from the camp also attended school in the community of Pueblo Nuevo with Afro–Costa Rican pupils (Pacheco 1989: 41, 44). Life at Pueblo Nuevo allowed Creoles to experience the bonds of racial and cultural solidarity with other Afro-Caribbeans, which was a source of comfort and social support denied to them in mestizo camps.

But beyond the comfort of taking refuge among family and friends, Pueblo Nuevo was not a nice place to be. After visiting in 1986, an expert on international refugee policy wrote that Pueblo Nuevo "had the worst physical conditions of any camp I saw in Central America" (Loescher 1988: 316). The overcrowded camp had substandard sanitation and dilapidated housing, infectious diseases were widespread, and residents had little to occupy their time (Diaz and Achi 1989; Loescher 1988; Pacheco 1989). A 1988 study of the refugee population at Pueblo Nuevo indicates that 92 percent of camp residents surveyed reported a significant decline in their standard of living since their arrival (Pacheco 1989: 12).

Although Costa Rican authorities liberally granted political asylum to Nicaraguans between 1983 and 1987, the refugee population was not well received in the country (Basok 1990: 731). Honey suggests that "initial support" for refugees turned into "near hysteria" as the population grew and the country slipped into economic recession (1994: 154). A massive external debt combined with falling prices for coffee and sugar led Costa Rica to seek assistance from the U.S. government and the IMF in the early 1980s. Economic aid from the United States increased from $15.2 million in 1981 to $214.2 million in 1983, but the country was still forced to adopt IMF structural adjustment policies, which had a disproportionate impact on the working poor (Ferris 1987: 18, 74–75). As poverty and crime rates climbed, Costa Ricans began to view the refugees as a drain on government coffers, unwelcome competition for scarce jobs, and a threat to national security. Many Costa Ricans also held racist and xenophobic beliefs about Nicaraguans, whom they saw as prone to delinquency, substance abuse, and violent behavior (Caulfield Vásconez 1987:61; Larson 1993:69). Even though the Costa Rican state distrusted the Sandinistas, tolerated a contra presence on national territory, and extended refugee status to Nicaraguans fleeing the war, there was intense xenophobia toward the refugee population that was fueled by economic crisis and rising fears about crime and violence (Caulfield Vásconez 1987: 61; Ferris 1987: 69–71).

These attitudes were evident at Pueblo Nuevo where residents said that camp officials routinely abused their positions of authority. Camp residents reported feeling dependent, confined, imprisoned, and subject to "an environment of institutional control," which caused them great distress and anxiety (Pacheco 1989: 28, 43). They directed the majority of their complaints at security personnel who were quick to use force against refugees in the camp. One male resident at Pueblo Nuevo said, "The most difficult thing of all is to be closed in. You feel like a prisoner. To leave and enter, you have to show and ask for permission, as if we were jailed convicts" (Ibid.: 59). Camp security personnel reportedly cultivated this kind of carceral environment. Another man described their practices in more detail: "For any little thing they'll handcuff you, and in recent days it's been worse. We've gone to complain, and the administration people tell us that they have nothing to do with guards, that there's nothing they can do" (Ibid.).

Young male refugees at Pueblo Nuevo had frequent conflicts with guards and police. Ex-combatants from Monkey Point recount incidents when police indiscriminately arrested and jailed large groups of men for a range of alleged offenses. There was a sizable population of young single men in the camp who traveled to Costa Rica without their families.[2] The Costa Rican police saw the displaced men as security threats and targeted them for arbitrary arrest and detention. This was due in part to the ambiguous status of the men, who because of their age, gender, race, and national origin were assumed to be potential combatants or delinquents prone to violence and agitation.

Some sources suggest that hundreds of young men in Costa Rican camps were, in fact, active contras (Fagen 1987: 115; Larson 1993: 74; Weiss Fagen 1988: 71). But contrary to these reports, men from Monkey Point who sought refuge at Pueblo Nuevo say that they did so only when they were ready to join the civilian population permanently. Some of these men, such as Rolando and Leonardo, were reluctant or forced recruits who, in their efforts to avoid Patriotic Military Service, became contras. Others fought willingly for the duration of the war and, after significant hardship, were anxious to leave combat roles and rebuild their lives. Regardless of their individual circumstances, young men from the community *as a group* were subject to forms of coercion, violence, and securitization that brought them into frequent contact with the Sandinista military, contra groups, and Costa Rican security forces throughout the 1980s.

For those men who fought, camp life signaled a shift in status from political refugee–demobilized combatant to security threat–delinquent. The shift illustrates how economic crisis, confinement in camps, national security concerns, militarization on the border, and racism and xenophobia in Costa Rica helped recast contra combatants into common criminals as the conflict began to ebb. The transition reflects a regionwide shift from political preoccupations with wartime violence to new neoliberal discourses about postwar security. Cold War–era conflict followed sharp ideological rifts and wartime violence was public, communal, and political, whereas postwar security involved more complex engagements with state and imperial power, often coding violence as private, individual, and apolitical (Moodie 2010). The emphasis on apolitical crime and delinquency reflects a model of neoliberal governance that "pins praise or blame for social conditions on individual actors," obscuring the historical roots and "systemic constitution of much violence and suffering" in postwar Central America (Benson, Thomas, and Fisher 2011: 142; O'Neill and Thomas 2011).

For some men, transitioning from combatant to civilian involved donning civilian clothing, registering as a refugee, and finding local employment. For others, the process was more fraught. Junior stayed at Pueblo Nuevo for only a short time. When he arrived, he said there was a group of young men who made trouble in the camp. "So, when the Costa Rica government come," he explained, "them take up everybody, innocent or not." Junior was rounded up with a group of about thirty-five men, and his status changed from demobilized combatant and refugee to criminal suspect, incarcerated inmate, and later deportee. After his arrest, he said, "They carry us in a bad jailhouse which part, it look like not even for the animal them. Later on, them took we from there and them carry us to San José." The men stayed in the capital for more than a month before they were deported to Nicaragua. Junior told me, "They didn't sending us with a recommendation letter from government to government, you know. Them sending us like, throwing us over the frontier for the Sandinista them to destroy us or something like that."

The deported men crossed into Nicaragua at the Peñas Blancas border crossing. Sandinista security forces took the group to a military post near the frontier, where Junior said, "Them start to investigate us one by one . . . because they really didn't sure who we are, because we didn't have no kind of document nor no bag nor nothing like that. We just passing through from the refuge." Later, they were taken to La Granja, near Granada on the Pacific side of the country, where the men spent some time in jail before they were allowed to return to Bluefields. "And after that," he recalled, "everybody was okay, home again with them family." Junior was able to get back his old job at the municipal wharf in Bluefields. After three years fighting in the bush with the contras, he was called up to train for the SMR with his co-workers. He told me, "And well them take us and give us uniform, weapon, and carry us to the airport, down below the airport, a base they had down there. And them go training us to shoot and thing like that." Junior already knew how to make war, but much to his relief he didn't have to fight. Service with Sandinista reserve forces, he explained, "was just to say hold a job. If you no go, you going to lose your work," and by that time armed conflict had begun to abate in the region.

Leonardo crossed into Costa Rica at Peñas Blancas not long before his older brother Junior was jailed and deported. When they entered the country, the Costa Rican authorities questioned Leonardo's group at length. He said that the immigration officials asked them, "You are Sandinista or contra?"

They told them neither: "We are civilian."

"You are not civilian, because we know how civilian walk, different from warrior," the officials replied. "You all is warrior. Tell us the truth, or we going to send you back over."

"Yeah, we was with the contra them," the men finally admitted.

With this admission, they were allowed into the country. Leonardo and his group were taken to a refugee reception center called Boca Arenal in north central Costa Rica. When he got there, someone told him that Junior had been at Santa Rosa. But by the time Leonardo was able to visit Santa Rosa, Junior had already left for Limón. Leonardo hadn't seen his brother for the duration of the war, and he was eager to reunite with him and other family members at Pueblo Nuevo. The refugees that he lived with at Boca Arenal were almost entirely mestizo. "Hardly Creole people you see," Leonardo said. "Where the black people go is Port Limón. They are looking the black-speaking people, the Creole." Rolando was also in a mestizo camp for a time before he was deported to Nicaragua and remembered it as a hostile environment where they were fed corn tortillas three times a day. He said they told the camp officials, "We don't eat them thing. We no eat coffee, tortilla in the morning, tortilla in the evening, in the night tortilla." Former combatants from Monkey Point who stayed in mestizo camps all reported trying to secure a transfer to Limón because they wanted to be with family and friends and because they experienced racial hostility from mestizos in the camps (Pacheco 1989: 43).

Once he settled in at Pueblo Nuevo, Leonardo was recruited to work on a nearby banana plantation at Matina called Finca la Luisa. He had been eager to continue his studies, which had been prematurely interrupted by the war, but, with no financial support from family, Leonardo was forced to take a job on the plantation. Official refugee status ensured basic access to shelter, food, and medical care, but material aid to refugees was meager, and many sought work outside of the camps to better their standard of living (Larson 1992: 337). The shift from an independent livelihood in Nicaragua to dependence on (often hostile) camp officials for housing, income, and food was demoralizing for residents (Pacheco 1989: 17), and Leonardo jumped at the chance to become self-sufficient. On the finca, he told me, "I used to plant banana. Afterward, them put me to cut banana." Later he was promoted to head of a work crew and was able to secure a job for his older brother Ricardo.

Other Creole men like Cow found work fishing lobster and doing construction while living at Pueblo Nuevo. Camp officials issued the men day passes that let them work in the informal sector on a temporary basis (Ibid.: 42). Cow told me, "Them used to go in the refuge and beg for workers. Them say all who want go out, go work and thing, but with we orders, sign a paper, so them could go out. We used to go out, go work, work so much time, and then coming back." Political asylum restricted employment opportunities for Nicaraguans as refugee policy was designed to protect the Costa Rican work-force from foreign workers (Larson 1992: 326–327).[3] The restrictions confined refugees to low-paid, unskilled, temporary work in the agricultural or infor-mal sector, making it difficult for them to become upwardly mobile (Pacheco 1989: 42). Although there was a tendency to assume Nicaraguans were eco-nomic migrants looking to benefit from higher wages and improved living standards in Costa Rica, in reality, resettlement brought forms of dependency, destitution, and institutional control that refugees had not experienced at home (Ibid.: 70). Despite these challenges, many Creoles from Monkey Point made decent lives for themselves in Limón after leaving the camp. Leonardo came home to Sammy and Lucille in 1991, but his brother Ricardo stayed on in Costa Rica. Jumbo and Cow's parents also remained in Limón after their sons returned to Nicaragua in the 1990s.

The Rise of the Drug Trade

The first time Jumbo saw crack cocaine was in 1987 at a house in Limón where contra fighters used to congregate. An Italian man who was involved in the arms trade with Colombia showed the men how to cook powder cocaine into crack, and some of them developed a habit for the drug. Rolando told me that he began to see crack in Bluefields a year or two later: "Some guys what was in Costa Rica, what was using the crack down there, one time they make a fight with the army. And well, [Costa Rican President] Óscar Arias say all who used crack and fighting with crack, cocaine, he going to take them out of the country, and he send them back home. He sent forty-nine of them back home, them is warrior, rebels. They come with it nasty." As the men indi-cate, the emergence of powder cocaine and crack use on the south coast in the late 1980s is entangled with the war. Although fisherman found jettisoned cocaine at sea and sacks of cocaine began to wash up on community beaches with some regularity in the decade after the war, cocaine was first introduced through contra participation in drug trafficking on the southern front and the contraband trade in arms and consumer goods with Colombia—activities that coincided with the growing power of Colombian drug cartels throughout the hemisphere in the 1980s.

According to Jumbo, drug trafficking on the southern front was an open secret among some contras. As early as 1983, he claims to have seen transshipments of cocaine brought to Colorado Bar, south of the San Juan River. He said the cocaine was taken up the Colorado River to the contra base Tango. From there, he had no idea where the drugs were sent. A number of community men say that the Sandinistas also participated in the drug trade. This accusation figured centrally in the Reagan administration's propaganda campaign against Latin American leftists, which attempted to link socialism with lawlessness and narcoterrorism in the region (Scott and Marshall 1991: 23–24). The historical record provides far more evidence that U.S.-backed contras and CIA assets in Costa Rica, Panama, and Honduras were trafficking cocaine in the mid-1980s (Cockburn 1987; Honey 1994; Johnston 2010; Scott and Marshall 1991). Scott and Marshall write, "Whatever Nicaragua's true relationship to the international drug trade (not one country in the region has managed to escape involvement), it is surely small compared to the historical involvement of the CIA" (1991: 102).

The drug trade in Costa Rica was not fully controlled by contras, and not all contra leaders were complicit. But contra networks were perhaps the largest and most organized cocaine traffickers in Costa Rica, and U.S.-funded militarization contributed to the growth of the trade in the region (Honey 1994: 356; Scott and Marshall 1991). Honduras and Costa Rica—two centers of contra activity—together accounted for some 30 percent of all cocaine entering the United States in the 1980s (Scott and Marshall 1991: 186). U.S. aid to the contras provided the conditions for a "cocaine-military symbiosis" in which militarization, arms smuggling, and intelligence alliances with unscrupulous actors promoted the drug trade and flow of cocaine northward (Ibid.: 186–191). After the war, the Nicaraguan and Costa Rican economies were in crisis, trafficking networks continued to proliferate, and the region was flooded with military-style weapons, all of which created an environment ripe for drug abuse and drug-related violence in Atlantic coast communities on both sides of the border.

The majority of the cocaine trafficked by contra networks appears to have been moved by plane to contra landing strips in northern Costa Rica between 1984 and 1986 (Honey 1994: 406; Scott and Marshall 1991). If cocaine was moved by boat up the coast as Jumbo suggests, it may have represented a smaller portion of the wartime trade. Some Creole fighters from Nicaragua who remained in Costa Rica in the late 1980s became involved with the drug trade, in part because they were skilled *pangueros* (skiff pilots) accustomed to sea travel. "Only Creole guys stay in that trafficking," Jumbo explained. "The Spaniard [mestizos] them used to work to the base to the back because Spaniard don't like too much sea business." Throughout the war, arms and supplies for the contras were offloaded at the Limón harbor and taken by skiff up the coast to Tortuguero and Colorado Bar. From there, contra pilots took the supplies by sea to combatants in Nicaragua. Limón was a hub for arms trafficking during the mid-1980s, and there was a significant population of indigenous and Creole combatants who settled there after the fighting was over (Honey 1994: 205–206). Jumbo told me that some of these men traveled to Colombia in the late 1980s to smuggle arms and were introduced to the drug trade.[4] When they returned to Nicaragua in the 1990s, they brought these connections with them.

Muche grew up in Corn Island and similarly suggests that the clandestine trade in arms and consumer goods with Colombia facilitated the introduction of cocaine to the island in the 1980s. As a teenager, Muche participated in the sale of arms to Colombian smugglers who visited the island during the war. He said that a Sandinista military officer stationed at Corn Island provided access to the arms. This was how he was first introduced to cocaine. The contraband lobster trade was also a significant factor in the early influx of the drug to the island. During the 1980s, the Sandinista state controlled the lucrative lobster industry on Corn Island, and local fishermen were paid for their catch in badly inflated Nicaraguan currency. This along with diminished access to consumer goods promoted the contraband lobster trade with Colombians who paid in U.S. dollars.

Local people also bought consumer goods from the Colombian smugglers. Muche explained, "What them used to use for change for lobster was to bring *grabadora* [tape recorders], they used to bring beers, they used to bring slippers, they used to bring sugar, they used to bring rice, chicken, tennis [shoes], milk. Yeah, you know, they used to bring that kinda thing and when you sell a little lobster, then you buy the thing from they." A Bluefields Creole who worked in Corn Island as the price manager for the state-run seafood plant also suggests that the contraband lobster trade led to the introduction of cocaine. He described his experiences working at the plant in 1986: "The minute I got to Corn Island I saw that lobster contraband was a big problem and that this illegal trade was opening the road for bigger problems to reach the place. Drugs were just starting to come in, through these same people who were dealing with Colombians whether to get condensed milk or spare-parts" (Campbell Hooker 2005: 217). In those days, very few people on Corn Island knew how to use cocaine or make money trafficking the drug. Muche told me, "After this, cocaine start to drift, then the people them find it out to sea, out to sea when they go fishining. But they don't know how to use it, I tell you." Just a few men learned to profit from the jettisoned cocaine that they found at sea by transporting it to the Cayman Islands on fishing boats that frequented the island. "And they is the one that used to make big money off of it," Muche said.

The testimony indicates that Creoles were introduced to drugs through historical processes tied to militarization and economic crisis in the late 1980s. Those with direct involvement in the trade were mostly small-time or opportunistic participants. They fell into transporting cocaine due to their familiarity with sea navigation and association with Colombian smugglers, or they found cocaine at sea while fishing and sought to make a profit from this new and unconventional catch. The details of how Creoles were exposed to cocaine, however, should not be mistaken for the idea that they were responsible for the introduction of the drug or that mestizos on the Atlantic coast and in other parts of the country were not involved in the trade. People far more powerful than Creoles were responsible for the rise of the drug trade in Nicaragua. By the mid-1980s, the Medellín and Cali cartels were expansive organizations that controlled sophisticated operations throughout Central America, Mexico, and the United States. It is more accurate to understand Creole involvement in the drug trade as one of the multidimensional effects of economic crisis, political violence, and U.S.-funded militarization in the region.

After the war, when people began to return to Monkey Point, drug-related violence and counternarcotics policing were on the rise; by the late 1990s, they increasingly shaped community life. In 1996, Allen came home to a community that was subject to frequent military incursions. He had left Bluefields for Limón shortly after his brother Johnny's death. When he returned to Monkey Point, he said, "The military used to go in there often and every time them go they used to got everybody running . . . They try to intimidate you so them can take what them like. And just saying they looking drugs, drugs they're looking, and they looking drugs. They say everybody got drugs down here." Allen recalled instances of physical violence too. "One of the time," he said, "when them gone down there them wan handle up everybody. And I was there, and I said, 'This foolishness have to stop some day.'" He told me community people were frightened by the soldiers and warned him, "No bwoy, them 'a kill you. Them is law."

But Allen did not return to Nicaragua with a wartime mentality. Costa Rica has a long history of democratic pluralism, attention to social welfare, and respect for human rights, and Allen returned with a different mind-set and a new set of expectations. He was also influenced by trade unionism and leftist labor politics when he was a stevedore in Limón. "Them all time talking about right," he told me, "what right you have as human, what right you have as laborer, what right you have as children, what right you have as woman, and what right you have as human being. And that used to be something constantly." These experiences influenced how he understood democratic process and abuses of state power after his return. "So when I come from there, I come with my principle of right," he explained. "I have right, not nobody supposed to get my right. And in Nicaragua, them supposed to got something what give you right. We not now in no more war. We just fighting now with mouth, paper, and pencil."

So Allen began to challenge the harassment using his principle of right and the same political tactics that community leaders would later refine. After one particularly bad confrontation, he remembers telling a soldier who had shoved him with an automatic rifle, "No problem, do what unu want, but I going to Bluefields tomorrow and I going to the radio station and I saying all what unu doing down here." Thus, as people began to rebuild community life after the war, demands for autonomous rights became fused with resistance to remilitarization and state violence. By the time I began working with Monkey Point in 2001, insecurity was the most immediate and tangible threat to community life, and preoccupations with military harassment and drug-related violence punctuated most meetings about autonomous rights.

Postwar Security and Self-Defense

Monkey Point existed in what can only be described as a state of extreme rural neglect in the late 1990s and early 2000s. There was no commercial transport to the community, and travel was often an improvised affair. The primary school was still a windowless cement casing, lacking materials and rarely in use. Monkey Point had no shops to buy basic foodstuffs and no electricity, infrastructure, or services. There were no police in the community, and local residents were often targets of intermittent drug-related violence. Mestizo colonists continued to settle communal lands, and the only evidence of a state presence was a poorly funded government health clinic staffed by Miss Pearl. But for all its marginality, Monkey Point was highly visible in the public sphere as the projected dry canal port and as a dangerous place, a purported hotbed of the south coast drug trade and a haven for traffickers and delinquents.

Like a bellwether of things to come, moral panic about drugs, delinquency, and crime settled over the coast like a slow-moving storm front after the war. The homicide rate in the region was still quite low in the decade following the revolution. At just fifteen homicides per 100,000 inhabitants in 1998, the rate for the south coast matched the national average, which continues to be one of the lowest in Central America (Policía Nacional de Nicaragua 2002; United Nations Office on Drugs and Crime 2011). By 2005, however, homicides had tripled, and the south coast became the most violent department in the nation (Policía Nacional de Nicaragua 2010). With a homicide rate that rivaled Guatemala, it was now three times the national average (United Nations Office on Drugs and Crime 2011). Militarization and a spike in drug seizures accompanied or perhaps precipitated the rising homicide rate, which has held steady for the last decade. The remilitarization of Central America under the auspices of the drug war meant that young black and brown men were once again foot soldiers on the frontlines of battle.

After the war, the Atlantic coast emerged early on as a focal point for drug interdiction operations in Nicaragua. The geography, low population density, and limited police and military presence made it a convenient maritime transit route and refueling stop for Colombian traffickers moving their product northward. In the area of drug enforcement, the United States took a lead role in restructuring Nicaraguan drug policy, funding and training counternarcotics forces, and directing drug interdiction operations from the late 1990s onward. The inauguration of a Drug Enforcement Agency (DEA) office in Managua in 1998 was followed by reforms and bilateral agreements that modernized criminal codes, increased penalties for trafficking and drug-related offenses, and secured the U.S. role in counternarcotics policing (United States Department of State 2000, 2001, 2002, 2003, 2004). Glossing the Reagan administration's covert aid to the contras, U.S. narcotics reports from the period associate the rise of the drug trade on the Atlantic coast with the Contra War and a "well-armed" and "ethnically and culturally distinct" coastal population more inclined to cooperate with foreign traffickers than with their own government's security forces. No longer Reagan's glorified

Figure 4.1 Auto-nomía.

SOURCE: Manuel Guillén (M. Guillén), editorial cartoon, *La Prensa*, July 21, 2002. Reprinted with permission.

freedom fighters, black and indigenous people now showed signs of an "incipient 'narco-culture,'" which made them new racialized security threats to the United States (United States Department of State 2003).

Similarly, political cartoons in Nicaraguan newspapers in the early 2000s depicted how Nicaraguans viewed drug trafficking on the Atlantic coast as a problem rooted in blackness, cultural difference, and regional separatism. For instance, the Sambo-like caricature in Figure 4.1 of a politically active Creole holds an Autonomy banner and declares, "The Coast is for Costeños!" To the right stands a perplexed and apprehensive mestizo. Atlantic coast autonomy is represented as a conflict between a black Creole wearing dreadlocks and Rastafarian knit cap (both associated with drug use) and a white (or near-white) mestizo *campesino* hard at work. The cartoonist takes the binary a step further with a word play on autonomy. The word *Auto* in bold letters flanking the Creole literally translates as "Self," whereas the words *No Mía* over the mestizo mean "Not Mine." Autonomy is thus cast as a selfish black demand that remains irrelevant to the mestizo majority.

Figure 4.2 Mapa de Nicaragua.

SOURCE: Manuel Guillén (M. Guillén), editorial cartoon, *La Prensa*, and supplement cover for "El Azote," May 9, 2004. Reprinted with permission.

A second cartoon entitled "Map of Nicaragua (according to the political class)" shows how nationalist preoccupations with Atlantic coast autonomy morph into a fear of drug trafficking and organized crime (see Figure 4.2). Labeled the "Black Zone," the coast is represented as a separate landmass. The protruding signpost reads, "Region ceded to narco-trafficking." Coconuts and cocaine are listed as south coast produce. The words *cocos* and *coca* lining the shore allude to a derogative mestizo term for Creoles, *come coco* or "coconut eater," suggesting that they have also developed a taste for cocaine. The figure

Figure 4.3 Be Very Careful!

SOURCE: Pedro X. Molina, editorial cartoon, *El Nuevo Diario*, April 23, 2009. Reprinted with permission.

of the drug trafficker is a representative of a Colombian mafia who has found safe haven on the coast.

Unlike the first two, the cartoon in Figure 4.3 was published in a left-leaning newspaper. Entitled "Be Very Careful," it depicts Nicaragua as a troubled interracial union between a mestizo male Pacific and a black female Atlantic. Political contention between the two groups is set within the intimate fantasy space of *mestizaje* and heterosexual domesticity. The raised wooden house, typical of coastal communities, is positioned to mirror the geography of the country: The light Pacific façade appears in the western frame, while the shadowed Atlantic back appears in the eastern frame. The Pacific husband lazily snoozes in a hammock as his neglected Atlantic wife reaches out to a Colombian drug trafficker with whom she is considering an extramarital affair. The narco attempts to convince her with sweet talk and a sexualized allusion to economic fulfillment: "You haven't decided? Has he forgotten about you? What a disgrace! Leave him, my queen, and come with me so that I can give you what you want!"

The images demonstrate how, from the mestizo nationalist perspective, the drug trade on the Atlantic coast is a product of racial difference and a source of anxiety about regional autonomy. One of my most memorable conversations in the mid-2000s was with a venerable mestiza figure in the Sandinista resistance to the Somoza dictatorship. She lamented that the autonomy process remained incomplete partly due to the rise of the drug trade. She noted that most of the nation had been spared the violence that gripped El Salvador, Honduras, and Guatemala and praised the more rehabilitative track that Nicaraguan police have taken with gang youth on the Pacific side of the country. The problem on the Atlantic coast, however, was more complex and intransigent because, she claimed, "Whole communities were involved in drugs." Drug trafficking had become a problem of communal collusion in black and indigenous communities rather than just a few young sons of the nation gone astray. Her assertion reflected a prominent assumption on both the Sandinista left and neoliberal right that drug traffickers had found a "*base social*" or social base in Atlantic coast communities. A Nicaraguan colleague from the region also once heard the defense minister for the Alemán administration refer to these same communities as "*narco-comunidades*." From this point of view, all black and indigenous people from the region are security threats and complicit in the drug trade.

Needless to say, everyone from Monkey Point was not involved in drug trafficking, and many local people felt unfairly targeted, dehumanized, and defenseless. In response to deteriorating security, community leaders submitted a series of petitions to the Bluefields police in the early 2000s asking them to deputize a volunteer police force made up of local men. The police denied the requests, and rumor had it that they dismissed the idea as absurd: Why would they deputize drug traffickers in Monkey Point? Community people saw the response as part of a wider state strategy to depopulate the region and divest them of their territorial rights in order to develop the canal project free from local resistance. I remember a community assembly when Miss Helen, trembling with emotion, declared: "They don't understand we're human. They think we is animal. With the security they leave us to ourself with no protection because they want the people them to leave." The other attendees nodded in agreement.

Despite U.S. intervention in drug enforcement, Sandinista military officers still had influence in counternarcotics policing in the early 2000s, creating continuity in wartime and postwar experiences with the military in

Monkey Point. Some of the same Sandinista officers who fought contra forces led counternarcotics operations on the south coast or had other positions in the regional government after the war. "Many of them right in Bluefields here walking," Rolando told me. "All those guy them that have hand in my brother life, them walking right on the streets. They give them work, big work they have." In my first year of research, one such individual—an Army officer who served in the EPS during the war—organized a small paramilitary group that traveled to Monkey Point in search of drugs. Rumors circulated in Bluefields that this individual had accrued significant wealth by requisitioning and selling jettisoned cocaine from the coastal trade. These types of allegations were common at the time, and reports in the national press occasionally implicated police and military from the Bluefields region in the drug trade (Fernández 2002; Potoy y Sergio 2003). Community men also claimed that this officer had a hand in Johnny's death and blamed him for other alleged war crimes during the 1980s.[5]

The incident occurred one evening in July 2002. I was on a short research hiatus, but Carla was working as the radio operator and gave me a detailed account of what she witnessed. I have heard additional accounts of the incident from other participants who confirm her story. Carla told me that the men who arrived with the military officer were not complete strangers. She knew one of them because he was married to her cousin, and Allen recognized another from Pancasán, the neighborhood where he lived in Bluefields. When I asked her if these men were in the military, she replied, "No, Jennifer, them is thief." Everybody knew that. They were looking for cocaine, she said. "Them goal was to hijack the *supuestamente* [supposed] people what them say have drugs."

"So when you say 'hijack,'" I asked her, "what do you mean?"

"Well, take all the drugs from the people, passing as the law them," she explained, "or intimidate them and say by them is the law, well, give them the drugs and them keep free."

"But not arrest them?"

"Not arrest them."

Carla said that the officer came to the clinic and requested access to the radio, which she happened to be using at the time. She told me, "And well, how him figure him was like, I don't know, like Elvis Presley, him want I lend him the radio right away." The two had an argument, and he left angry. A few hours later, four men returned without the officer and anchored their panga in the inlet below the health clinic for the night. Apprehension spread throughout the tiny settlement. Allen radioed the civil defense office in Bluefields to ask if the military had any operations in the area. When he heard they did not, he devised a plan to disarm the men.

Allen told Carla and his sister Mimi, "You going to be the *carnada* [bait] and *entretener* [distract] them." The women agreed to the plan. "So, the boy them reach," Carla said, "them say goodnight. We tell them goodnight. Well, we was talking, talking, talking, making love to we, telling we things." The flirting was interrupted when armed men from the community surrounded the visitors. Carla said, "They point the gun on them and tell them, 'Don't move!' Then they catch them and they tie them up." They also disarmed the men who stayed down in the harbor with the panga. "We have to beg for they," she recalled. "Then them tie them up and have them in the kitchen, and you know fly biting them up whole night. I was sorry for them, but I say, *la mayoría gana* [the majority wins]."

The next morning the police came down from Bluefields with the officer to release the men. Community leaders cooperated but took the men's arms and refused to return them. Carla said that the officer denied knowing the men. "Him start talking all kinda lie and things," she said, "like I was on the radio making transaction with the drugs dealer them. That's why I never wan lend him the radio." Angered by the false accusation, Carla told me she lost her temper: "And then there was where I get vexed, and I box him."

"You hit him in his face with your fist?" I asked her.

"Yeah," she said, "so then he say—"

"Wait, you hit him in front of the police?"

"No!" she said with a hint of exasperation. She wasn't a fool.

Still stinging from the red mark Carla left on his face, she claimed that he asked her, "You know what you do?"

"Yes, I know what I doing," Carla replied. Still she confessed to me, "But then afterward, you know, I was feel like nervous, but I didn't let him see it." She said Allen reassured her, "You know something, don't worry about that. Thing will come out good."

As soon as he returned to Bluefield, Allen embarked on a major publicity campaign against the men and their ringleader. His first stop was the Procuraduría de Derechos Humanos, the state-sponsored human rights office, where he filed a complaint against the men. He then got on the radio and local television news and denounced them by name. But when he arrived at the

Bluefields police station to report the incident, he was told there was a warrant out for his arrest. If he didn't return the arms, the police would take him into custody. The men they had disarmed also initiated civil suits against community members, Carla included. As tensions mounted, Allen traveled to Managua to enlist the support of CENIDH. Both CENIDH and the community's legal representative Dr. Acosta denounced the paramilitary group, and their statements were reported in the national press. The community eventually returned the arms. As with other confrontations in the past, the civil cases and arrest warrants were eventually dropped, the tensions subsided, and the incident blew over. The press and civil society provided a safety net for community activists, but neither could stem remilitarization, state corruption, and drug-related violence.

By the time I left Nicaragua in 2004, the government had begun to establish military posts in coastal communities like Tasbapauni and Monkey Point where involvement in the drug trade was purportedly high. During this same period, naval forces created checkpoints along the main coastal water routes where they searched commercial and private vessels for drugs. After 2004, drug interdiction records show sharp annual increases in cocaine seizures, and by 2007 seizures had reached ten times the number recorded in 2003 (Observatorio Centroamericano sobre Violencia 2008). Military search and surveillance operations at key transit points along the coastline, as well as tightened airport security for internal air travel, led to frequent complaints about the racial profiling of black travelers (Jarquín 2003; Lewin 2004). Creole women have complained of being sexually groped by mestizo security forces while traveling. The policing of urban space in Bluefields also intensified as special antiriot forces with blue-black uniforms and semiautomatic rifles began to patrol the city streets. They were much more menacing than local police, who wore light blue short-sleeved shirts and routinely traveled through the city center unarmed.

On a return trip to Monkey Point in 2009, I witnessed the full extent of five years of remilitarization. This trip was punctuated by a range of new search and surveillance tactics that I had not witnessed in my decade of sea travel on the Atlantic coast. Local people now must travel with *cédulas* (identity cards) and foreigners with passports, which are carefully recorded on a *zarpe* (travel clearance document) before embarkation. As we set out from Bluefields, the commercial panga made a detour east to the barrier island between the bay and sea where the regional naval command is headquartered. We sat in the

Figure 4.4 Soldiers stationed at Monkey Point search luggage on commercial pangas.
SOURCE: Jennifer Goett, 2009.

sweltering sun for nearly an hour as soldiers reviewed the *zarpe* and searched our luggage. The soldiers had Allen and an elderly Creole man from Devil's Creek step out of the panga to give their identification and belongings special scrutiny. After receiving travel clearance, the panga turned south toward Monkey Point only to be stopped fifteen minutes later on the open sea by five armed soldiers who again checked the *zarpe* and searched our luggage. As we bobbed from wave to wave, Allen asked for my camera and began to snap photos of the scowling soldiers in the military panga. As he reversed the surveillance gaze, he told me, "It's good to make them know we watching them too." On our arrival at Monkey Point an hour later, we were subject to a final search by soldiers stationed at the post before gaining permission to disembark (see Figure 4.4).

According to community leaders, the irony of such search and surveillance tactics is that individuals engaged in the traffic of jettisoned cocaine do not tend to move it in luggage on commercial pangas but find more clandestine means of transport that bypass military checkpoints. The result is that everyday forms of search and surveillance target individuals who are unlikely to be engaged in drug trafficking and thus work to regulate minority spaces, reproduce spatial hierarchies between the mestizo state and community people, and interpellate racialized bodies engaged in mundane forms of local travel as potentially criminal. Such everyday experiences are a part of postwar securitized social reproduction; combined with the violence that men and women continue to experience, these practices inform a community politics of self-defense and security. In the postwar period, security politics are deeply enmeshed in demands for territorial rights and political autonomy such that they often became animating forces for political action in Monkey Point. The final chapter of the book examines state sexual violence and the gendered politics of autonomous self-defense as community people began to confront abuses under military occupation after they gained title to their territory in 2009.

5 Sexual Violence and Autonomous Politics

THE LONG PROCESS OF MOBILIZATION FOR DEMARCATION culminated in a title to a massive multiethnic territory stretching from the southern reaches of Bluefields to the Costa Rican border in December 2009. Allen said that President Ortega tried to shake his hand at the ceremony to turn over the title, but Allen ignored the gesture. Miss Pearl admonished him, "Go back and shake the man hand, man!" When he turned back to the president, Allen said Ortega told him, "Anything, we are here to defend you. We are hand in hand with the community of Monkey Point." Allen told me rather sardonically, "I tell him, 'Yeah.'" But less than a year after the encounter, a conflict with the Sandinista state over the military's sexual abuse of local girls threw the community back into the national spotlight. The allegations came in the form of a complaint from the Rama-Kriol Territorial Government to the head of the South Atlantic Naval District in November 2010. Embellished with the GTR-K seal and the signatures of the new territorial authorities, the document accuses mestizo soldiers stationed in Monkey Point of sexually abusing a dozen mestiza and Creole girls between the ages of nine and sixteen. Later testimony revealed that the violence was not contained to girls but that soldiers were sexually aggressive toward local women and sought to dominate and sexually humiliate local men. The sexual aggression also had a spatial expression: Soldiers bathed nude in public settings, propositioned women at their traditional washing site, and followed girls along secluded paths as they went to fetch water. Despite Ortega's assurances, ordinary life for men, women, and children under military occupation was saturated with state violence.

Although the abuse occurred over the course of six years, the complaint marks the moment it took on a political life beyond the community, leading to a yearlong battle between communal leaders and the Nicaraguan military. As president of the communal government, Allen and his younger brother Harley, who held the position of first vocal, led the campaign against the military. After publicizing the details of the abuse in the press, the community gained the support of human rights organizations in Managua. And, in October 2011, a group of mestiza feminists from the Pacific side of the country introduced the case to the Inter-American Commission on Human Rights (IACHR), during a hearing on sexual violence in Nicaragua. The case itself provoked dramatically distinct discourses of injury that were mobilized for different political ends by male Creole leaders and mestiza feminists, troubling any satisfactory form of redress for the girls involved in the abuse. Although the government eventually agreed to relocate the post to a more peripheral part of the community, no official charges or sanctions against the soldiers ever resulted from the case.

The longevity of the abuse and the failure to hold the soldiers accountable reflect the challenges that women and girls throughout Latin America face when confronting sexual violence. Feminist scholars who document sexual violence against indigenous women living under military occupation in Latin America note how hard it is to find redress for these crimes (Boesten 2010; Franco 2007; Hastings 2002). Like other kinds of rape, state sexual violence is notoriously difficult to prosecute and often remains embedded in the private realm with tenuous connections to wider political debates. Moreover, violence against women and girls is endemic in societies that suffer from multiple forms of insecurity (Merry 2009; Sanford 2008), making it difficult to parse the relationship between sexual assault and rape as tactics of political power and other forms of gender-based violence in a given society. Violence against women and girls in Monkey Point is similarly hard to locate within the framework of autonomous politics because it is both private and pervasive. It remains an ordinary intimate injury that Creole women and girls often suffer on their own (Morris 2012). The politicization of the sexual abuse case, however, reveals subtle shifts in discourse that mark a transition from the normalization of gender-based violence to a collective confrontation with the state under the banner of autonomous rights. If we take this shift to be indicative of a transformation in political consciousness on the ground, it is worth investigating how this actually happens. What are the conditions and discursive cues that mark a transition from ordinary and expected violence to exceptional and politicized violence?

This chapter examines the everyday politics of sexual violence under military occupation and the emergence of organized resistance to the state in the wake of the violence. I argue that the racial and gendered articulation of violence in the community is central to the postwar project of state securitization in the region as well as the nature and form of resistance that emerged in response to the state. In a political system where mestizo racial patriarchy shapes sexual norms, ideological constructions of the family, the exercise of authority, and the monopoly on legitimate violence, state power interpenetrates the intimate, domestic, and political domains of life. Ethnographic attention to these points of interplay reveals how socially differentiated subjects are caught up in the systems of racial and patriarchal power that animate the state security project, inciting varied forms of resistance in the process. Politically engaged feminist ethnography attuned to multiple forms of power, inequality, and resistance can help map socially differentiated sites of struggle in the interest of political praxis. Tracking the conditions that support and undermine collective resistance and coalitional struggle can provide critical political knowledge to activists working toward egalitarian change. Reading across the discourses of injury that violence generates might be seen then as an act of translation between aligned but power-differentiated groups that can lay the groundwork for a more expansive politics of liberation (Haraway 1991: 187).

The following sections of the chapter are based on written and videotaped witness testimony that Monkey Point leaders collected in January 2011 and my own interviews and informal conversations with community people in July and August of the same year. I name community leaders and those who gave interviews after the resolution of the case but leave individuals who gave testimony against soldiers as the case unfolded anonymous. I avoid delving into the details of the children's abuse to protect the identity of the girls and their families. Altogether, the chapter draws on testimony from seventeen adult community members, including four mestizas, six Creole women, and seven Creole men.

Experiencing the State

Leaders estimate that as many as 250 soldiers have been stationed in Monkey Point since 2004. The men were deployed in rotating detachments of ten soldiers with a single commanding officer. This rotational policy is in part an anticorruption measure designed to prevent low-paid soldiers from becoming involved with drug trafficking (United States Department of State 2001). An unanticipated effect of the policy is the blurring of individual soldiers—who wore no identifying nameplates on their navy blue fatigues—into a group of undifferentiated agents of the state. In their testimony, witnesses refer to individual soldiers as "the military," "the guard," "the army," "the navy," and even on occasion simply "the law." As representatives of the state, soldiers assumed the role of petty sovereigns in an isolated community setting. Petty sovereigns reign "in the midst of bureaucratic army institutions mobilized by aims and tactics of power they [do] not inaugurate or fully control. And yet such figures are delegated with the power to render unilateral decisions, accountable to no law and without any legitimate authority," in Judith Butler's words (2004: 56).

And indeed the soldiers had prerogative power to act outside of the law but with the force of the sovereign state behind them. Wendy Brown points out that state agents most frequently commit acts of sexual violence in the context of prerogative power, which is derived from the state's legitimate arbitrary power in policy making and monopoly on violence (1992: 14). This discretionary form of state power has "heavily extralegal, adventurous, violent, and sexual characteristics" (Ibid.: 22–23) and is often justified through political appeals to territorial sovereignty and security. Unlike rational tactics of government that aim to regulate bodies and populations, power in the name of sovereignty is excessive, self-justificatory, and recursive. Its highest purpose is its own legitimation, gaining meaning and force through its threatened violation and continual reassertion (Foucault 1991: 95). As petty sovereigns, soldiers took advantage of their arbitrary power to act outside of the law and to randomly enforce the law when they saw fit. They unself-consciously exercised erotic power by aggressively sexualizing women, openly engaging in sexual relationships with girls, and threatening and physically assaulting the men who challenged them. Their sexual conduct was so routinized that it fused violent heterosexual masculinity with the daily operations of military occupation such that each worked to animate and empower the other.

So who are these petty sovereigns? Most are young men in their late teens and early twenties who were born and raised in Pacific or interior departments of the country (see Figure 5.1). Some are from urban centers such as Managua, Leon, Chinandega, Granada, and Rivas, and some are *campesinos* from the countryside. All are Spanish-speaking mestizos of modest education

Figure 5.1 An armed soldier at Monkey Point. A weathered sign to the right of the soldier warns that sexual exploitation is a punishable crime.

SOURCE: Jennifer Goett, 2009.

and class standing. The demographic composition of the detachments is not surprising given the military's role as an institution of masculine socialization grounded in mestizo racial patriarchy. Military service works to institutionally harness youthful and potentially delinquent masculinity—or surplus masculinity (Cowen and Siciliano 2011)—for state ends by providing a means of upward mobility to mestizo men who are economically disenfranchised and might otherwise be unemployed or committing crimes in their communities of origin. Local people signal this process at work when they refer to the soldiers in a more personal register as "*vagos*" (unemployed men in the street), "gangsters," and "glue sniffers" from Managua.

In the early years of occupation, clear patterns of gendered and sexual violence emerged between soldiers and local people. This violence and the conflicts that followed framed their daily experience of the state and thus produced the state as a certain kind of social subject for community people (Aretxaga 2003: 393). Women and men experienced the state in distinct ways even as the occupation subjected all community spaces and bodies to forms of domination that were sexual. For community women, the state was sexually aggressive and predatory. Almost all have witnessed soldiers' sexualized speech acts, which include calling *piropos* (flirtatious remarks), making "vulgar" or sexually explicit comments, and hissing at women and girls as they walked along the path that follows the perimeter of the military compound. Before the military moved the post to a more peripheral site, the compound was located in the central sector of Monkey Point, making it impossible for women and girls to avoid harassing speech as they moved about the community.

Women say that soldiers also made direct social and sexual overtures, and some women willingly had friendships and sexual relationships with them over the years. Most women, however, did not choose to have relationships with soldiers and felt threatened and offended by the men's advances. A local mestiza gave testimony about an officer's sexual advances, which she satirized and turned into a story of women's agency:

> One of them fell in love with me, and I was passing by the post to go eat mango. I was walking eating mango, and he said to me, "Hi," he said. "How are you?" "Good and you?" Then he said to me, "Give me a piece of mango." I said, "Take it then." Then he came over by me and started to sweet talk and from there he said, "Give me a chance." So how I was walking with a machete, I said to him, "This is the chance I can give you," I said to him, "with this machete."

Other women reported being propositioned for sex by soldiers, in some cases in exchange for money. Local people found these advances to be especially insulting when directed at older women or women who were married with children as they showed a lack of deference for basic social conventions.

In the long list of injuries reported, the soldiers' use of the *pila* was of particular offense. The *pila* is a cool natural spring that bubbles up from a rocky outcrop in a semisecluded part of the community. Women and men go there to collect drinking water, wash clothing, and bathe in sex-segregated groups, but never entirely disrobed. When women are at the *pila*, men remain at a respectful distance, waiting until they are done to use it. Harley told me, "We as native people, we go and we find a group of women washing there and thing, we will haul off, you know, and we will keep away until they finish . . . That's our custom then." Community people testified that soldiers approached women who were alone at the *pila* to proposition them for sex and would bathe there nude. One mestiza noted in her testimony, "I have a girl of thirteen, and there's a band of them chasing after her. Here, when she carries water from the *pila* along the path, I notice that they are always behind her following." This sexual occupation made spaces that were once folded into the domestic domain of women and girls into newly threatening sites. Soldiers who drank to the point of inebriation and discharged guns in communal spaces heightened this sense of threatening and unpredictable spatial power. These same soldiers monitored local people's movements, searched their personal belongings for drugs when they disembarked from boats, and patrolled the beaches where Creole fishermen hauled in their catch.

The aggressive sexualization of women, girls, and communal spaces also translated into efforts to dominate and sexually humiliate men, signaling how patriarchal violence structures hierarchies among men. An oft-repeated case in the witness testimony involved an adult mestizo from the community who was wearing military fatigue pants. Since the occupation began, many local men wear castoff military fatigues acquired from soldiers stationed at the post. In this particular instance, a group of soldiers stopped the man and demanded that he remove his pants. He asked them to let him go home to change and promised to return the pants afterward. When the soldiers refused, he disrobed reluctantly as he was wearing badly torn underwear. The man was forced to walk home in this state of undress in front of women and children causing him considerable humiliation and distress. This assertion of state power underscores the precarious line between state and nonstate actors: All of the men involved in the incident were mestizos from modest backgrounds. The only difference lies in the soldiers' access to the symbolic and institutional power of the state fetishized here in the form of military fatigue pants. Soldiers arbitrarily asserted their prerogative in ways that made sexual humiliation and the spectacle it generated a mundane, but no less real, act of sovereign state power.

The most heated conflicts between men were about women and erupted when soldiers made sexual advances toward local men's wives, daughters, and female relatives. For instance, Allen confronted a soldier after he made a pass at his wife. He told the man, "Look that's my wife. And look I not like the rest of the people them down here . . . Look on my children them, and do like you no see them. You look on my wife, and do like you no see her. And you look on my niece them and my sister them, and do like you no see them because then you getting in serious problem and with me." He went on to describe how the commanding officer would tell newly arrived soldiers to stay away from his female relatives, that they were not fair game like the others, presumably because they had a male relative in a position of authority. Here prerogative state power comes up against an alternative masculine power grounded in autonomous communal authority and men's paternalism within families.

Fights between Creole men and mestizo soldiers over women were frequent. Another Creole man, who also held a leadership position in the communal government, returned home from a fishing trip to hear rumors that his wife had had sexual relations with a soldier in his absence. He went to confront the soldier. The encounter ended with another soldier drawing a gun on him and holding it to his chest. Describing this moment, the man explained, "Well I just ease up. I just ease up because, well, since I have no right[s], I just have to cool down, understand? But is wrong what they doing." The man and his wife continued to fight and separated shortly after the incident. His father testified that this had happened before with other couples: "And you have them what disturbing a matrimony and mashing up people life, well, because I experience it with my son. Them even take away my son wife and take away many others." A third Creole man described a similar situation that occurred in his family: "Just the other day here, I got one ex-sister-in-law. What they do? Beat up her husband. Send him away, just to be with the girl. You think that's right?"

What emerges from these accounts is a multilayered struggle over female sexuality. Most women rejected the sexual advances of soldiers. A few chose to engage in sexual relationships with soldiers. These relationships often created strife within the community. Adult women had more agency in their interactions with soldiers, but girls and adolescents were particularly vulnerable to sexual abuse. Despite these diverse responses and vulnerabilities, the military occupation worked to sexualize and objectify community women and girls as a group. This objectification was manifest in repetitive sexual advances and the sexualized occupation of spaces that once fell under their domain. For men, it was most evident in confrontations with soldiers over advances toward daughters, nieces, sisters, girlfriends, and wives and the violence that followed. The conflicts represent a power struggle between soldiers and local men that underscores how patriarchal privilege mutually structures heterosexual intimacy, paternalism in families, and the exercise of political authority. In fact, the most heated conflicts were between soldiers and local men in leadership positions, demonstrating how the ability to wield political power and authority were closely tied to efforts to protect, control, or violate female sexuality (Brown 1992: 25).

These battles were critical for community men invested in the autonomous process and struggling to assert their authority in the face of an expansive and jealous mestizo state. Although it is tempting to attribute a woman-centered consciousness to the Creole men who led the effort to politicize the abuse, their actions were driven by a desire for political autonomy that was grounded in expressions of patriarchal privilege and masculine authority. The men's politics left few openings to question their own investments in patriarchal power or to examine how preexisting patterns of gendered violence set the stage for the sexual abuse and contributed to its longevity. Women and girls were left to navigate the fraught spaces between patriarchal relations within their own community and mestizo state patriarchy. Their agency and resistance to sexual violence should thus be read through the multiple expressions of power that condition their experiences of patriarchy and masculine violence.

Community Patriarchy and Women's Resistance

Under military occupation, women's sexual autonomy did not always align with men's efforts to consolidate autonomous political authority in the community. Sexual autonomy can be broadly defined as control over one's own body and the ability to freely pursue sexual interests and desires. This can involve the choice to have sex or not have sex. An effort to keep a woman from having sex with a soldier when she chooses to does not support a woman's sexual autonomy, whereas an effort to protect her right to decline does. Men from Monkey Point made both kinds of interventions. It is also useful to consider how sexual autonomy might be constrained in other realms of social life, where there are clear asymmetries between the freedoms accorded to men and women. Most men are presumed to have full sexual autonomy. It may not be an overreach to say that sexual autonomy is understood to be an inherent masculine privilege, even a natural physical compulsion, with few social constraints. For instance, men often pursue sexual relations outside of their primary relationships and resist women's efforts to limit their freedom. But most people understand women's sexual autonomy to be legitimately constrained by marriage, economic dependence, and the norms of respectable feminine behavior.

Witness testimony and my own ethnographic research suggest that the sexual abuse of local girls by soldiers initially followed established patterns of gendered violence in the community. Female sexuality was a daily site of struggle before military occupation, and violence had long served as a mechanism of masculine control. For instance, some community men engaged in statutory rape of adolescent girls, rumors of acquaintance rape occasionally circulated among women, and intimate partner violence was a common masculine response to the real or perceived infidelity of wives and girlfriends. These incidents rarely resulted in formal complaints, police investigations, or court interventions and thus did not take on a political life beyond the community. They are ordinary forms of violence that underpin gender relations and are woven into the deeper fabric of structural violence that women and girls suffer.

For men, many of these forms of gendered violence were normalized. This was evidenced by their willingness to talk openly with me about their acts of battery toward wives and girlfriends and their relationships with underage girls. Men described hitting and fighting with women partners who were "too jealous" or attempted to control their drinking or drug use and socializing outside the home. Conversely, many men are quick to assert their right to control their wives and girlfriends, by demanding that women spend their time at home, limit their contact with friends, and avoid talking to or socializing with other men. For instance, Muche told me that his efforts to control his girlfriend's social interactions with men were a reaction to past experiences of infidelity. He explained, "I get so much burn from woman now I kinda little jealous, you know. If I see a boy talking to her, to my girlfriend, I just say, 'Eh, why you talking to him,' you know." And although it is not common behavior, some community men have also engaged in sexual relationships with girls under the age of consent with little criticism from their peers. Muche, who is now in his early forties, told me, "I had a lot of girlfriend down here since I come here, Jenny. I come here I take a girl thirteen years old—young girl—when I had three days down here. And we live together for just a month and change and her mother take her away from me." The soldiers' behavior toward local girls did not initially depart from these norms. Still, local men contested the soldiers' actions because they were agents of the mestizo state rather than social intimates.

Patriarchal relations and domestic violence within families also made it more difficult to politicize and challenge state sexual violence. Witness testimony indicated that a few families were complicit in the abuse, although most were not. Two cases reportedly happened with the knowledge and, some said, consent of families. Interviewees described instances when family members beat an adolescent girl and a young woman after rumors circulated that they had been with soldiers. A few women felt implicated in the abuse for allowing it to happen, others denied the abuse or refused to press charges to protect family propriety, and almost everyone feared military retaliation. Courtney Morris has found Nicaraguan Creole women reluctant to share experiences of sexual violence or seek institutional redress for rape. Social shame and stigma contribute to silence, but Creole women must also contend with a profound lack of state resources and institutional will to prosecute sexual violence as well as racist discourses that position them as exotic, "hot" or hypersexual, always available, and thus inherently rapable (Morris 2012: 284–285, 311). This does not mean that women are passive victims or accommodating agents of sexual assault and rape but that, like men, they are caught up in extraordinarily complex interpersonal and political dynamics that are textured by racism, patriarchal power, and violence. Individual efforts to negotiate these dynamics varied tremendously: Some women were vocal and proactive opponents to the abuse, and some were not. Almost all, however, relied on the same forms of female sociality and mutual aid that women have always used to deal with gendered violence.

Women rarely speak openly about their own experiences of violence, but they can be strong advocates for others who suffer abuse by providing life-affirming social safety nets. These mutual aid networks are buttressed by the intense sociality of women's lives and the prevalence of homosociality. One case of women's mutual aid that I witnessed in the early 2000s illustrates how women's sociality helps counter gendered violence. The case involved a seventeen-year-old indigenous girl from a neighboring community who did domestic work for a local family. She had become pregnant by the father of the family who was also physically abusive. I met her when she came to the health clinic bruised and suffering from anemia and a kidney infection. Community women urged her to leave, but she stayed until her baby was born. When the man began to abuse her baby girl, she left for Bluefields, where community women fostered her and the baby and accompanied her to the hospital.

The tradition of fostering children from families that are neglectful or violent remains strong among Creole women. Even as this case unfolded, another local woman was raising a child from the same household to protect the girl from her father's violence. She explained to me, "So the father like to ill-treat this little baby when she was small. Like to beat the little baby. Don't like she. He like all the rest. You see how things does happen?" She went to see the girl's mother and told her, "Better you give me your little girl because the papa don't like her, and he beat she up more than the balance them [the others]." The violence that occurred in this family was so egregious and unrelenting that community leaders intervened by reporting the man to the police in Bluefields. Allen went so far as to alert the police by radio when the man made a trip up to Bluefields in the hope that they would meet him at the wharf and take him into custody. The man eventually relocated his family to a more remote part of the territory south of Monkey Point. More than a decade later, the Bluefields police finally arrested him for the sexual and physical abuse of one of his adult daughters.

Under military occupation, women employed a wide range of strategies to protect children from abuse. Women recounted instances when soldiers passed notes to their female children or attempted to "convince" the girls when they were unsupervised by parents. They also described how they kept a close eye on their girls and carefully monitored their movements outside of the household. The most successful forms of everyday resistance involved communication and solidarity between women. Women reported what they saw to each other, and the news traveled fast in this small community. One Creole woman described how she learned of abuse toward her daughter from other women in the community. She said, "I would be right on them side for talk because I know what she tell me the military them do to me daughter. I no see, but she see then. Just like I see when some next parents no see. What happen to them own I see, you understand?"

Some women took a more direct approach by confronting soldiers and making complaints to the commanding officer at the post. Another Creole woman testified that she complained as early as 2005 after a soldier made advances toward her daughter. She explained what transpired when she addressed the issue with the soldier directly:

> When I find out about that I went and talk with him and tell him, "I don't like them things." And he tell me, "It no going to happen again." He wait till I gone to Bluefields and come over to this health center here, telling her he want meet her in the night out. And she tell my sister about it. So when I come down, I gone and me and him have a fight about that. Because I tell him, "I already talk to you about this." My daughter had fourteen years, I say, and I never did want she to get onto no military because, "Unu no wan hand nothing to nobody [you all don't do anything good for anybody]."

This confrontation turned into an ongoing antagonism between the two that was resolved only when the soldier rotated out of the community.

Despite these forms of everyday resistance, I found that only exceptional forms of sexual violence—those that stood outside the depressing normality of everyday abuse—provoked a demand for institutional redress beyond the community. Communal leaders moved to politicize the abuse, at the urging of community men and women, only after allegations emerged that three soldiers had raped an adolescent girl. Her case provoked a sense of collective outrage because the violence of a gang rape was a shocking departure from more mundane forms of sexual abuse and statutory rape. As Allen pointed out to me, after the rape, local people felt that "the military them passing the limit." This sense of "passing the limit" signals the moment that ordinary gender violence becomes an exceptional violence, creating a rupture in the status quo and inciting collective indignation and political action. After this event, community people began to formulate a political strategy to challenge the abuse they had witnessed for years. Their testimony serves as an archive that records the transformation of everyday resistance into a collective refusal grounded in autonomous politics.

Politicizing Sexual Violence

The official allegations of abuse that emerged at this point fall into a range of legal designations, including rape, statutory rape, and sexual abuse.[1] The majority of girls involved in the case were between the ages of thirteen and fifteen, although witnesses say that soldiers publically engaged in sexual behavior with younger girls. In fact, they testified that soldiers made little effort to conceal their advances toward the girls or the sexual relationships that followed. As Harley put it, "Them did got it like say them is them woman, okay, and them could'a do anything all about here. People see them kissing up or standing around. In the night, the military drinking rum with the girl them." A middle-aged mestiza noted similar kinds of public openness in her testimony:

> What I know and what I have seen is that it's very true that the soldiers, the army go around a lot with underage girls. This is what I've seen. I've seen them bathing in the sea, going to bathe at the *pila*. They pass the entire day with the girls, and this is not right . . . because they are eleven- and ten-year-old girls. They are in the sea all of the blessed day bathing with the girls hanging off of their necks, and this is not right.

Here witnesses describe how soldiers unselfconsciously exercised erotic power in a range of public spaces. The behavior signals a colonial logic that eroticizes military occupation and political domination. For these petty sovereigns, racial and sexual advantage fueled a "cult of imperial masculinity" in which hierarchy feels sexually satisfying and politically empowering for occupying forces (Gregory 2007: 133).

A number of women testified that some of the girls were "done a woman" or had already been sexually active by the time they became involved with soldiers. The same woman who testified in the preceding paragraph pointed out that this should not detract from the charges against the soldiers: "They are girls that, even though maybe some say they have had men already, this is not normal for a girl of this age." This rhetorical move shifts the blame from girls to soldiers and politicizes the power differentials that exist between the two. Witnesses struggle to make sense of teenage girls' sexual agency in their relations with soldiers. Outside the military abuse case, girls past the age of puberty are usually accorded a high degree of sexual agency and viewed as willing partners to older men. This same idea is not attributed to girls before they reach sexual maturity. Once they mature, however, discourses of blame shift from the adult male to the girl, who then becomes responsible for her early sexual activity.

Notably, this interpretation of adolescent sexual agency is absent in the witness testimony, which marks a shift from normalizing discourses about gendered violence to newly politicized ways of understanding the violence. The significant power differential between soldiers and children living under military occupation reorients community interpretations toward a discourse of collective injury that would not be readily apparent otherwise. The following testimony points to the girls' compromised sexual agency and is noteworthy because sympathetic readings of female sexuality are so rare to begin with:

> Yes, I was here for all of that and they always keep doing this crime, abusing underage girls. It's true that they don't hit them or anything, but they convince them because they are just girls and their minds are weak. (Mestiza)

> In certain case, them man got fault because, well, the girl them is underage girl, and you just can't come in a way to be authority and just come and try to put thing in their head to be with them. That's something wrong, against the law. (Creole man)

They don't respect the young girl what is innocent just because, well, they have the power, they the government, they do what them want. You know they destroy up a lot of young girl down here. (Creole man)

The witnesses use language to signal the political nature of the abuse—such as "crime," "authority," "power," and "law"—as they work to position girls as sexually and politically "innocent" and subject to an unequal and illegitimate exercise of power.

Leaders also drew on the nascent institutionality of the communal government to challenge the abuse in the early years of occupation. For instance, two or three years before the complaint, leaders enacted an internal law prohibiting contact between soldiers and women and girls. The law drew clear social and spatial divisions between military personnel and community life by stipulating that civilians were not allowed in the post and soldiers were not allowed in local residences. Leaders invited commanding officers from the post to communal assemblies to inform them of the internal law, but their efforts were ineffective due to noncompliance and the frequent rotation of soldiers stationed at the post. The soldiers also dismissed the notion that communal leaders had the authority to create laws that would hold them accountable for their behavior. A Creole man who served on the communal government described his efforts to challenge soldiers for their violation of the internal law in the following way: "I tell them about that law. So well them say, them under no law because them *is* the law and them is who make the law, you understand me?"

These efforts reflect an emerging political consciousness about how sexual violence articulates with other forms of injury local people experience under military occupation and mestizo colonization. Harley explained, "Okay, I am convinced, I am overconvinced as native and communal leader we have the authority here for rule in our community. And I believe toward them, them is here for their own purpose, you know?" His older brother Allen concurred with the assessment: "Them say was to stop the drugs, *them say*. But that is not why. What they want to do is try to see how they can control the whole country, handle the country. That's why you see they no want to move from [here] because them idea is not to give no security to nobody. It's just to keep the control." They see the military presence and abuses of state power as part of a larger state strategy to consolidate territorial sovereignty and assert mestizo state power in a racially and culturally distinct region with longstanding seditious tendencies.

These perspectives are embedded in a deep aversion to the mestizo state and its racial underpinnings. Most Creoles believe that soldiers have little capacity for multicultural governance but instead work to promote mestizo solidarity and dominance. Several Creole men gave me accounts of incidents when locals sought help from soldiers to settle disputes with mestizo land colonists. These men noted that soldiers always supported mestizos over Creoles regardless of the circumstances or law. Harley pointed out, "Whether them wrong or them right, them always there to protect them people." By the same token, they believe that mestizo soldiers are unwilling to help or protect Creoles when they are in need. Another Creole man suggested that soldiers harbored so much racial animosity that they wished Creoles harm. He imagined when fights broke out in the community between Creoles that soldiers said to each other, "Make them kill up one another. Make one die then, you know?" The prevailing sentiment was that soldiers based their actions on racial antipathy toward Creoles and racial solidarity with mestizos. This relationship of antipathy set the conditions for the conflict between communal leaders and the military once the sexual abuse allegations were made public.

Confronting the State

After hearing the rumors that three soldiers raped an adolescent girl, Allen met with Dr. Acosta, who wrote a formal letter to the military high command denouncing the last six years of abuse. This confrontational moment quickly escalated into a national scandal and full-blown battle between communal leaders and the military. As the scandal unfolded, the opposing sides harnessed the institutional resources they had available to buttress their cases. Communal leaders used the media to publicize the abuse, found allies in human rights and feminist NGOs, and employed the institutionality of the territorial government by issuing formal complaints on letterhead with official seals, collecting written and videotaped testimony, and speaking in the name of their constituents. The military used the law and the mestizo justice system as instruments of the state to surveil and intimidate the leaders, drawing on racialized security discourses to further undermine the communal government and justify military occupation.

A few days after the community issued the complaint, the top military official for the south Atlantic region met with communal leaders to discuss the allegations. According to Allen, the commander had a violent reaction to the charges: "The man rail up and want to know if anyone can prove that. Did I see the military put it in the little girl and take it back out?" Indeed, the commander told a reporter from a local radio station something similar: "Look, these accusations are too heavy, you could say. They must be substantiated by something . . . They must be proven with clear and convincing evidence and not just because he says so." He assured the reporter that the military took the charges seriously, even as he minimized and individualized the abuse. "We are very serious in this situation," he said. "It's very delicate, very embarrassing that we are involved and that they call us rapists when we are actually the protectors of children's rights. It could be that there is an isolated case."

Soon after the meeting, Allen left for Managua to attend a forum on ethnic rights. During the trip, he visited CENIDH, which later sent a representative to the community to investigate the charges. Based on conversations with local people, CENIDH found the charges to be credible and thus became a central institutional advocate for the children. The military also took trips to the community to investigate and found that there was no credible evidence that the abuse occurred. The state proceeded from the position that if the abuse happened, the children and parents would freely share the details with police, court, and military officials. But the community's nurse explained in her witness testimony, "Community members are afraid, and when they see that the same military arrive to investigate, they stay quiet out of fear because they believe that they were the same ones that committed the acts now under investigation." Moreover, the accused soldiers were stationed just meters from their homes. These men still searched their personal belongings for drugs when they returned home from visits to Bluefields and sauntered by their front porches in military fatigues with assault rifles slung over their shoulders. The fear of military reprisals became an embodied state effect that produced a massive intensification of mestizo racial patriarchy, limiting local people's ability to institutionally confront state sexual violence. As they navigated diverse expressions of state power that alternately violate, adjudicate, protect, and discipline, community people fell silent, choosing not to testify to state officials and reserving their candor for human rights advocates and communal leaders.

The second incident occurred in the midst of these events, becoming entangled with the claims and counterclaims of the opposing parties. In mid-December, Allen and a Creole leader from Greytown stopped at Monkey Point on a journey south to the Costa Rican border. The men had been drinking. Although the hired driver was sober, the military detained them at

Monkey Point and took away their identification cards and *zarpe* (travel clearance document). Allen vigorously protested, and the confrontation devolved into a physical fight between soldiers and Allen and his family members. The same military commander described the event to Radio Zinica: "Then with a lack of maturity and due to the effects of alcohol he called the population to the military post. With this attitude and disrespect for the law—because he was confronting the institutionality of the state—and with machete in hand, he tried to assault the post." To calm a volatile situation, the officer in charge released the documents and allowed the men to continue on their journey.

A couple of days later, Allen returned to Monkey Point with a delegation from the American Embassy. Military personnel in a patrol boat stopped them on the high seas, demanded to see their identification, and questioned their motives for travel. According to Allen's version of events, the sergeant in charge threatened his life. In response, Allen upped the ante by submitting a complaint to the Bluefields Court of Appeals against the military officers for illegal detention and threats made against his person. In the final weeks of December, communal leaders worked diligently to document the allegations and mobilize public sympathy for their case. They gave interviews to local television and radio outlets and collected written and video testimony from community people, which they sent to regional and national human rights NGOs, the national Ombudsman for Women, and the Army and Navy high commands. The chief naval officer for the Atlantic region responded by initiating a slander case against Allen, which required that he report every two weeks to court officials for the next six months.

Little happened during these long months leading up to the IACHR hearing in October 2011. Allen unfailingly reported to the court and continued his work with the territorial government, traveling frequently between Monkey Point and Bluefields, where his domestic partner and young children live. That summer, I spent two months on the coast. It was the height of the slander case against Allen, and the strain of the conflict was wearing on him. The previous week, a Creole leader from Bluefields had been murdered over a land conflict, and images of his badly mutilated body had appeared on the evening news. Allen was agitated and exhausted. We met on a dusky evening and walked the streets of Bluefields together. I noticed that he carried a gun in his waistband and intentionally accentuated its outline beneath his long T-shirt as he leaned up against the gate of my hotel. After a decade, our friendship had matured, and for the first time he spoke to me of his death. I felt an aching anxious fear for him. A few weeks later we traveled to Monkey Point and disembarked under the hostile glares of soldiers. I felt a lump rise in my throat and that queasy ache return to the pit of my stomach.

Stasis and fear were the order of the day, providing the backdrop for an official response to the charges that emphasized militarization as a national security imperative. In the process, the abuse charges were embedded in a mestizo nationalist script that associates Atlantic coast blackness with drug trafficking and criminality. I argue elsewhere that this script now shapes most debates about the region and has become one of the principal ways that racial difference is produced in the Nicaraguan political imaginary (Goett 2011). The following exchange between a local journalist and the head of the South Atlantic Naval Command illustrates the official response to the abuse charges in its nascent stages:

> *Commander:* There may have been some abuses on the part of a few *compañeros* in years past. But I don't know why in that moment they didn't denounce it . . . and because they are only denouncing it now, it gives the impression that there are dark . . . interests motivating Mr. Clair.
>
> *Reporter:* What could those be?
>
> *Commander:* I'll leave it there for analysis. Well, because the truth of it is that there are dark interests here and you all know that in reality we are fighting narcotrafficking and there are people who are involved in this. Well, I am not saying that this man [is involved], but he could be.

Here the commander implicates Allen in criminal activity, not by suggesting he has committed a crime but by pointing out that he is precisely the *kind* of person who might. Once deemed a threat, Allen and other men like him necessitate the presence of a vigilant security state. Months later, a spokesperson for the Armed Forces responded to the abuse charges in the national press by reaffirming the security imperative: "The truth is that we cannot withdraw from the zone. Our presence is necessary, given that this is an intersection for narco-activity in the region" (*El Nuevo Diario* 2011).

Although the official rationale for the militarization of the Atlantic coast is the drug trade, the Nicaraguan military is central to the maintenance of mestizo racial rule in the region. Monkey Point leaders posed a threat to the mestizo state, not as drug traffickers but because they sought to usurp its territorial authority. Military officials tried to discredit the leaders as unreliable witnesses due to their presumed involvement in drug trafficking, but the men's previous brushes with the law had happened when they asserted autonomous control over land or defended themselves from the paramilitary incursion. The sexual abuse case was fused with these earlier conflicts over territorial autonomy and security. Once the soldiers arrived, they attempted to exercise the prerogatives of an occupying force, protecting and violating in ways that affirmed mestizo masculinity and sovereign state power.

Redress? The IACHR Hearing

On October 24, 2011, representatives from the Nicaraguan autonomous women's movement and transnational NGOs presented the abuse case at the Inter-American Commission on Human Rights in Washington, DC. The abuse allegations served as one of two emblematic cases for a hearing on sexual violence against women in Nicaragua. It was held on the eve of the November elections that returned Ortega to office for his third presidential term. Under pressure from the upcoming elections and the impending IACHR hearing, the military had entered into negotiations with Monkey Point leaders and as a conciliatory gesture agreed to move the post to a more peripheral part of the community.

Although Monkey Point served as an emblematic case, the hearing was meant to denounce the state's failure to guarantee the rights of women and girls who are subject to sexual violence in Nicaragua, rather than resolve conflicts with the state that were specific to the community. The petitioners condemned the abuse of girls in Monkey Point, but they did not challenge military occupation or the violation of Afrodescendant rights. Their testimony reflected a separate field of political contention that was structured around long-standing conflicts between the autonomous women's movement and the postrevolutionary Sandinista Party. Demands for two legislative reforms provided the backdrop for the testimony: the passage of the Comprehensive Law against Violence toward Women (Law 779), which focuses on procedural and penal reforms such as more stringent sentencing guidelines for offenders; and the repeal of the therapeutic abortion ban, which criminalizes all abortions in Nicaragua regardless of circumstance.[2]

Focused on the mestizo Pacific side of the country, the autonomous women's movement formed as an independent network of feminist activists after the Sandinista Revolution, becoming increasingly alienated from the Sandinista Party in the last two decades (Kampwirth 2008: 126–127). A pivotal moment in this alienation occurred when key figures from the movement supported Daniel Ortega's stepdaughter after she accused him in 1998 of sexually abusing her from the age of eleven. Ortega avoided prosecution due to his immunity as a member of the National Assembly, although the accusations tarnished his political credibility among women's groups throughout the region (Kampwirth 2011: 11). More recently, feminist organizations have vigorously challenged Sandinista support for a total abortion ban. In an effort to curry favor from the religious right, Sandinista representatives to the National Assembly voted to support a ban on therapeutic abortion during the run up to the 2006 elections that returned Ortega to power after a long hiatus from the presidency (Kampwirth 2008: 123). The ban would not have passed without Sandinista support, cementing an alliance between the Sandinista Party and the "profamily" Christian right on women's issues.

The petitioners' testimony at the hearing focused on the alarming rates of sexual violence against women and girls in Nicaragua. Rape and statutory rape of girls and adolescents are widespread and dramatically underreported, often coming to light only when they result in pregnancy (Amnesty International 2010). The statistics on early pregnancy for girls and adolescents are staggering. Nicaragua has the highest adolescent birth rate in Latin America and the Caribbean. According to a 2012 Nicaraguan Ministry of Health report, girls and adolescents between the ages of ten and nineteen accounted for 27 percent of recorded births between 2000 and 2009 (Silva 2012). Although the majority of these births are to adolescents between fifteen and nineteen, the country clearly stands as a statistical outlier for pregnancy among girls fourteen and under.[3] Moreover, Amnesty International reports that between 1998 and 2008 more than two-thirds of Nicaraguan rape victims were minors, and almost half were girls younger than fourteen (Disterhoft 2010).

The women's twenty-minute presentation detailed these statistics and described the many obstacles survivors face in prosecuting such cases. The legal system gives few dispensations to survivors of sexual violence in Nicaragua. Women and girls must contend with insensitive and poorly trained police and court officers as well as a prolonged and expensive legal process. They are frequently blamed for their victimization and find that they are unable to sufficiently prove that rape occurred when cases go to trial. A lack of state-run shelters, mental and reproductive health services, and public education campaigns about sexual violence make it harder for them to find support and legal redress after rape (Amnesty International 2010). The petitioners added that the total ban on abortions and the criminalization of women who seek abortions subordinate women's political rights to their reproductive function in the family and thus promote another form of institutionalized violence toward women. The testimony supported the petitioners' assertion that women and girls are essentially "defenseless" in the Nicaraguan justice system, which fails to guarantee their rights and promotes impunity for men who commit acts of sexual violence.

A representative from the Women's Autonomous Movement (MAM, Movimiento Autónomo de Mujeres) presented the two emblematic cases during the final four minutes of petitioner testimony. After outlining the charges from the communal government's complaint to the Navy, she gave a few details from the case to illustrate the severity of the charges. She read from a prepared statement:

> In one of the cases, a mother reported that her daughter, a mentally disabled youth, was forced from the year 2004 to have sexual relations with a sergeant. When the mother complained, the response was: "The Army has more power than the president himself." Indeed, the authorities never punished this sergeant. Another youth, also, had been forced to have relations with another soldier who had her lodge in the post, and now the youth works in a brothel . . . No form of investigation has been initiated in respect to the sexual violations made public. (Comisión Interamericana de Derechos Humanos 2011a)

Her statement did not politicize military occupation or Afrodescendant rights but focused on gendered abuses of state power and the failure to investigate and punish men who commit sexual violence. The other emblematic case drove home this theme. It involved a young woman from Managua who accused her former co-worker of rape. His trial was marked by irregularities that the victim and her family blame on his social and familial ties to Sandinista Party officials.

A female representative opened the state's rebuttal with the assertion that sexual violence affects the entire globe and that Nicaragua, like any other place, has not escaped this phenomenon. This effort to normalize sexual violence ignores the fact that rates of sexual violence against women and girls vary dramatically from country to country and from urban to rural populations (World Health Organization 2005). She followed with a barrage of laws, penal codes, programs, and services in place to address sexual violence, all of which, she carefully noted, originated with Ortega's return to power in 2007. Sandinista antiviolence initiatives with names like "For Family Love and

Unity" prioritize the nuclear family unit and further embed the violation of women's rights within the private realm.

Later in the hearing, IACHR officials questioned the idea that family programs can sufficiently provide equal protection under the law to women and girls. The feminist petitioners, however, took the argument a step further by suggesting that the state itself is a gendered political system that promotes masculine violence toward women. They cast the state as an assailant. Rank and file military men, even the president himself, stand accused of criminal acts but are not prosecuted by state institutions because they *are* the state. Women and girls are defenseless in front of this state, which reproduces violent masculinity through its very laws, governing institutions, and flesh-and-blood officials. The implications of the testimony were not lost on the male state representative who sputtered in protest: "Many times we have economic problems, social problems, there are cultural problems, but we cannot speak of women's complete defenselessness because Nicaragua does not, does not, does not *favor* sexual violence against women" (Comisión Interamericana de Derechos Humanos 2011a).

His comments regarding the case put the matter to rest for the duration of the hearing:

> The prosecutor for the Attorney General's office in the southern region, in coordination with the local National Police, appointed a police investigator, who traveled to the community of Monkey Point to investigate the allegations . . . and they were not able to formalize a single complaint or identify victims . . . we must also remember that the community of Monkey Point is located in a geographic point that is one of the preeminent trafficking routes with the greatest incidence of narco-activity. (Comisión Interamericana de Derechos Humanos 2011a)

This official response was well rehearsed by the time the case reached the IACHR. Over time and through repetition, it fused the operations of racial and gendered state power to set the discursive boundaries of political debate, suturing over state sexual violence with allusions to racially coded security threats. The narrative in its entirety goes something like this: The sexual abuse of children in Monkey Point does not warrant serious attention. We can find no credible evidence that it occurred, and if it did it was an isolated incident from the past. More important, we should remember that Monkey Point is a center for drug trafficking. Military occupation of the zone is vital to national security. Also keep in mind that communal leaders may have ties to drug traffickers and cannot be trusted to represent the children. Thankfully, the military is there to protect the population and secure the zone.

When confronted with this state narrative, mestiza feminists had no political language to challenge its racial logics, and discourses about black criminality on the Atlantic coast were left unchallenged, legitimating military occupation and promoting impunity for the sexual abuse of Creole and mestiza girls. So while a gender critique of the state is crucial, the girls involved in the abuse get only partial traction through this political discourse. The inadvertent outcome is the production of another form of ideological cover—a racialized escape hatch, so to speak—for patriarchal state power.

In the final analysis, the petitioners' presentation of the case and the state's institutional response trouble any adequate resolution to the abuse charges. As the case moved from a local field of contention to the arena of international law and human rights, it was removed from the racialized power relations that conditioned the abuse. Sally Merry documents how women's rights advocates have successfully worked to translate or vernacularize human rights discourse at the grassroots level. She observes, however, that "international perspectives are translated 'down' more than grassroots perspectives are translated 'up.'" The danger is "that women's own experiences are alienated in the process" (Merry 2006: 216). I argue that not only were local experiences alienated as the case worked its way up to the IACHR but that this was because mestiza feminist petitioners reframed or even revernacularized the abuse to fit their own subjective experience of the state. It was not a universal language of human rights that masked the racial logics of the sexual abuse but a tacit feminist narrative of the universal Nicaraguan mestiza, whose rights can (presumably) be addressed with no reference to mestizo racism or the neocolonial state.

My point is not to dismiss the women's testimony due to their inability to see race or mestizo state racism. I am far more interested in finding ways to speak across difference that are politically productive. Feminist petitioners provide a gendered critique of the patriarchal state that is vital to women and girls in Nicaragua, a critique that Creole male leaders are unlikely to endorse in their public politics. But this is not enough. Their testimony reveals that Donna Haraway's now classic appeal for a new feminist politics is as urgent today as it was two decades ago. We must insist on better, richer, more critical, and power-savvy accounts of the world that have the ability to translate situated knowledges across power-differentiated communities (1991: 187).

What might a better, more critical, power-savvy response have looked like? One possible model comes from Afrodescendant women activists, whose voices remained absent in the politicization of the Monkey Point abuse case. Just four days after the hearing, members of the Network of Afro-Latin American, Afro-Caribbean, and African Diasporic Women laid out a platform for action on racial and gender inequality at an IACHR hearing on Afrodescendant Women's Human Rights in Latin America. Speaking from the standpoint that disenfranchised women share a common struggle to survive in societies structured by interlocking forms of inequality, a woman representative from Puerto Rico opened with this statement: "We must remember that to be a black woman, indigenous woman, poor woman, migrant woman in patriarchal, racist, homophobic, and neoliberal society is to live in a corporal, affective, spiritual, and material territory in continual dispute with hegemonic groups that seek to model society in the interests of men, whites, heterosexuals, and those who control resources" (Comisión Interamericana de Derechos Humanos 2011b). She and other petitioners emphasized the multiple and intersecting character of oppressive systems, pointing out that effective institutional remedies require this kind of analysis. The women outlined the varied forms of racial, gender, and structural violence that Afrodescendants in Latin America face, including the violation of territorial rights, forced displacements, criminalization of youth, overrepresentation in penitentiary systems, the traffic of young women for sexual labor, and sexual violence toward women and girls. Even though they do not provide a full picture of events in Monkey Point, they emphasize the specificity of African diasporic experiences and situate sexual violence against women and girls within a continuum, showing how diverse forms of violence operate through webs of association and collusion (Scheper-Hughes and Bourgois 2004). In doing so, they model a transnational rights language that offers a more comprehensive account of the multiple forms of oppression that Afro-Nicaraguan communities experience.

Conclusion

In the summer of 2012, when I returned to the coast, the military base had been moved to a more peripheral part of Monkey Point, and tensions between soldiers and communal leaders had abated. Like other political flare-ups, the sexual abuse scandal had run its course and no longer generated the kind of animus or fear that it had the previous summer. But it remained a critical event in community politics that had an afterlife of sorts, at least to the degree that it generated new types of political knowledge about gender, violence, and the state. The abuse led communal leaders to tentatively acknowledge the relationship between gender equality and autonomous rights in ways they had not before. As Harley told me, "The thing is like this, this is our home then, this is not a market for young girls . . . Even if it was so before, we trying to make them know now that no continue with us then. Them children have them right, and them have them national right and them communal right, and they have the international right too then." Just as the John Vogel affair empowered new expressions of autonomy and territoriality a decade before, the sexual abuse and resulting confrontation with the state added another layer of experience to the radicalization of community politics.

This period of quiescence dovetailed with national legal reforms regarding gender-based violence. Shortly after Ortega won his third presidential term, the National Assembly approved the Comprehensive Law against Violence toward Women (Law 779) in January 2012. The signs of reform were everywhere. Media outlets debated the impact of the new law on women and girls in the autonomous regions, and billboards and posters funded by a host of international organizations like UNICEF interrupted public space in Bluefields with educational messages about sexual violence. My personal favorite is located in the vestibule of the Bluefields airport—*We Don't Permit Sexual Exploitation of Boys, Girls, and Adolescents*—which to my eyes reads more as a daily affirmation for a dysfunctional state than a warning to potential abusers. That summer the IACHR Rapporteur for the Rights of Women, Tracy Robinson, visited Nicaragua on the International Day of Action for Women's Health. She praised Law 779 as an important milestone but urged the state to seriously confront impunity for gender-based violence, which remains a chronic problem in Nicaragua (IPAS 2012).

Both Law 779 and the mestiza feminist movement have emphasized reform to the criminal justice system as a frontline approach to gender-based violence in Nicaragua. Even though reform is necessary, it is critical that we develop responses to gender-based violence in Afrodescendant communities that do not rely on the mestizo state for resolution. These communities already have a fraught relationship with the Nicaraguan justice system and suffer from systemic inequality and violence that is reinforced by mestizo state policies. Moreover, individualistic punitive methods of combating gendered violence do little to address the relationship between interpersonal violence, mestizo state racism, militarization, land dispossession, and capitalist intensification in Afrodescendant communities. Policing and incarceration can exacerbate inequality and violence, as illustrated by Monkey Point's experiences with counternarcotics militarization. Sandinista antiviolence initiatives that focus on mediation and nuclear family cohesion as an alternative to incarceration are similarly problematic in that they reproduce the patriarchal power of the state, deny women autonomous personhood, further embed gender violence in the private realm, and leave survivors vulnerable to retribution from their assailants.

More holistic strategies that ensure the safety of survivors and promote social justice and nonviolent egalitarian relationships in place of universalizing agendas and neoliberal carceral containment are vital for marginalized communities (INCITE! Women of Color against Violence 2001). This suggests a real need for stronger coalitions between differentially positioned activists and new community-based approaches to politicizing and confronting gendered violence and abuses of state power. Politically engaged feminist ethnographers who work in collaboration with marginalized communities can contribute strategic knowledge to these endeavors by showing how interlocking systems of power shape insecurity and by supporting coalitional alliances for more egalitarian, comprehensive, and locally appropriate responses to violence.

Epilogue

IN ONE DECADE, THE COMMUNITY OF MONKEY POINT underwent a transformation from a marginal settlement with little political legitimacy to a self-governing territory with a reputation for radical politics and a record of direct resistance to the state. But, in many respects, the story is just beginning. Monkey Point people continue to live under conditions of great precarity, and it remains unclear what will happen if the Chinese build the Interoceanic Grand Canal just a few miles to the south of the community. At this stage, I cannot predict whether the canal will be built, but even if it is not, the Rama-Kriol Territory will continue to grapple with capitalist intensification, land enclosures, and environmental degradation in the future. The potential for conflict and violence is high, as competition for land drives more and more mestizos into the region and the illegal traffic in land, logs, and narcotics continues apace.

As the process unfolds, territorial recognition and multicultural citizenship offer political opportunities and potential entrapments. In this book, I have approached autonomy as a set of vernacular practices based on solidarities and social values that exist in tension with official multicultural recognition, always vulnerable to contradiction and compromise, even co-optation by state and capitalist power, but grounded in self-valorizing principles that are not reducible to a contest with the state for rights. Autonomous activism has found its footing within wider movements for territorial recognition, but it draws much of its political force from more intimate social and experiential realms. Although Monkey Point people have a generally positive valuation of multicultural rights as an asset in the struggle to secure and maintain territory, they continue to reject the state as a viable agent of egalitarian change. From their vantage point, the state is a self-interested entity that maximizes power in the hands of the president and offers public officials an easy path to enrichment in exchange for their loyalty.

Scholars have similarly noted that the Sandinista state is highly centralized, even hyperpresidential. Party interests dominate political decision making, and "the spoils of office" are the prize for electoral success (Martí i Puig and Close 2012: 292). In the midst of the sexual abuse scandal, Harley explained to me that the Sandinista Party now controls all state institutions in Nicaragua and many civil society organizations in Bluefields. "Okay, all of them, all of them, all of them link up with the Sandinista Party them," he said, "and they manipulated by them. You understand me?" Referencing the judiciary and military, he told me, "The president own them institution, him create them institution, and him still believe them things is not for the country. Them thing is for him and his party." The question remains as to whether Ortega will be able to successfully co-opt territorial governments in the same way that he has been able to consolidate power throughout the rest of the country. There are indications that this process is well underway throughout the Atlantic coast, and, in the Rama-Kriol Territory, state efforts to co-opt and divide territorial and community leadership have led to significant strife.

A conflict over community leadership in Monkey Point in September 2013 illustrates how vulnerable the system of territorial governance established under Law 445 is to state power and the expansion of capital into newly titled territories. But this vulnerability is not new nor has recognition necessarily pacified community leaders. When I first began to work with Monkey Point, an internal struggle over leadership had been brewing since women elders had deposed the standing *síndico* for collaborating with land speculators. Ever since this event took place, a cluster of families and their allies have controlled the communal government, resulting in continuity in leadership since the early 2000s. The continuity has generated resentment among some sectors, including the family members of the deposed *síndico* in Bluefields.

Such resentments have frequently bubbled to the surface, and community people routinely argue the merits and failings of their leaders. Family rivalries and past slights shape the debate. At some point, I came to regard these quarrels as a part of the communal process. Harmony and consensus are hard to come by in politics. Add a large and outspoken family living in both Monkey Point and Bluefields to the mix, and community politics are sure to be fractious at least some of the time. What mattered, I thought, were the kinds of social solidarity that held this large and unwieldy collectivity together, binding community people to this place and to one another. Disputes over leadership rarely took on a life beyond the community, and I came to view them as background static: interruptive and distracting but not the central storyline.

But a challenge to the standing leadership has high political stakes these days. As the territorial government gained institutional legitimacy in the mid-2000s, a formal leadership position in the GTR-K began to accord new prestige and access to the political power structure in Bluefields. After the National Assembly authorized the canal concession (Law 840) in June 2013, the debates over whether current leaders adequately and justly represent the community took on new import. Community resistance to the canal is an obstacle for the Sandinista state. A new leadership, a more compliant leadership, a leadership with less political experience and conviction, would be a welcome change for the state. At least this is how community leaders interpreted the challenge to their standing in September 2013.

The codification of communal leadership in indigenous and Afrodescendant communities on the south coast began in earnest in the late 1930s after Anastasio Somoza García came to power. At that time, the *jefe político* (Liberal Party boss) in Bluefields certified directive boards and *síndicos* whose political legitimacy now rested, at least in part, on state recognition. Formal leadership positions brought the Nicaraguan state, particularly the Liberal Party, into the communal sphere where other sources of local authority, such as community elders and the Moravian Church, still held more influence. But directive boards were often contested and inactive entities charged with administrative duties that had little practical application in small communities. The *síndico*, however, became a respected authority in many places and a key intermediary for the Liberal Party.

Law 445 established a new set of governing mechanisms for indigenous and Afrodescendant territories in the early 2000s. At least in spirit, the law preferences local practices over state-imposed procedures by allowing communities to follow their own customs, which vary from place to place. In practice, however, the governance model outlined in Law 445 loosely follows the older model established during the Somoza era, with directive boards and *síndicos* who are now democratically elected and then certified by the Autonomous Regional Council in Bluefields. As in years past, the codification of indigenous and Afrodescendant leadership brings the multicultural state, or more precisely the Sandinista Party, into the communal sphere. But the vernacular practices that shape racial solidarity and oppositional politics in Monkey Point are not so easily codified. Recognition has emboldened these practices, even as territorial governance remains highly susceptible to state intervention.

The most recent episode in the community's conflict over leadership erupted when several men in Bluefields who were allied with the former *síndico* began to lobby for an election to select new communal leaders. Community bylaws require elections every five years, and the current leadership had only completed four years of their five-year term. Still, the aspiring candidates had decided to capitalize on a call from the Autonomous Regional Council in Bluefields to set all communal elections in the region to coterminous four-year cycles for the purpose of bureaucratic efficiency. Advocates suggested that the proposed regulation was an administrative reform that would benefit everyone involved in the process. Many Monkey Point people, however, saw the initiative as a political maneuver masked in a cloak of bureaucratic rationality, arguing that it would open the communal process to a greater degree of outside manipulation. They felt that local variability was a positive mechanism to resist state intervention. Moreover, the five-year cycle they had outlined in the community bylaws was their prerogative. The Autonomous Regional Council had no authority to change Monkey Point's bylaws or to schedule elections for the communal government.

During the week preceding the confrontation, the upstart faction made the rounds in Bluefields appealing to Sandinista Party officials, regional council members, and territorial leaders to support their demand for a new election. One of the men even got on a local radio station to denounce the current leadership and invite community people in Bluefields to travel to Monkey Point to participate in the election the following weekend. Rumor had it that he had received funding from the Sandinista Party to buy gas for transport to Monkey Point and that regional council members would accompany his group to witness and authorize the election.

As the challenge gained momentum, the standing leadership made copies of the community's bylaws and submitted them to the Autonomous Regional Council. They had a solid constituency in Monkey Point and began to mobilize their large social base in Bluefields. The day before the scheduled election, I traveled with Allen and a group of his siblings, cousins, nieces, and nephews

Figure E.1 Community people confront members of the Autonomous Regional Council in Monkey Point. The electoral bylaws for the communal government are posted in the background.
SOURCE: Jennifer Goett, 2013.

to Monkey Point. The women sat up late into the night, joking, telling stories about family feuds, and spinning conspiratorial theories about the effort to depose their leaders. The next day, a group of women wrote passages from the community bylaws and Law 445 on large pieces of poster board and affixed them to posts near the wharf.

By midmorning, most of the community had assembled down by the wharf to greet a panga carrying two Creole Sandinista members of the Autonomous Regional Council in Bluefields. Community people surrounded the men, each taking a turn to denounce the interference in their affairs (see Figure E.1). Allen told the councilmen that Ortega would have to come and kill each and every one of them before they would let him build a canal on their land. "And if I is the last one," he declared, "them have to kill me behind the rest of them!" Another women shouted out, "We is cattle, and I feel like they milking me. They milking me to feed them baby in Bluefields or feed them baby in Managua." Her daughter told the councilmen that she warned one of the aspiring candidates in Bluefields, "Money come, money go. No love money. Love unu land!"

The councilman from Corn Island was quick to set the record straight: "We no come here for check nothing about the canal. We no got no interest in seeing 'bout the canal. You understand?" They had just come to witness the process, he told the crowd, not to interfere in communal affairs. When he attempted to explain the bureaucratic rationale for four-year election cycles, a community man spoke over him, loudly interjecting, "We no obligated for that!" The councilman conceded that indeed there was no obligation to change the bylaws. "The law only give we one faculty: come to observe and certify," he acknowledged. "That's the onliest faculty we got for do, and that's what we here doing. We can't change nobody in no community."

With the matter settled, the councilmen got back in their panga and headed back to Bluefields. Hours later, the aspiring challengers arrived with a large group of their family members only to learn that the councilmen had departed. Exhausted from the long sea journey, they mingled with their relatives from the community before returning home to Bluefields. A year later, Monkey Point reelected the same leadership to the communal government, following the time line established in their bylaws.

More troubling efforts to co-opt leaders, interfere in elections, and create parallel communal governments have occurred in Bluefields and the Rama-Kriol Territory since Monkey Point thwarted the attempt to change their leadership in 2013. The most recent development was in May 2016 when Sandinista state representatives brought a group of leaders from the Rama-Kriol Territory together to sign a free, prior, and informed consent agreement that outlines the lease of 263 square kilometers of communal lands for canal development. This kind of perpetual lease—or one that cannot be broken and may last into perpetuity—violates the terms of Law 445, which grants indigenous and Afrodescendant people absolute ownership and inalienable rights to their communal lands. The material result of this arrangement would be permanent dispossession (see González 2016). A significant number of communal leaders from the territory remain in opposition to the consent agreement, including the majority of Monkey Point people. They say the state has failed to follow the minimum standards for consultation outlined in national and international law, pressured and bribed communal leaders to sign the agreement, and denied them the right to have their legal representative review the document.

Monkey Point remains a stronghold of resistance to the canal, but the community has its vulnerabilities, as evidenced by the fact that two leaders have broken with the communal government and approved the agreement. Still, the example illustrates that territorial recognition is an open process that can both support oppositional politics and promote compromise with the state and capital. Formal recognition can expand the strategic resources that communities have to fight back in the political and legal spheres even as it may facilitate the manipulation and co-optation of communal leaders. The tensions between these effects now shape autonomous politics in the territory.

I have argued throughout this book that the radical potential and force behind black autonomy is not premised on recognition but stems from intimate spheres of social life that remain peripheral in most studies of grassroots social movements. In these everyday spheres of self-valorization, community people draw on a reservoir of political knowledge and oppositional subjectivity grounded in a shared black diasporic experience and gendered cultural practices. Black autonomy as an achieved state is a utopian aspiration given the racial violence and compromised political conditions that community people must negotiate on a daily basis. But black autonomy does exist as a real and vibrant social practice rooted in working-class Creole culture that is resistant to racial hierarchies and capitalist values even as it sometimes remains in contradictory tension with patriarchy. In this postwar epoch of intensified violence in Central America, it is tempting to conclude that the neoliberal state, capitalist intensification, and drug war militarization generate politically disabled subjects who are skilled in the arts of survival but can hardly challenge the structures of domination that condition their lives. This account of Afrodescendant activism suggests otherwise.

Notes

Introduction

1. The Atlantic coast is home to seven formally recognized ethnic groups, including: indigenous Miskitu, Mayangna (Panamahka and Tuahka), Rama, and Ulwa; Afrodescendant Creole and Garifuna; and Indo-Hispanic mestizo. After decades of land colonization, mestizos who are originally from other parts of the country are now the demographic majority in the region (Instituto de Estadísticas y Censos 2005).

2. Ley del Régimen de Propiedad Comunal de los Pueblos Indígenas y Comunidades Étnicas de las Regiones Autónomas de la Costa Atlántica de Nicaragua y de los Ríos Bocay, Coco, Indio y Maíz.

3. Two proposals to build an interoceanic dry canal led by the Nicaragua Interoceanic Canal Consortium (CINN, Consorcio del Canal Interoceánico de Nicaragua) and the Global Intermodal Transport System (SIT-Global, Sistema Intermodal de Transporte Global) emerged in the late 1990s and early 2000s, during the Alemán and Bolaños administrations.

4. The current canal route follows the Punta Gorda and Tule Rivers from the Atlantic coast eastward, traverses Lake Nicaragua south of Ometepe Island, and terminates via the Brito River on the Pacific coast (HKND Group 2014: 1).

Chapter 1

1. A Nicaraguan Executive Decree created the *síndico* position in 1919, but it did not become institutionalized on the south coast until the first years of the Somoza regime. The *síndico* is an important Miskitu and Mayangna leadership position charged with the management of communal lands and natural resources. Rama, Garifuna, and some Creole communities do not have a *síndico* tradition.

2. Liberal and Conservative Party factionalism shaped political competition between Nicaraguan elites in the nineteenth and early twentieth centuries. This factionalism characterized Central American politics after independence. Booth, Wade, and Walker distinguish the competing factions in the following way: "Conservatives advocated authoritarian, centralized government (sometimes even monarchy), greater economic regulation, and a continuation of special privileges for the Catholic Church. Liberals espoused limited representative democracy, decentralized government", free trade and reduced economic regulation, and a separation of church and state" (2010: 51–52.)

3. William B. Sorsby, U.S. Consul, San Juan del Norte, Nicaragua, to David J. Hill, Assistant Secretary of State, Washington, DC, December, 29, 1900, Confidential No. 439, U.S. Consul Despatches, San Juan del Norte, Vol. 18.

4. A. L. M. Gottschalk, U.S. Consul, San Juan del Norte, Nicaragua, to David J. Hill, Assistant Secretary of State, Washington, DC, December 14, 1902, Confidential No. 89, U.S. Consul Despatches, San Juan del Norte, Vol. 20; John Todd Hill, U.S. Consul, San Juan del Norte, Nicaragua, to Francis B. Loomis, Assistant Secretary of State, Washington, DC, February 8, 1905, No. 50, U.S. Consul Despatches, San Juan del Norte, Vol. 21.

5. Manifesto del Gral. J. S. Zelaya al Pueblo Nicaragüense, Managua, diciembre de 1909, p. 14, Crowdell Archives, CIDCA-UCA, Bluefields.

6. British colonial authorities and Zambo Miskitu made several attempts to abolish the indigenous slave trade in the eighteenth century, but a decree issued at Pearl Lagoon by Miskitu King Robert Charles Frederick in 1832 outlawing indigenous slave raiding by "pain of Death" suggests that raids continued into the 1830s. The decree does not question the legality of indigenous slavery, declaring, "All Indian Slaves prior to this date may remain in that state." Robert Charles Frederick, King of the Mosquito Nation, Pearl Key Lagoon, October 26, 1832, PRO FO 53/7: 275.

7. The Abolition Act of 1833 marked the end of slavery throughout the British Empire, although it was replaced by a mandatory and unremunerated (or quasi-slavery) system of apprenticeship lasting until 1838.

8. *Quequisque* (Spanish) or malanga (English).

9. PRO FO 371/1922 (1914) Note 74283/14, November 24, 1914.

10. *Breadkind* refers to starchy agricultural produce such as green banana, plantain, cassava, malanga, sweet potatoes, yams, and breadfruit.

11. Carey or Hawksbill turtles.

12. The Guardia or the Nicaraguan National Guard was the Somoza regime's military and police force. The U.S. government created the Guardia during the Marine occupation of Nicaragua in the 1930s.

Chapter 2

1. John Bodden may have been a relative of Rachel and Hutchin Jr.'s friend Hafford Bodden, although the surname is common in the Cayman Islands.

2. The name refers to the story of Judah Maccabee and his Jewish rebel warriors. References to Maccabee are relatively common in reggae music, and artists from the United Kingdom and the Caribbean have taken variations of the name as stage names.

3. *Givenot* (*agouti paca*, also known in Spanish as *guardatinaja* or *tepescuintle*) is a kind of "bush meat."

Chapter 3

1. Fab 5 lyrics, written by A. Grub Cooper, reproduced courtesy of Stage Records Publishing © 1999.

2. Similar claims about working-class African diasporic communities have been advanced, critiqued, and complicated in academic scholarship about male marginalization in the Caribbean (Barriteau 2003; Chevannes 2001; Miller 1991) and the feminization of labor in the Caribbean and Latin America (Freeman 2000; Hite and Viterna 2005; Mills 2003; Safa 1995).

3. Cleaver points out that "mainstream bourgeois social theory" has sought to characterize this kind of informal, unintegrated, and unmanageable autonomy as disorganized, backward, underdeveloped, deficient, deviant, criminal, and schizophrenic (1992: 124).

4. The informal sector swelled during the revolutionary years, and by the mid-1980s, unofficial-market commercial activities had become a more lucrative prospect for the urban poor than the scarce jobs in the formal sector, where there was a steady decline in real wages (Stahler-Sholk 1990: 74–75). The state responded by cracking down on speculative commerce in the informal sector and raising official market prices to stimulate rural production and remove artificial price controls, resulting in a rise in the cost of basic foodstuffs for the urban poor (Ryan 1995: 169–170). These measures had the unanticipated effect of alienating the nonsalaried urban poor—an important sector of the Sandinista base—at a time when mandatory draft policies conscripted young men from these same communities in ever greater numbers (Ibid.: 168).

5. Despite a dip in revenue after the global economic recession of 2007–2008 began, the 2014 figures represent an annual compound growth rate of 7 percent since 1990, when fewer than 4 million passengers went on cruise vacations (Cruise Market Watch 2015).

6. In 2014, the Cruise Lines International Association calculated that 55.1 percent of cruise passengers were from the United States, 30.1 percent were from Europe,

and 14.8 percent were from the rest of the world (Cruise Lines International Association 2014).

7. Structural adjustment began under the Sandinistas in response to the economic crisis in the mid-1980s but floundered due to heavy deficit spending and a severe lack of foreign exchange (Arana 1997: 82).

8. MINSA estimates that 94 percent of HIV infections result from heterosexual contact, and USAID reports that housewives in Chinandega, Nicaragua, are now twice as likely as sex workers to be infected with HIV (Shedlin et al. 2008: 270).

Chapter 4

1. Creole women go to jail for drug-related crimes but at dramatically lower rates than men. For instance, the national police detained forty-three women and 632 men in the RACCS in 2011 (Policía Nacional de Nicaragua 2011: 118–119). These figures indicate that men have a deeper entanglement with the police, exposing them to violent dynamics that underpin masculine subject formation.

2. Diaz and Achi report that there were 125 families with 650 members as well as 100 single men at the camp in January 1986 (1989: 115).

3. Although many believed refugees created unwelcomed competition, they often labored in low-wage agricultural jobs that Costa Ricans found less desirable. The agricultural export economy also benefited from low-paid undocumented and refugee workers by reducing labor costs and maintaining competitiveness in the world market. One consequence of these restrictive employment policies was that undocumented Nicaraguan migrants, who might have qualified for refugee status, had better access to jobs because they were unencumbered by the labor restrictions placed on formally recognized refugees (Wiley 1995).

4. Colombian guerrilla groups obtained arms from the Nicaraguan black market that had been funneled into Central America at the behest of the Reagan administration (Louise 1995: 6). Godnick, Muggah, and Waszink further document the involvement of Nicaraguan ex-combatants in the Costa Rican drug and arms trade after the war but suggest this group was disproportionately blamed for the rise in violent crime (2002: 9). During the war, approximately 2 million small military arms were in circulation in Nicaragua (Lira, in Moser and Winton 2002: 22).

5. Leftist states and guerilla groups in Central America showed restraint in their use of violence, particularly toward civilians, during the civil conflicts of the 1980s. U.S.-backed right-wing militaries and death squads committed the overwhelming majority of human rights abuses (see, for instance, Commission on the Truth for El Salvador 1993; Human Rights Office, Archdiocese of Guatemala 1999). In Nicaragua, the EPS did not engage in widespread systematic human rights abuses like their right-wing counterparts in El Salvador and Guatemala (Cruz 2011: 13). They did, however,

commit some abuses of human rights on the Atlantic coast, although contra forces are better known for war crimes and terrorizing civilian populations (Booth, Wade, and Walker 2010: 91, 95).

Chapter 5

1. The Nicaraguan Penal Code designates sex with children under fourteen as rape due to the child's inability to give consent. The law grants adolescents fourteen and older the ability to give consent and establishes statutory rape as consensual sex with minors between the ages of fourteen and sixteen. It defines sexual abuse as lewd acts or sexual touching without consent with the proviso that children under fourteen and the mentally disabled are unable to give consent (República de Nicaragua, Código Penal, Ley No. 641: Artículos 168, 170, 172).

2. The Nicaraguan National Assembly unanimously passed Law 779 in 2012. Under pressure from the Christian right, the National Assembly reformed the law in 2013, removing some of its most significant provisions. In 2014, Daniel Ortega unilaterally decreed new guidelines for the implementation of the law, emphasizing the integrity of the nuclear family and further weakening legal protections for women (De Cicco 2014). The 2006 ban on therapeutic abortion outlaws abortion in cases where fetal abnormalities are present or the pregnancy poses a threat to the health of the mother. Before the ban, abortion was also legal in cases of documented rape (Kampwirth 2008: 132).

3. To give some comparative perspective, 1.16 percent (1,448) of children born in public health institutions in 2008 were to girls fourteen and under. The same year in Canada, just 0.035 percent (134) of total births were to girls in the same age range. A bit closer to home, 0.59 percent (2,209) of Guatemalan births in 2006 were to girls fourteen and under (United Nations Statistics Division 2010).

References

Abu-Lughod, Lila. 1990. "The Romance of Resistance: Tracing Transformations of Power through Bedouin Women." *American Ethnologist* 17 (1): 41–55.

Acevedo, Adolfo. 2013. "The Canal and the Illusion of Development." *Envío* 385, August. Retrieved on January 15, 2015, from www.envio.org.ni/articulo/4932.

———. 2014. "Questions about the Canal's Economic 'Viability.'" *Envío* 399, October. Retrieved on January 15, 2015, from www.envio.org.ni/articulo/4736.

Agamben, Giorgio. 1998. *Homo Sacer: Sovereign Power and Bare Life.* Stanford, CA: Stanford University Press.

Amnesty International. 2010. "Nicaragua: Listen to Their Voices and Act. Stop the Rape and Sexual Abuse of Girls in Nicaragua." November 25. Retrieved on July 29, 2013, from www.amnestyusa.org/research/reports/nicaragua-listen-to-their-voices-and-act-stop-the-rape-and-sexual-abuse-of-girls-in-nicaragua.

Anderson, Mark. 2007. "When Afro Becomes (Like) Indigenous: Garifuna and Afro-Indigenous Politics in Honduras." *Journal of Latin American and Caribbean Anthropology* 12 (2): 384–413.

———. 2009. *Black and Indigenous: Garifuna Activism and Consumer Culture in Honduras.* Minneapolis: University of Minnesota Press.

Anglin, Mary K. 2013. "Learning Social Justice and Activist Ethnography from Women with Breast Cancer." In *Feminist Activist Ethnography: Counterpoints to Neoliberalism in North America,* eds. Christa Craven and Dána-Ain Davis, 39–52. Lanham, MD: Lexington Books.

Arana, Mario. 1997. "General Economic Policy." In *Nicaragua without Illusions: Regime Transition and Structural Adjustment in the 1990s,* ed. Thomas W. Walker, 81–96. Wilmington, DE: SR Books.

Aretxaga, Begoña. 1997. *Shattering Silence: Women, Nationalism, and Political Subjectivity in Northern Ireland*. Princeton, NJ: Princeton University Press.

——. 2001. "The Sexual Games of the Body Politic: Fantasy and State Violence in Northern Ireland." *Culture, Medicine, and Psychiatry* 25 (1): 1–27.

——. 2003. "Maddening States." *Annual Review of Anthropology* 32: 393–410.

Bagley, Bruce Michael. 1988. "The New Hundred Years War? US National Security and the War on Drugs in Latin America." *Journal of Interamerican Studies and World Affairs* 30 (1): 161–182.

Barriteau, Eudine. 2003. "Requiem for the Male Marginalization Thesis in the Caribbean: Death of a Non-Theory." In *Confronting Power, Theorizing Gender: Interdisciplinary Perspectives in the Caribbean*, ed. Eudine Barriteau, 324–355. Kingston: University of West Indies Press.

Basok, Tanya. 1990. "Welcome Some and Reject Others: Constraints and Interests Influencing Costa Rican Policies on Refugees." *International Migration Review* 24 (4): 722–747.

Bell, Charles N. 1989. *Tangweera: Life and Adventures among Gentle Savages*. Austin: University of Texas Press. (Originally published in 1899)

Belli, Gioconda. 2002. *The Country under My Skin: A Memoir of Love and War*. New York: Anchor Books.

Benson, Peter, Kendron Thomas, and Edward E. Fisher. 2011. "Guatemala's New Violence as Structural Violence: Notes from the Highlands." In *Securing the City: Neoliberalism, Space, and Insecurity in Postwar Guatemala*, eds. Kevin Lewis O'Neill and Kendron Thomas, 127–145. Durham, NC: Duke University Press.

Besson, Jean. 1984. "Land Tenure in the Free Villages of Trelawny, Jamaica: A Case Study in the Caribbean Peasant Response to Emancipation." *Slavery and Abolition* 5 (1): 3–23.

——. 2002. *Martha Brae's Two Histories: European Expansion and Caribbean Culture-Building in Jamaica*. Chapel Hill: University of North Carolina.

Bickham Mendez, Jennifer. 2005. *From the Revolution to the Maquiladoras: Gender, Labor, and Globalization in Nicaragua*. Durham, NC: Duke University Press.

——. 2008. "Globalizing Scholar Activism: Opportunities and Dilemmas through a Feminist Lens." In *Engaging Contradictions: Theory, Politics, and Methods of Activist Scholarship*, ed. Charles R. Hale, 136–163. Berkeley: University of California Press.

Boesten, Jelke. 2010. "Analyzing Rape Regimes at the Interface of War and Peace in Peru." *The International Journal of Transitional Justice* 4 (1): 110–129.

Böhm, Steffen, Ana C. Dinerstein, and André Spicer. 2010. "(Im)possibilities of Autonomy: Social Movements in and beyond Capital, the State, and Development." *Social Movement Studies: Journal of Social, Cultural, and Political Protest* 9 (1): 17–32.

Booth, John A., Christine J. Wade, and Thomas W. Walker. 2010. *Understanding Central America: Global Forces, Rebellion, and Change.* Boulder, CO: Westview Press.

Bourgois, Philippe. 1986. "The Miskitu of Nicaragua: Politicized Ethnicity." *Anthropology Today* 2 (2): 4–9.

Brown, Wendy. 1992. "Finding the Man in the State." *Feminist Studies* 18 (1): 7–34.

Bryan, Joe. 2012. "Rethinking Territory: Social Justice and Neoliberalism in Latin America's Territorial Turn." *Geography Compass* 6 (4): 215–226.

Bullington, Bruce, and Alan A. Block. 1990. "A Trojan Horse: Anti-Communism and the War on Drugs." *Contemporary Crises* 14 (1): 39–55.

Burbach, Roger. 2009. "Et Tu, Daniel? The Sandinista Revolution Betrayed." *NACLA Report on the Americas* 42 (2): 33–43.

Burt, Al. 1965. "Cuban Exiles: The Mirage of Havana." *The Nation* 2000 (4): 76–79.

Butler, Judith. 2004. *Precarious Life: The Powers of Mourning and Violence.* London: Verso.

Caldwell, Kia Lilly. 2007. *Negras in Brazil: Re-Envisioning Black Women, Citizenship, and the Politics of Identity.* New Brunswick, NJ: Rutgers University Press.

Campbell Hooker, Noel Hilberto. 2005. "We Can Live with Mistakes." In *The Times and Life of Bluefields: An Intergenerational Dialogue*, ed. Deborah Robb Taylor, 206–219. Managua: Academia de Geografía e Historia de Nicaragua.

Cárdenas, Roosbelinda. 2012. *Articulations of Blackness: Journeys of an Emplaced Politics in Colombia.* PhD dissertation, Department of Anthropology, University of California, Santa Cruz.

Caulfield Vásconez, Kimberly. 1987. *Costa Rica: A Country Profile.* Washington, DC: The Office of U.S. Foreign Disaster Assistance.

Chevannes, Barry. 2001. *Learning to Be a Man: Culture, Socialization, and Gender Identity in Five Caribbean Communities.* Kingston: University of West Indies Press.

Chin, Christine B. N. 2008. *Cruising in the Global Economy: Profits, Pleasure, and Work at Sea.* Aldershot, UK: Ashgate.

Clarke, Edith. 1953. "Land Tenure and the Family in Four Selected Communities in Jamaica." *Social and Economic Studies* 1 (4): 81–118.

———. 1957. *My Mother Who Fathered Me: A Study of the Family in Three Selected Communities in Jamaica.* Oxford, UK: Humanities Press.

Cleaver, Harry. 1992. "The Inversion of Class Perspective in Marxian Theory: From Valorization to Self-Valorization." In *Open Marxism, Volume II: Theory and Practice*, eds. Werner Bonefeld, Richard Gunn, and Kosmas Psychopedis, 106–144. London: Pluto Press.

Cockburn, Cynthia. 2004. "The Continuum of Violence: A Gender Perspective on War and Peace." In *Sites of Violence: Gender and Conflict Zones*, eds. Wenona Giles and Jennifer Hyndman, 24–44. Berkeley: University of California Press.

Cockburn, Leslie. 1987. *Out of Control: The Story of the Reagan Administration's Secret War in Nicaragua, the Illegal Arms Pipeline, and the Contra Drug Connection.* New York: Atlantic Monthly Press.

Collins, Patricia Hill. 2009. *Black Feminist Thought: Knowledge, Consciousness, and the Politics of Empowerment.* New York: Routledge.

Comaroff, Jean, and John L. Comaroff. 2001. "Millennial Capitalism: First Thoughts on a Second Coming." *Public Culture* 12 (2): 291–343.

Comaroff, John L., and Jean Comaroff. 2006. "Law and Disorder in the Postcolony: An Introduction." In *Law and Disorder in the Postcolony*, eds. Jean Comaroff and John L. Comaroff, 1–56. Chicago: The University of Chicago Press.

Comisión de Liquidación del Ferrocarril de Nicaragua. 1997. *El Ferrocarril de Nicaragua: Historia y Liquidación.* Managua: Comisión de Liquidación del Ferrocarril de Nicaragua.

Comisión Interamericana de Derechos Humanos. 2011a. "Audiencia: Situación de los derechos de las mujeres en Nicaragua." October 24. Retrieved on July 15, 2012, from www.oas.org/OASPage/videosasf/2011/10/102411_RubenDario_V2_11am.wmv.

———. 2011b. "Audiencia: Situación de los derechos humanos de las mujeres afrodescendientes en América Latina." October 28. Retrieved on July 15, 2012, from www.oas.org/OASPage/videosasf/2011/10/102811_RB_S2.wmv.

Comisión Nacional de Demarcación y Titulación. 2013. "Informe Ejecutivo de la CONADETI y las CIDT's al 30 de Junio del año 2013." Bilwi, June 30. Retrieved on February 15, 2015, from http://www.poderjudicial.gob.ni/pjupload/costacaribe/pdf/informe_costacaribe3006.pdf.

Commission on the Truth for El Salvador. 1993. *From Madness to Hope: The Twelve-Year War in El Salvador.* New York: United Nations.

Comunidad Negra Creole Indígena de Bluefields. 2012. *Diagnóstico del Territorio de la Comunidad Negra Creole Indígena de Bluefields.* Bluefields, RAAS: Author.

Conzemius, Eduard. 1932. *Ethnographical Survey of the Miskito and Sumu Indians of Honduras and Nicaragua.* Washington, DC: Smithsonian Institution, Bureau of American Ethnology.

Cooper, Carolyn. 2004. *Sound Clash: Jamaican Dancehall Culture at Large.* New York: Palgrave Macmillan.

Corte Interamericana de Derechos Humanos. 2001. *Caso de la comunidad Mayangna (Sumo) Awas Tingni vs. Nicaragua: Sentencia de 31 Agosto de 2001.* Retrieved on March 15, 2015, from www.corteidh.or.cr/docs/casos/articulos/Seriec_79_esp.pdf.

Cotera, Maria Eugenia. 2004. "All My Relatives Are Noble: Recovering the Feminine in Ella Cara Deloria's *Waterlily*." *American Indian Quarterly* 28 (1–2): 52–72.

Cowen, Deborah, and Amy Siciliano. 2011. "Surplus Masculinities and Security." *Antipode* 43 (5): 1516–1541.

Craven, Christa. 2013. "Reproductive Rights in a Consumer Rights Era: Toward the Value of 'Constructive' Critique." In *Feminist Activist Ethnography: Counterpoints to Neoliberalism in North America*, eds. Christa Craven and Dána-Ain Davis, 101–118. Lanham, MD: Lexington Books.

Craven, Christa, and Dána-Ain Davis, eds. 2013. *Feminist Activist Ethnography: Counterpoints to Neoliberalism in North America*. Lanham, MD: Lexington Books.

Crichlow, Michaeline A. 1994. "An Alternative Approach to Family Land Tenure in the Anglophone Caribbean: The Case of St. Lucia." *New West Indian Guide* 68 (1–2): 77–99.

Cruise Lines International Association. 2014. "Annual State of the Industry Press Conference and Media Marketplace." February 9. Retrieved on June 12, 2014, from www.cruising.org/sites/default/files/pressroom/PressConferencePresentation .pdf.

Cruise Market Watch. 2015. "Growth." Retrieved on April 10, 2015, from www .cruisemarketwatch.com/growth/.

Cruz, José Miguel. 2011. "Criminal Violence and Democratization in Central America: The Survival of the Violent State." *Latin American Politics and Society* 53 (4): 1–33.

Davis, Dána-Ain. 2006. *Battered Black Women and Welfare Reform: Between a Rock and Hard Place*. Albany: State University of New York Press.

Dayan, Joan. 1995. *Haiti, History, and the Gods*. Berkeley: University of California Press.

De Cicco, Gabby. 2014. "Nicaragua: Decree to Implement Law on Violence against Women–A Setback for Women's Rights." Association for Women's Rights in Development, November 14. Retrieved on March 14, 2015, from www.awid.org/News-Analysis/Friday-Files/Nicaragua-Decree-to-Implement-Law-on-Violence-Against-Women-A-Setback-for-Women-s-Rights.

de la Cadena, Marisol. 1995. "Women Are More Indian: Gender and Ethnicity in a Community in Cuzco." In *Ethnicity, Markets, and Migration in the Andes: At the Crossroads of History and Anthropology*, eds. Brooke Larson, Olivia Harris, and Enrique Tandeter, 319–328. Durham, NC: Duke University Press.

Diaz, Theresa, and R. Achi. 1989. "Infectious Diseases in a Nicaraguan Refugee Camp in Costa Rica." *Tropical Doctor* 19: 14–17.

Díaz Polanco, Héctor, and Gilberto López y Rivas. 1986. *Nicaragua: Autonomía y Revolución*. México: Juan Pablos Editor.

Disterhoft, Jason. 2010. "Sexual Violence against Girls in Nicaragua Widespread." *Amnesty International: Human Rights Now Blog*, December 2. Retrieved on August 2, 2013, from http://blog.amnestyusa.org/americas/sexual-violence-against-girls-in-nicaragua-widespread/.

Ellis, Aimé J. 2011. *If We Must Die: From Bigger Thomas to Biggie Smalls*. Detroit: Wayne State University Press.

Enloe, Cynthia. 2014. *Bananas, Beaches, and Bases: Making Feminist Sense of International Politics*. Berkeley: University of California Press.

Envío Team. 1985a. "Nicaragua: Behind the State of Emergency." *Envío* 53, November. Retrieved on October 22, 2014, from www.envio.org.ni/articulo/3413.

———. 1985b. "Nicaragua: Both Sides Up the Ante." *Envío* 51, September. Retrieved on October 22, 2014, from www.envio.org.ni/articulo/3407.

———. 1985c. "Nicaragua: New Successes, Higher Stakes." *Envío* 48, June. Retrieved on October 22, 2014, from www.envio.org.ni/articulo/3399.

———. 1985d. "Nicaragua: The Atlantic Coast: War or Peace?" *Envío* 52, October. Retrieved on October 22, 2014, from www.envio.org.ni/articulo/3412.

———. 1988. "Nicaragua: The War Disabled: Wounds Still to Heal." *Envío* 85, July. Retrieved on October 22, 2014, from www.envio.org.ni/articulo/3059.

Escobar, Arturo, and Sonia E. Alvarez. 1992. *The Making of Social Movements in Latin America: Identity, Strategy, and Democracy*. Boulder, CO: Westview Press.

Fab 5. 1999. "Woman's Anthem." From *Shape*. New York: VP Records.

Fagen, Richard R. 1987. *Forging Peace: The Challenge of Central America*. New York: Basil Blackwell.

Fanon, Frantz. 1963. *The Wretched of the Earth*. Richard Philcox, trans. New York: Grove Press.

———. 1965. *A Dying Colonialism*. Haakon Chevalier, trans. New York: Grove Press.

Farmer, Paul. 2004. "The Anthropology of Structural Violence." *Current Anthropology* 45 (3): 305–325.

Farthing, Linda. 2007. "Everything Is Up For Discussion: A 40th Anniversary Conversation with Silvia Rivera Cusicanqui." *NACLA Report on the Americas* 40 (4): 4–9.

Federici, Silvia. 2012. *Revolution at Point Zero: Housework, Reproduction, and Feminist Struggle*. Oakland, CA: PM Press.

Fernández, Mariela. 2002. "Representante de Monkey Point Acusa a Mayor." *La Prensa*, July 23. Retrieved on June 25, 2014, from www.laprensa.com.ni/2002/07/23/nacionales/836387-representante-de-monkey-point-acusa-a-mayor.

Ferris, Elizabeth G. 1987. *The Central American Refugees*. New York: Praeger.

Finley-Brook, Mary, and Curtis Thomas. 2011. "Renewable Energy and Human Rights Violations: Illustrative Cases from Indigenous Territories in Panama." *Annals of the Association of American Geographers* 101 (4): 863–872.

Forum for Food Sovereignty. 2007. *Declaration of Nyéléni*. February 27. Retrieved on May 21, 2014, from www.nyeleni.org/IMG/pdf/DeclNyeleni-en.pdf.

Foucault, Michel. 1991. "Governmentality." In *The Foucault Effect: Studies in Governmentality*, eds. Graham Burchell, Colin Gordon, and Peter Miller, 87–104. Chicago: University of Chicago Press.

Franco, Jean. 2007. "Rape: A Weapon of War." *Social Text* 25 (2): 23–37.

Frazer, Elizabeth, and Kimberly Hutchings. 2008. "On Politics and Violence: Arendt Contra Fanon." *Contemporary Political Theory* 7 (1): 90–108.

Freeman, Carla. 2000. *High Tech and High Heels in the Global Economy: Women, Work, and Pink-Collar Identities in the Caribbean.* Durham, NC: Duke University Press.

Freire, Paulo. 2000. *Pedagogy of the Oppressed.* New York: Bloomsbury.

Fritz, Bruce W. 1995. *Southern Opposition Front in Costa Rica During the Contra War: 1980–1988.* MA thesis, Department of Latin American Studies, University of Kansas, Lawrence.

Gershon, Ilana. 2011. "Neoliberal Agency." *Current Anthropology* 52 (4): 537–555.

Godnick, William, Robert Muggah, and Camilla Waszink. 2002. *Stray Bullets: The Impact of Small Arms Misuse in Central America.* Geneva: Small Arms Survey, Graduate Institute of International Studies. Retrieved on October 29, 2014, from www.smallarmssurvey.org/fileadmin/docs/B-Occasional-papers/SAS-OP05-Central-America.pdf.

Goett, Jennifer. 2006a. *Diasporic Identities, Autochthonous Rights: Race, Gender, and the Cultural Politics of Creole Land Rights in Nicaragua.* PhD dissertation, Department of Anthropology, University of Texas at Austin.

———. 2006b. "La historia oral de las mujeres criollas de Monkey Point, Nicaragua." *Wani: Revista del Caribe Nicaragüense* 47: 10–36.

———. 2011. "Citizens or Anticitizens? Afro-Descendants and Counternarcotics Policing in Multicultural Nicaragua." *Journal of Latin American and Caribbean Anthropology* 16 (2): 354–379.

———. 2015. "Securing Social Difference: Militarization and Sexual Violence in an Afro-Nicaraguan Community." *American Ethnologist* 42 (3): 475–489.

Goldstein, Daniel M. 2010. "Toward a Critical Anthropology of Security." *Current Anthropology* 51 (4): 487–517.

———. 2012. *Outlawed: Between Security and Rights in a Bolivian City.* Durham, NC: Duke University Press.

———. 2014. "Laying the Body on the Line: Activist Anthropology and the Deportation of the Undocumented." *American Anthropologist* 116 (4): 839–842.

González, Miguel. 1997. *Gobiernos Pluriétnicos: La Constitución de Regiones Autónomas en Nicaragua.* México: Editorial Plaza y Valdés & URACCAN.

———. 2012. "Securing Rights in Tropical Lowlands: Communal Land Property Ownership in the Nicaraguan Autonomous Regime." *AlterNative: An International Journal of Indigenous Peoples* 8 (4): 426–446.

———. 2016. "Reality Check del Canal en Tierras Comunales." *Confidencial,* January 17. Retrieved on January 18, 2016, from http://confidencial.com.ni/reality-check-del-canal-en-tierras-comunales/.

Goodale, Mark, and Nancy Postero, eds. 2013. *Neoliberalism, Interrupted: Social Change and Contested Governance in Latin America*. Stanford, CA: Stanford University Press.

Gordon, Edmund T. 1998. *Disparate Diasporas: Identity and Politics in an African-Nicaraguan Community*. Austin: University of Texas Press.

Gordon, Edmund T., and Mark Anderson. 1999. "The African Diaspora: Toward an Ethnography of Diasporic Identification." *The Journal of American Folklore* 112 (445): 282–296.

Gordon, Edmund T., Galio C. Gurdián, and Charles R. Hale. 2003. "Rights, Resources, and the Social Memory of Struggle: Reflections on a Study of Indigenous and Black Community Land Rights on Nicaragua's Atlantic Coast." *Human Organization* 62 (4): 369–381.

Gould, Jeffery L. 1998. *To Die in this Way: Nicaraguan Indians and the Myth of Mestizaje, 1880–1965*. Durham, NC: Duke University Press.

Graeber, David. 2001. *Toward an Anthropological Theory of Value: The False Coin of Our Own Dreams*. New York: Palgrave.

———. 2004. *Fragments of an Anarchist Anthropology*. Chicago: Prickly Paradigm Press.

———. 2009. *Direct Action: An Ethnography*. Oakland, CA: AK Press.

Gregory, Steven. 2007. *The Devil behind the Mirror: Globalization and Politics in the Dominican Republic*. Berkeley: University of California Press.

Gross, Michael. 2014. "Will the Nicaragua Canal Connect or Divide?" *Current Biology* 24 (21): R1023–R1025.

Guha, Ranajit. 1999. *Elementary Aspects of Peasant Insurgency in Colonial India*. Durham, NC: Duke University Press.

Hale, Charles R. 1994. *Resistance and Contradiction: Miskitu Indians and the Nicaraguan State, 1894–1987*. Stanford, CA: Stanford University Press.

———. 2002. "Does Multiculturalism Menace? Governance, Cultural Rights and the Politics of Identity in Guatemala." *Journal of Latin American Studies* 34 (3): 485–524.

———. 2004. "Rethinking Indigenous Politics in the Era of the 'Indio Permitido.'" *NACLA Report on the Americas* 38 (1): 16–20.

———. 2005. "Neoliberal Multiculturalism: The Remaking of Cultural Rights and Racial Dominance in Central America." *PoLAR: Political and Legal Anthropology Review* 28 (1): 10–28.

———. 2006. "Activist Research v. Cultural Critique: Indigenous Land Rights and the Contradictions of Politically Engaged Anthropology." *Cultural Anthropology* 21 (1): 96–120.

———, ed. 2008. *Engaging Contradictions: Theory, Politics, and Methods of Activist Scholarship*. Berkeley: University of California Press.

————. 2011. "Resistencia para que? Territory, Autonomy, and Neoliberal Entangle-ments in the 'Empty Spaces' of Central America." *Economy and Society* 40 (2): 184–210.

Hall, Stuart, Chas Critcher, Tony Jefferson, John Clarke, and Brian Roberts. 1978. *Policing the Crisis: Mugging, the State, and Law and Order*. London: The Macmillan Press.

Haraway, Donna. 1991. *Simians, Cyborgs, and Women: The Reinvention of Nature*. New York: Routledge.

Hardt, Michael. 1999. "Affective Labor." *boundary 2* 26 (2): 89–100.

Harvey, David. 2003. *The New Imperialism*. Oxford, UK: Oxford University Press.

Hastings, Julie A. 2002. "Silencing State-Sponsored Rape in and beyond a Transna-tional Guatemalan Community." *Violence against Women* 8 (10): 1153–1181.

Hebdige, Dick. 1987. *Cut 'N' Mix: Culture, Identity and Caribbean Music*. London: Routledge.

Hernández Castillo, R. Aída. 2006. "Fratricidal War or Ethnocidal Strategy? Women's Experience with Political Violence in Chiapas." In *Engaged Observer: Anthro-pology, Advocacy, and Activism*, eds. Victoria Sanford and Asale Angel-Ajani, 149–169. New Brunswick, NJ: Rutgers University Press.

Herskovits, Melville J. 1990. *The Myth of the Negro Past*. Boston: Beacon Press.

Hite, Amy Bellone, and Jocelyn S. Viterna. 2005. "Gendering Class in Latin America: How Women Effect and Experience Change in the Class Structure." *Latin Ameri-can Research Review* 40 (2): 50–82.

HKND Group. 2014. "Nicaragua Canal Project Description." December. Re-trieved on January 28, 2015, from http://hknd-group.com/upload/pdf/20150105/Nicaragua_Canal_Project_Description_EN.pdf.

Holm, John. 1983. "Nicaragua's Miskito Coast Creole English." In *Central American English*, ed. John Holm, 95–130. Heidelberg: Groos.

Honey, Martha. 1994. *Hostile Acts: U.S. Policy in Costa Rica in the 1980s*. Gainsville: University of Florida Press.

Hooker, Juliet. 2005a. "'Beloved Enemies': Race and Official Mestizo Nationalism in Nicaragua." *Latin American Research Review* 40 (3): 14–39.

————. 2005b. "Indigenous Inclusion/Black Exclusion: Race, Ethnicity, and Multi-cultural Citizenship in Latin America." *Journal of Latin American Studies* 31 (1): 1–26.

hooks, bell. 1989. *Talking Back: Thinking Feminist, Thinking Black*. Cambridge, MA: South End Press.

————. 2004. *We Real Cool: Black Men and Masculinity*. New York: Routledge.

Huggins, Martha Knisely, Mika Haritos-Fatouros, and Philip G. Zimbardo. 2002. *Violence Workers: Police Torturers and Murderers Reconstruct Brazilian Atrocities*. Berkeley: University of California Press.

Human Rights Office, Archdiocese of Guatemala. 1999. *Guatemala, Never Again! REMHI, Recovery of Historical Memory Project.* Maryknoll, NY: Orbis Books.

Illich, Ivan. 1981. *Shadow Work.* Salem, NH: Marion Boyars.

Imai, Shin, Ladan Mehranvar, and Jennifer Sander. 2007. "Breaching Indigenous Law: Canadian Mining in Guatemala." *Indigenous Law Journal* 6 (1): 101–139.

INCITE! Women of Color against Violence. 2001. "INCITE! Critical Resistance Statement: Gender Violence and the Prison Industrial Complex." Retrieved on March 24, 2015, from www.incite-national.org/page/incite-critical-resistance-statement.

Inda, Jonathan Xavier. 2006. *Targeting Immigrants: Government, Technology, and Ethics.* Malden, MA: Blackwell Publishing.

Instituto de Estadísticas y Censos. 2005. *VII Censo de Población y IV de Vivienda: Resumen Censal.* Managua: Gobierno de Nicaragua.

Internacional de Resistentes a la Guerra. 1998. "Nicaragua." April 30. Retrieved on October 3, 2014, from http://wri-irg.org/es/co/rtba/nicaragua.htm.

International Centre for Prison Studies. 2016. "Nicaragua: World Prison Brief." Retrieved on January 29, 2016, from www.prisonstudies.org/country/nicaragua.

IPAS. 2012. "Rapporteur for Women's Rights Visits Nicaragua, Urges Reforms to Address Sexual Violence and Unsafe Abortion." July 16. Retrieved on September 12, 2013, from www.ipas.org/en/News/2012/July/Rapporteur-for-womens-rights-visits-Nicaragua--urges-reforms-to-address-sexual-violence-an.aspx.

Jacobs, Harriet. 2001. *Incidents in the Life of a Slave Girl.* Mineola, NY: Dover Publications.

Jarquín, Herberto. 2003. "¿Racismo en aeropuerto?" *La Prensa*, March 21. Retrieved on August 10, 2009, from www.laprensa.com.ni/archivo/2003/marzo/ 21/cartas/cartas-20030321-02.html.

———. 2008. "Rebelión en Monkey Point." *El Nuevo Diario*, March 9. Retrieved on April 7, 2015, from http://archivo.elnuevodiario.com.ni/nacional/233060-rebelion-monkey-point/.

Jensen, Bergholdt, and Claus Kjaerby. 2010. "Dinamarca apoya la titulación del territorio del Pueblo Rama." March 1. Retrieved on January 22, 2015, from http://ibisnicaragua.org/articles/dinamarca-apoya-la-titulacion-del-territorio-del-pueblo-rama/.

Johnston, Kevin. 2010. *The CIA, the Contras, and Cocaine: The Reagan Administration's Complicity in Drug Trafficking, 1981–1988.* MA thesis, Department of History, Dalhousie University, Halifax, Nova Scotia.

Juris, Jeffery S., and Alex Khasnabish, eds. 2013. *Insurgent Encounters: Transnational Activism, Ethnography, and the Political.* Durham, NC: Duke University Press.

Kampwirth, Karen. 2008. "Abortion, Antifeminism, and the Return of Daniel Ortega: In Nicaragua, Leftist Politics?" *Latin American Perspectives* 35 (6): 122–136.

————. 2011. *Latin America's New Left and the Politics of Gender: Lessons from Nicaragua*. New York: Springer.

Kempadoo, Kamala. 2004. *Sexing the Caribbean: Gender, Race, and Sexual Labor*. New York: Routledge.

Kerssen, Tanya M. 2013. *Grabbing Power: The New Struggles for Land, Food and Democracy in Northern Honduras*. Oakland, CA: Food First Books.

Kornbluh, Peter, and Malcolm Byrne, eds. 1993. *The Iran-Contra Scandal: The Declassified History*. New York: New Press.

Larson, Elizabeth M. 1992. "Costa Rican Government Policy on Refugee Employment and Integration, 1980–1990." *International Journal of Refugee Law* 4 (3): 326–342.

————. 1993. "Nicaraguan Refugees in Costa Rica from 1980–1993." *Yearbook. Conference of Latin Americanist Geographers* 19: 67–79.

Lewin, Gregory. 2004. "A Profiling: If You Are Black You Are a Drug Dealer in the Eyes of the Nicaraguan Government." *Bluefields Pulse*, October 22. Retrieved on August 10, 2009, from http://bluefieldspulse.com/profiling.htm.

Loescher, Gil. 1988. "Humanitarianism and Politics in Central America." *Political Science Quarterly* 103 (2): 295–320.

Loperena, Christopher A. 2012. *A Fragmented Paradise: The Politics of Development and Land Use on the Caribbean Coast of Honduras*. PhD dissertation, Department of Anthropology, University of Texas at Austin.

López, Iris. 2013. "Negotiating Different Worlds: An Integral Ethnography of Reproductive Freedom and Social Justice." In *Feminist Activist Ethnography: Counterpoints to Neoliberalism in North America*, eds. Christa Craven and Dána-Ain Davis, 145–164. Lanham, MD: Lexington Books.

López Baltodano, Monica. 2014. "Truths about the Canal Concession All Nicaraguans Should Know." *Envío* 390, January. Retrieved on January 21, 2015, from www.envio.org.ni/articulo/4805.

Louise, Christopher. 1995. *The Social Impacts of Light Weapons Availability and Proliferation*. Geneva: United Nations Research Institute for Social Development. Retrieved on October 29, 2014, from www.essex.ac.uk/armedcon/story_id/Social%20Impact%20.pdf.

Low, Setha M., and Sally Engle Merry. 2010. "Engaged Anthropology: Diversity and Dilemmas." *Current Anthropology* 51 (S2): S203–S226.

Mahmood, Saba. 2001. "Feminist Theory, Embodiment, and the Docile Agent: Some Reflections on the Egyptian Islamic Revival." *Cultural Anthropology* 16 (2): 202–236.

Martí i Puig, Salvador. 2013. "Nicaragua: La Consolidación de un Régimen Híbrido." *Revista de Ciencia Política* 33 (1): 269–286.

Martí i Puig, Salvador, and David Close. 2012. "The Nicaraguan Exception?" In *The Sandinistas and Nicaragua since 1979*, eds. David Close, Salvador Martí i Puig, and Shelly A. McConnell, 287–307. Boulder, CO: Lynne Rienner Publishers.

McClintock, Anne. 1993. *Imperial Leather: Race, Gender, and Sexuality in the Colonial Contest*. New York: Routledge.

Merry, Sally Engle. 2006. *Human Rights and Gender Violence*. Chicago: University of Chicago Press.

———. 2009. *Gender Violence: A Cultural Perspective*. Malden, MA: Wiley-Blackwell.

Metoyer, Cynthia Chavez. 2000. *Women and the State in Post-Sandinista Nicaragua*. Boulder, CO: Lynne Rienner Publishers.

Meyer, Axel, and Jorge A. Huete-Pérez. 2014. "Nicaragua Canal Could Wreak Environmental Ruin." *Nature* 506: 287–289.

Miller, Errol. 1991. *Men at Risk*. Kingston: Jamaica Publishing House.

Mills, Mary Beth. 2003. "Gender and Inequality in the Global Labor Force." *Annual Review of Anthropology* 32: 41–62.

Mintz, Sidney W., and Richard Price. 1992. *The Birth of African American Culture: An Anthropological Perspective*. Boston: Beacon Press.

Moodie, Ellen. 2010. *El Salvador in the Aftermath of Peace: Crime, Uncertainty, and the Transition to Democracy*. Philadelphia: University of Pennsylvania Press.

Morales, Waltraud Queiser. 1989. "The War on Drugs: A New US National Security Doctrine?" *Third World Quarterly* 11 (3): 147–169.

Morris, Courtney. 2012. *To Defend this Sunrise: Race, Place, and Creole Women's Political Subjectivity on the Caribbean Coast of Nicaragua*. PhD dissertation, Department of Anthropology, University of Texas at Austin.

Moser, Caroline, and Ailsa Winton. 2002. *Violence in the Central American Region: Towards an Integrated Framework for Violence Reduction*. London: Overseas Development Institute. Retrieved on October 28, 2014, from www.odi.org/sites/odi .org.uk/files/odi-assets/publications-opinion-files/1826.pdf.

Nagel, Joane. 1998. "Masculinity and Nationalism: Gender and Sexuality in the Making of Nations." *Ethnic and Racial Studies* 21 (2): 242–269.

Neumann, Pamela J. 2013. "The Gendered Burden of Development in Nicaragua." *Gender and Society* 27 (6): 43–73.

El Nuevo Diario. 2011. "Líder de Monkey Point acusado por el Ejército." *El Nuevo Diario*, May 4. Retrieved on June 17, 2012, from www.elnuevodiario.com.ni/ nacionales/101245.

———. 2013. "Madres y abuelas sin importar las distancias." May 29. Retrieved on June 12, 2014, from www.elnuevodiario.com.ni/especiales/287421-madres-abuelas-importar-distancias/.

Observatorio Centroamericano sobre Violencia. 2008. "Narcoactividad en Nicaragua, 2007." July 10. Retrieved on March 12, 2009, from www.ocavi.com/docs files/file 587.pdf.

Offen, Karl. 2003. "The Territorial Turn: Making Black Territories in Pacific Colombia." *Journal of Latin American Geography* 2 (1): 43–73.

Olwig, Karen Fog. 1995. "Caribbean Family Land: Communal Land in a Colonial Society." Paper presented at the Fifth Annual Common Property Conference of the International Association for the Study of Common Property, Bodø, Norway, May 24–28. Retrieved on March 15, 2015, from http://dlc.dlib.indiana.edu/dlc/bitstream/handle/10535/1060/Caribbean_Family_Land_Communal_Land_in_a_Colonial_Society.pdf?sequence=1.

O'Neill, Kevin Lewis, and Kendron Thomas, eds. 2011. *Securing the City: Neoliberalism, Space, and Insecurity in Postwar Guatemala.* Durham, NC: Duke University Press.

Pacheco, Gilda. 1989. *Nicaraguan Refugees in Costa Rica: Adjustment to Camp Life.* Washington, DC: Hemispheric Migration Project, Center for Immigration Policy and Refugee Assistance, Georgetown University.

Paley, Dawn. 2014. *Drug War Capitalism.* Oakland, CA: AK Press.

Perla, Héctor, and Héctor Cruz-Feliciano. 2013. "The Twenty-First Century Left in El Salvador and Nicaragua: Understanding Apparent Contradictions and Criticisms." *Latin American Perspectives* 40 (3): 83–106.

Perry, Keisha-Khan Y. 2013. *Black Women against the Land Grab: The Fight for Racial Justice in Brazil.* Minneapolis: University of Minnesota Press.

———. 2015. "State Violence and the Ethnographic Encounter: Feminist Research and Racial Embodiment." In *Bridging Scholarship and Activism: Reflections from the Frontlines of Collaborative Research*, eds. Bernd Reiter and Ulrich Oslender, 151–170. East Lansing: Michigan State University Press.

Pim, Bedford. 1863. *The Gate of the Pacific.* London: Lovell Reeve & Company.

Policía Nacional de Nicaragua. 2002. *Anuario Estadístico.* Retrieved on June 15, 2012, from www.policia.gob.ni/cedoc/sector/estd/ae2002.pdf.

———. 2010. *Anuario Estadístico.* Retrieved on June 15, 2012, from www.policia.gob.ni/cedoc/sector/estd/ae2010%20PN.pdf.

———. 2011. *Anuario Estadístico.* Retrieved on June 15, 2012, from www.policia.gob.ni/cedoc/sector/estd/ae2011%20PN.pdf.

Postero, Nancy Grey. 2007. *Now We Are Citizens: Indigenous Politics in Postmulticultural Bolivia.* Stanford, CA: Stanford University Press.

Potoy y Sergio, Freddy. 2003. "Narcos carcomen la policía." *La Prensa*, May 5. Retrieved on June 22, 2014, from www.laprensa.com.ni/2003/05/05/nacionales/861852-narcos-carcomen-la-polica.

Puente Sur. 2012. "Ortega defensor de los ricos: Dora María Téllez, Daniel Ortega y la revolución en Nicaragua." January 17. Retrieved on January 25, 2015, from http://puentesurarg.blogspot.com/2012/01/ortega-defensor-de-los-ricos-dora-maria.html.

Putnam, Lara. 2002. *The Company They Kept: Migrants and the Politics of Gender in Caribbean Costa Rica, 1870–1960.* Chapel Hill: University of North Carolina Press.

Ramírez, Sergio. 2012. *Adiós Muchachos: A Memoir of the Sandinista Revolution.* Durham, NC: Duke University Press.

Reiter, Bernd, and Ulrich Oslender, eds. 2015. *Bridging Scholarship and Activism: Reflections from the Frontlines of Collaborative Research.* East Lansing: Michigan State University Press.

República de Nicaragua. 2008. *Código Penal de Nicaragua, Ley No. 641.* Retrieved on May 4, 2013, from http://legislacion.asamblea.gob.ni/Normaweb.nsf/($All)/1F5B59264A8F00F906257540005EF77E?OpenDocument.

———. 2013. "Ley No. 840. Ley Especial para el Desarrollo de Infraestructura y Transporte Nicaragüense Atingente a El Canal, Zonas de Libre Comercio e Infraestructuras Asociadas." *La Gaceta: Diario Oficial* 117 (110): 4973–4983.

———. 2014. "Texto de la Constitución Política de la República de Nicaragua con sus Reformas Incorporadas." *La Gaceta: Diario Oficial* 118 (32): 1254–1284.

Richards, Patricia, and Jeffery A. Gardner. 2013. "Still Seeking Recognition: Mapuche Demands, State Violence, and Discrimination in Democratic Chile." *Latin American and Caribbean Ethnic Studies* 8 (3): 255–279.

Robinson, Cedric J. 2000. *Black Marxism: The Making of the Black Radical Tradition.* Chapel Hill: The University of North Carolina Press.

Robinson, William I. 1997. "Nicaragua and the World: A Globalization Perspective." In *Nicaragua without Illusions: Regime Transition and Structural Adjustment in the 1990s,* ed. Thomas W. Walker, 23–42. Wilmington, DE: SR Books.

———. 2003. *Transnational Conflicts: Central America, Social Change, and Globalization.* London: Verso.

Rodgers, Tim. 2012. "Ortega: Nicaragua Is Winning the War on Drugs." *Nicaragua Dispatch,* September 8. Retrieved on December 3, 2013, from www.nicaraguadispatch.com/news/2012/09/ortega-nicaragua-is-winning-the-war-on-drugs/5169.

Rodríquez, Dylan. 2007. "Forced Passages." In *Warfare in the American Homeland: Policing and Prison in a Penal Democracy,* ed. Joy James, 35–57. Durham, NC: Duke University Press.

Rose, Nikolas. 1999. *Powers of Freedom: Reframing Political Thought.* Cambridge, UK: Cambridge University Press.

Ryan, Phil. 1995. *The Fall and Rise of the Market in Sandinista Nicaragua.* Montreal: McGill-Queen's University Press.

Safa, Helen I. 1995. *The Myth of the Male Breadwinner: Women and Industrialization in the Caribbean*. Boulder, CO: Westview Press.

———. 2005. "The Matrifocal Family and Patriarchal Ideology in Cuba and the Caribbean." *Journal of Latin American Anthropology* 10 (2): 314–338.

Salinas Maldonado, Carlos, and Iván Olivares. 2015. "HKND contratará en total 25 mil empleados extranjeros: 12,500 chinos para construir el canal." *Confidencial*, January 6. Retrieved on January 23, 2015, from www.confidencial.com.ni/articulo/20594/12-500-chinos-para-construir-el-canal.

Sanford, Victoria. 2008. "From Genocide to Feminicide: Impunity and Human Rights in Twenty-First Century Guatemala." *Journal of Human Rights* 7 (2): 104–122.

Sanford, Victoria, and Asale Angel-Ajani, eds. 2006. *Engaged Observer: Anthropology, Advocacy, and Activism*. New Brunswick, NJ: Rutgers University Press.

Schehl, Ed, and Katherine Knight, dirs. 2000. *Our Land, Our Future*. Santa Cruz, CA: Earth Links and Three Americas (formerly the Coalition for Nicaragua).

Scheper-Hughes, Nancy, and Philippe Bourgois. 2004. "Introduction: Making Sense of Violence." In *Violence in War and Peace*, eds. Nancy Scheper-Hughes and Philippe Bourgois, 1–31. Malden, MA: Blackwell Publishing.

Scott, David. 1999. *Refashioning Futures: Criticism after Postcoloniality*. Princeton, NJ: Princeton University Press.

Scott, James C. 2012. *Two Cheers for Anarchism*. Princeton, NJ: Princeton University Press.

Scott, Peter Dale, and Jonathan Marshall. 1991. *Cocaine Politics: Drugs, Armies, and the CIA in Central America*. Berkeley: University of California Press.

Shedlin, Michele G., Rita Arauz, Pascual Ortells, Mariana Aburto, and Danilo Norori. 2008. "Factors Influencing Drug Use and HIV Risk in Two Nicaraguan Cities." In *Geography and Drug Addiction*, eds. Yonette F. Thomas, Douglas Richardson, and Ivan Cheung, 267–286. Berlin: Springer Science and Business Media.

Silva, José Adán. 2012. "Pregnant Nicaraguan Girls Forced to Become Mothers." *Inter Press Service News Agency*, August 22. Retrieved on August 2, 2013, from www.ipsnews.net/2012/08/pregnant-nicaraguan-girls-forced-to-become-mothers/.

Smith, Christen A. 2015. "Between Soapboxes and Shadows: Activism, Theory, and the Politics of Life and Death in Salvador, Bahia, Brazil." In *Bridging Scholarship and Activism: Reflections from the Frontlines of Collaborative Research*, eds. Bernd Reiter and Ulrich Oslender, 135–149. East Lansing: Michigan State University Press.

Smith, Raymond T. 1996. *The Matrifocal Family: Power, Pluralism, and Politics*. New York: Routledge.

Spalding, Rose J. 2011. "Poverty Politics." In *The Sandinistas and Nicaragua since 1979*, eds. David Close, Salvador Martí i Puig, and Shelly A. McConnell, 215–243. Boulder, CO: Lynne Rienner Publishers.

Speed, Shannon. 2006. "Indigenous Women and Gendered Resistance in the Wake of Acteal: A Feminist Activist Research Perspective." In *Engaged Observer: Anthropology, Advocacy, and Activism*, eds. Victoria Sanford and Asale Angel-Ajani, 170–188. New Brunswick, NJ: Rutgers University Press.

Stahler-Sholk, Richard. 1990. "Stabilization, Destabilization, and the Popular Classes in Nicaragua, 1979–1988." *Latin American Research Review* 25 (3): 55–88.

Stoler, Ann Laura. 2007. "Affective States." In *A Companion to the Anthropology of Politics*, eds. David Nugent and Joan Vincent, 4–20. Malden, MA: Blackwell Publishing.

Thomas, Deborah. 2004. *Modern Blackness: Nationalism, Globalization, and the Politics of Culture in Jamaica*. Durham, NC: Duke University Press.

Trouillot, Michel-Rolph. 2001. "The Anthropology of the State in the Age of Globalization." *Current Anthropology* 42 (1): 125–138.

United Nations Office on Drugs and Crime. 2011. *Global Study on Homicide*. Vienna: UNODC. Retrieved on April 23, 2013, from www.unodc.org/documents/data-and-analysis/statistics/Homicide/Globa_study_on_homicide_2011_web.pdf.

———. 2013. *Global Study on Homicide*. Vienna: UNODC. Retrieved on December 12, 2015, from www.unodc.org/documents/gsh/pdfs/2014_GLOBAL_HOMICIDE_BOOK_web.pdf.

United Nations Statistics Division. 2010. "Live Births by Age of Mother and Sex of Child, General and Age-Specific Fertility Rates: Latest Available Year, 2000–2009." *Demographic Yearbook 2009-2010*. Retrieved on August 5, 2013, from http://unstats.un.org/unsd/demographic/products/dyb/dyb2009-2010/Table10.pdf.

United States Department of State. 2000. *1999 International Narcotics Control Strategy Report: Canada, Mexico, and Central America*, March 1. Retrieved on February 6, 2009, from www.state.gov/p/inl/rls/nrcrpt/1999/920.htm.

———. 2001, *2000 International Narcotics Control Strategy Report: Canada, Mexico, and Central America*, March 1. Retrieved on February 6, 2009, from www.state.gov/p/inl/rls/nrcrpt/2000/888.htm.

———. 2002. *2001 International Narcotics Control Strategy Report: Canada, Mexico, and Central America*, March 1. Retrieved on February 6, 2009, from www.state.gov/p/inl/rls/nrcrpt/2001/rpt/8478.htm.

———. 2003. *2002 International Narcotics Control Strategy Report: Canada, Mexico, and Central America*, March 1. Retrieved on February 6, 2009, from www.state.gov/p/inl/rls/nrcrpt/2002/html/17941.htm.

———. 2004. *2003 International Narcotics Control Strategy Report: Canada, Mexico, and Central America*, March 1. Retrieved on February 6, 2009, from www.state.gov/p/inl/rls/nrcrpt/2003/vol1/html/29833.htm.

Van Cott, Donna Lee. 2001. "Explaining Ethnic Autonomy Regimes in Latin America." *Comparative International Development* 35 (4): 30–58.

Visweswaran, Kamala. 1994. *Fictions of Feminist Ethnography*. Minneapolis: University of Minnesota Press.

Walker, Thomas W. 1997. "Introduction: Historical Setting and Important Issues." In *Nicaragua without Illusions: Regime Transition and Structural Adjustment in the 1990s*, ed. Thomas W. Walker, 1–19. Wilmington, DE: SR Books.

Weis, Jennifer R. 2013. "Feminist Ethnography with Domestic Violence Shelter Advocates: Negotiating the Neoliberal Era." In *Feminist Activist Ethnography: Counterpoints to Neoliberalism in North America*, eds. Christa Craven and Dána-Ain Davis, 53–68. Lanham, MD: Lexington Books.

Weiss Fagen, Patricia. 1988. "Central American Refugees and U.S. Policy." In *Crisis in Central America: Regional Dynamics and U.S. Policy in the 1980s*, eds. Nora Hamilton, Jeffry A. Frieden, Linda Fuller, and Manuel Pastor Jr., 59–76. Boulder, CO: Westview Press.

Wekker, Gloria. 2006. *The Politics of Passion: Women's Sexual Culture in the Afro-Surinamese Diaspora*. New York: Columbia University Press.

White, Aronette M. 2007. "All the Men Are Fighting for Freedom, All the Women Are Mourning Their Men, but Some of Us Carried Guns: A Race-Gendered Analysis of Fanon's Psychological Perspectives on War." *SIGNS: Journal of Women and Culture in Society* 32 (4): 857–884.

Wiley, James. 1995. "Undocumented Aliens and Recognized Refugees: The Right to Work in Costa Rica." *The International Migration Review* 29 (2): 423–440.

Williams, Randall. 2010. *The Divided World: Human Rights and Its Violence*. Minneapolis: University of Minnesota Press.

Winant, Howard. 2009. *The World Is a Ghetto: Race and Democracy Since World War II*. New York: Basic Books.

Wood, Robert E. 2000. "Caribbean Cruise Tourism: Globalization at Sea." *Annals of Tourism Research* 27 (2): 345–370.

———. 2004. "Global Currents: Cruise Ships in the Caribbean Sea." In *Tourism in the Caribbean: Trends, Development, Prospects*, ed. David Timothy Duval, 152–171. New York: Routledge.

World Health Organization. 2005. *Summary Report: WHO Multi-Country Study on Women's Health and Domestic Violence against Women*. Geneva: World Health Organization. Retrieved on August 12, 2013, from www.who.int/gender/violence/who_multicountry_study/en/.

Yuval-Davis, Nira, and Floya Anthias. 1989. *Woman-Nation-State*. New York: Palgrave Macmillan.

Zilberg, Elana. 2013. "Gangster, Soldier, Cop: Masculinity and Violence between the Americas." Paper presented at the 112th American Anthropological Association Annual Meeting, Chicago, November 20–24.

Index

Aaron, 105–6
Abolition Act of 1833, 188n7
abortion ban, 170, 171–72, 191n2
Abu-Lughod, Lila, 4
Acevedo, Adolfo, 15
Achi, R., 131, 190n2
Acosta, María Luisa, 76, 79, 148, 166
adolescent girls: birth rate among, 171, 191n3;
    sexuality of, 70, 102, 161, 164, 171; sexual
    violence against, 158, 160, 161, 163,
    164–65, 166–75, 171
affective labor, 65, 91, 92
Afrodescendant people, 5, 12, 13, 15,
    16, 17, 18; Afro–Costa Ricans, 131;
    Afro-Surinamese women, 90, 91; as
    identifying with African diaspora, 3,
    10, 24, 26, 31, 36, 39, 53–54, 73, 185; vs.
    indigenous people, 30, 48–49; and Law
    445, 7–8, 181, 184; slavery of, 10, 24, 30,
    36–38, 39, 43, 45, 91. *See also* Creoles;
    Garifuna; vernacular practices
Agamben, Giorgio, 83
Alan, 125
Alemán, Arnoldo, 7, 34, 76, 145, 187n3;
    and land speculation, 52, 56; policies
    regarding multicultural rights, 14
Algeria under French colonialism, 57–61
Allen. *See* Clair, Allen
Alvarez, Sonia E., 76
Amnesty International, 171
anarchist principles, 20, 81
Anderson, Mark, 5, 10, 30

Angel-Ajani, Asale, 20
Anglin, Mary K., 20
Anthias, Floya, 77
Arana, Mario, 10, 109, 190n7
Archdiocese of Guatemala: Human Rights
    Office, 190n5
ARDE (Alianza Revolucionaria
    Democrática), 117, 122, 129, 130
Aretxaga, Begoña, 4, 21, 155
Argentina, 11
Arias, Óscar, 136
arms trafficking, 136, 137, 138, 190n4
Atlantic Railroad. *See* Monkey Point–San
    Miguelito Railroad
autonomous activism, 11, 26, 152; among
    women, 24, 25, 30, 31–32, 77–79
Autonomous Regional Council of the South
    Caribbean Coast, 32, 74, 181, 182, 183–84
Awas Tingni, 8; Mayangna community, 7

Bagley, Bruce Michael, 120
Bangkukuk Taik, 33
Barriteau, Eudine, 189n2
Basok, Tanya, 124, 132
Bay of Pigs invasion, 2, 49
Beenie Man, 67
Bell, Charles Napier, 13, 45
Belli, Gioconda, 13
Benson, Peter, 133
Besson, Jean, 29, 30
Bickham Mendez, Jennifer, 20, 21
Bilwi (Puerto Cabezas), 49